RAPHAEL

Jean-Pierre Cuzin

Raphael

His Life and Works

CHARTWELL BOOKS, INC.

Frontispiece. *Study of a landscape with ancient mines.* About 1512-13. Metal-point heightened with white, on pink prepared paper. 21 x 14.1 cm. Windsor, Royal Library.

This intensely poetic drawing can be related to Marcantonio Raimondi's engraving of *The Plague of Phrygia*, known as the *Morbetto*, which features a similar motif.

Published by
CHARTWELL BOOKS, INC.
A Division of **BOOK SALES, INC.**
110 Enterprise Avenue
Secaucus, New Jersey 07094

© 1983 Office Du Livre

Translation by Sarah Brown

Translation © Office Du Livre 1985

Reprinted with permission by William S. Konecky Associates, Inc.

ISBN 0-89009-841-7

Printed and bound in Israel.

Table of Contents

O Gottes Welt, o Mutter, ist so schön!
Lass mich nich, fleh'ich, eh' die Stunde schlägt,
Zu jenen schwarzen Schatten niedersteigen!

Heinrich von Kleist,
The Prince of Hamburg, III, 5

Introduction

Will Raphael ever again be regarded as the greatest of all painters? This may seem a strange question to ask, suggesting as it does the idea of a hierarchy of painters which is no longer considered important. Today we look for different qualities in an artist — the expression of his individuality, the coherence or diversity of his style — rather than attempting to place him on a scale of excellence. Yet for centuries past no one would have dreamed of denying that Raphael was the greatest painter who had ever lived; in the world of art he stood for all that was most accomplished and beautiful. Who would now accord him this honor? For more than a hundred years he has not always been placed in the very front rank of painters. He is acclaimed as a "perfect" artist, but lacking in those qualities of mystery or violence which are now regarded as a sign of true creativity; Leonardo da Vinci and Michelangelo, who with Raphael are considered the artistic giants of the Renaissance, seem more attractive in this respect. Raphael still represents the highest achievement of the Italian Renaissance in terms of sweetness and perfect balance, and nothing can detract from this. Yet it seems that the very fame of his works has made them turn stale. They have been reproduced so many times, in so many places, in painted or drawn copies of every possible format, engravings of every possible technique, and even photographs, with their slickly achieved, blandly "impartial" images. There have been Raphaels in porcelain, enamel, stained glass, tapestry, bas-relief even set in gold which we know too well and which form part of our heritage of images. And so there developed the idea of an over-sweet, glossy painter, his works almost sickeningly familiar. Exploited, misunderstood, the victim of his own reputation, this most famous of artists has become the most difficult to appreciate.

· Apart from all these obstacles and difficulties, there is a more insidious and serious problem which is bound up with dangerous notions of "originality" in the two senses in which the word is used when applied to art. It is generally accepted that the early paintings, before Raphael's departure for Florence, are so steeped in the influence of Perugino that he has not yet found his own, independent voice; and that after his murals in the *Stanza dell'Incendio,* his paintings and frescoes were largely executed by pupils, and so cannot be considered as "authentic" Raphaels. Of his twenty years' work as a painter, ten can in some respects be set aside. Moreover, it cannot be denied that throughout his artistic career Raphael was drawn like a magnet to contemporary developments in painting which he absorbed, assimilated, and experimented with in his own works. Can this, then, be considered as true creativity? Perhaps Raphael should be regarded as a gifted eclectic or sublime plagiarist? These very questions seem to condemn his achievement; yet the twentieth century is preoccupied with such problems of authenticity and artistic borrowing, and they must be asked.

In addition, the frequent reproduction of Raphael's works has two unpleasant aspects and creates another difficulty; in the teaching of fine art, Raphael the diligent student — "at the top of his class" as Roberto Longhi amusingly puts it — has become Raphael the professor, for generations of students who are compelled to copy his works. He has also become a revered figure in the Catholic religion and it is hardly necessary to describe the fate of those works in whose figures the faithful see the true features of holiness. There is nothing in art more to be distrusted than those elements which encourage an over-academic, dryly scholastic approach, or which seem to invite an excess of religious sentiment. On top of all this Raphael has an almost irritatingly perfect image: an orphan, highly gifted, a willing pupil and diligent worker, admired for his talents and universally loved, who died at a romantically early age. His physical appearance remains vague and almost insipid; various portraits of long-haired young men have been taken at different times to show the artist himself, a far cry from the images of a wizard or the fighter associated with da Vinci and Michelangelo.

Now, on the five hundredth anniversary of his birth, the opportunity presents itself for a new study of Raphael's work, a study which seems especially valuable in that it can adopt an essentially

1 *Marcantonio Raimondi.* Portrait, said to be of Raphael. Engraving. 13.9 x 10.6 cm.

Although the sitter in this portrait has been identified through the centuries as Raphael, it is fashionable today to see this artist in his studio surrounded by the tools of his profession as a self-portrait showing Marcantonio Raimondi. There may, however, be some substance in the traditional identification: there is certainly a powerful feeling of presence about the engraving.

new approach. In the last few years, several important "lost" works have been restored to Raphael's *oeuvre*. Major paintings previously considered to be copies have been revealed as originals — for example, the *Madonna del Loreto*, the *Julius II* and the *Lorenzo de' Medici*. A newly-identified fragment of the *Altarpiece of St. Nicholas* enables us to form a clearer impression of Raphael's first known painting. Careful studies of the drawings have resulted in many important discoveries. Historical research has thrown new light on every aspect of Raphael's art, deciphering its iconography, questioning its chronological sequence and strengthening attributions.

These fresh approaches by art historians have slowly chipped away at Raphael's image, creating it anew, shorn of age-old myths and misunderstandings and its association with the kind of pious *vignettes* seen at a first communion. In recent years the work of restorers has also radically altered the traditional image of Raphael; one after another his paintings have been stripped of the yellow varnish which obscured them, revealing their true, often breathtaking, colors; consequently, we can now have some idea of how works, as yet unrestored, must originally have looked and how Raphael's color sense developed. The recent restoration of the Vatican's *Transfiguration* which revealed a startlingly flamboyant use of color, was crucial in this respect. And so Raphael's *oeuvre* is now more complete; we are particularly fortunate today in that we can appreciate his extraordinary achievement more clearly than at any time in the past.

Will he then be revered once again despite current suspicions that his paintings are too accessible, too imbued with an old-fashioned grace and tenderness, given our preference for more abrupt, disjointed and stressful works? It is significant that Malraux' *Musée Imaginaire* refused a place to Guido Reni and Murillo and accepted Raphael only grudgingly. Perhaps his works will one day inspire an untroubled sense of wonder as evoked by the work of those "unknown," faceless painters, Piero della Francesca and Georges de la Tour. In any case, it is time to reexamine his art afresh.

I. Urbino and Perugia 1483–1504: Apprenticeship

Raphael was 17 years old when in December 1500 Andrea Baroncio, about whom nothing else is known, commissioned an altarpiece for his family chapel in the Church of Sant' Agostino at Città di Castello. It was to be delivered in September of the following year. Two painters are mentioned in the documents — the young Raphael and Evangelista da Pian di Meleto who had previously worked with Raphael's father Giovanni Santi. This work was almost certainly the great *Coronation of St. Nicholas of Tolentino*; its presence in the Church is recorded in the seventeenth and eighteenth centuries. Unfortunately, only four fragments remain of this enormous painting, originally almost four meters high. In 1789 an earthquake destroyed a large part of the Church of Sant' Agostino and its adjoining monastery, and the altarpiece was sold in order to finance their reconstruction by the Augustinian monks. Pope Pius VI purchased it for what is thought to have been a huge sum of money. It was at this time that the large panel was broken up; the earthquake had left some areas irreparably damaged and so it was presumably considered impossible to restore as a whole. Questions of taste may also have played some part in the decision. Very little about it is known; however, the four remaining fragments reveal that an attempt was made to preserve such principal figures as were undamaged and refashion them into separate paintings.

Nothing seems to have survived of the central figure of St. Nicholas. Two fragments of the upper part of the work, the Virgin and the figure of God the Father, are now in Naples at the Museo Nazionale; and two of the angels surrounding the saint are now in the Pinacoteca Tosio Martinengo at Brescia and in the Louvre (the latter recently identified by Sylvie Béguin and subsequently acquired by the Museum). These surviving fragments, together with some preparatory drawings, early descriptions of the work and one late eighteenth century copy (unfortunately incomplete and lacking in detail) give us some idea of the original appearance of what was probably Raphael's first major work. It was a tall panel, arched at the top. In front of a wide, vaulted hall, opening onto a landscape and decorated with grotesques in the antique style (described by one eighteenth century historian as 'Mantegnesque'), there was a symmetrical composition; at the center, the tall and sombre figure of St. Nicholas, in a simple homespun robe, holding a crucifix and an open book, and the black, batwinged man-devil which he is crushing beneath his feet; surrounding him, four dancing angels in iridescent robes, carrying scrolls. In the upper section, three half-length figures in front of the hall look downwards, each one holding out a crown to St. Nicholas; at the center, God the Father, surrounded by a *mandorla* decorated with small angel heads, with the Virgin to the left and St. Augustine to the right.

The remaining sections of this work are all the more precious in that they constitute, with the preparatory drawings now in the museums at Lille and Oxford (Ashmolean), the earliest firm evidence of Raphael's activity as a painter and enable us to study the work of a very young artist at a precise moment in his career. Although mentioned by name in the contract for the altarpiece, Evangelista da Pian di Meleto, a little-known painter who specialized in gilding and armorial bearings, would not seem to have played an important part in its execution. The drawings at Lille and Oxford are accepted as being the work of Raphael. Perhaps Evangelista confined himself to painting according to Raphael's design a few relatively unimportant sections such as the architecture and its grotesque decoration and the heads of the cherubim surrounding God the Father; the latter, judging by the painting's present condition, appear to have been rather dryly executed. It is in any case likely that he was responsible for the many gilded areas. Otherwise, the fragments — including the two now in Naples, often doubted because of their bad state of preservation — appear to be essentially the work of the young Raphael.

Vasari mentions only Pietro Vanucci, commonly known as Perugino (c.1448–1523), as the young Raphael's master and the composition of this work, with the figures placed symmetrically within an architectural framework, is entirely Peruginesque, as is the division into terrestrial and celestial regions and the idea of surrounding a divine figure with a *mandorla* containing the heads of cherubim. More precisely, the placing of the principal figure of an altarpiece in front of a luminous sky visible through a large archway is often found in Perugino's works; for instance, his *Virgin and Saints* of 1493 (Florence, Uffizi) and of 1497 (Fano, Santa Maria Nuova).

2 *Compositional study for the altarpiece of St. Nicholas of Tolentino.* 1500-01. Black Chalk. 39.5 x 25 cm. Lille, Musée des Beaux-Arts.

This, the most important drawing relating to the altarpiece, shows the whole composition close to the final form of the painting itself. St. Nicholas, in the center trampling on the demon, is lightly but firmly sketched in, his nude body indicated under his robe. On the left is just one of the four angels surrounding the saint — the one corresponding to the fragment in the Louvre. In the upper part the figures of God the Father and the Virgin, corresponding to the fragments in Naples, are drawn from models in contemporary dress. On the right, the figure of St. Augustine appears as it probably did in the finished painting.

3 *Studies for the Altarpiece of St. Nicholas of Tolentino: St. Augustine, an angel, the arm of God the Father.* Black chalk. 37.9 × 24.5 cm. Oxford, Ashmolean Museum.

This drawing seems to be contemporary with the great sheet of studies in Lille, perhaps slightly earlier in view of the fact that the latter shows St. Augustine as he appears in the painting. Here he is shown full-length, and the gesture of the hand holding the crown is only very roughly indicated. In life drawings such as this, each light, supple line flows into the next with a kind of nervous delicacy. The other side of the sheet also contains studies for the same picture, notably for hands.

Despite these analogies, there are significant differences when the main elements of the altarpiece are compared with similar areas or individual figures in the works of Perugino. A comparison of the half-length God the Father painted by Raphael with that painted by Perugino in an exactly contemporary work, the *Ascension of Vallombrosa* (1500, Florence, Uffizi), is revealing. In Raphael's work the robe, with its large folds enveloping the shape of the body, is markedly different from Perugino's flatter and less substantial garment. The firm placing of the arms, gently curved and reaching forward with the large, well-formed hands holding the crown, displays the ease with which Raphael is already positioning his figures in three-dimensional space rather than simply describing them as Perugino did on the surface of the painting. Moreover, the face of God the Father has a strength verging on harshness in the precise rendering of its well-defined features, quite different from the rather insipid sweetness of Perugino.

Of the remaining fragments of the altarpiece it is, however, the *Angel* now in the Louvre which is the most instructive in this respect. The Peruginesque line, evident in Raphael's fluid treatment of the scroll and the backward tilt of the head on its supple neck, is immediately striking but a more enduring impression is made by the sheer volume of the forms, the solidity of the face with its accentuated jaw, the strong, short hands. All this, together with the vividly contrasting colors and the vigorous, at times almost brutal, technique clearly reveals a use of paint and brushstroke still further from Perugino's style.

It is now possible to attempt a reconstruction of the *Altarpiece of St. Nicholas* with its decorative arabesques and gold highlights providing a backdrop to the large, sombre silhouettes of saint and demon — its rich, deep blues and vermilions with, here and there, the white or bronze of an angel's tunic. The painting must have been very tall and more narrow than is suggested by the Lille drawing; the figures would have been placed closer to the center than has been previously thought, with the fairly compact group of four angels surrounding the dark form of the saint, crushing the demon like a small and brilliantly colored hemicycle, entwined with the dancing ribbons of their unfurled scrolls. The composition might appear to have been disjointed, with the three truncated figures in the upper section, but the imposing architecture would have had the effect of balancing the strong, bright colors and a sense of unity would have been imparted by the imperious gaze of the three celestial beings at the face of St. Nicholas. The eyes of the *Angel* in the Louvre, raised to heaven, would have linked the celestial and terrestrial spheres — a technique Raphael derived from Perugino.

Despite its clear debt to Perugino, however, the painting contains so many elements — of design, color and treatment of form

— which represent a significant break with Perugino's style that we can only marvel at the very young artist's independence while speculating on the other influences which may have contributed to the evolution of his art.

This is the moment to consider Raphael's father, Giovanni Santi. Born in about 1440, he was probably the pupil of Melozzo da Forlì, whose style he carried to Urbino and its surroundings, bringing

5 *Head of an angel,* fragment from the *Altarpiece of St. Nicholas of Tolentino.* Oil on panel. 1501. 31 × 27 cm. Brescia, Pinacoteca Tosio Martinengo.

The angel was positioned immediately to the right of the saint; in the upper left corner part of the open book which he was holding out to the faithful is visible. The freshness and vivacity of expression and boldness of the color contrasts recall Pinturicchio. But the strong, harmonious interweaving of sinuous lines with the strands of hair blown by the wind could only be Raphael's. The work was identified by Fischel in 1912 at the same time as the two fragments in Naples.

4 *God the Father surrounded by cherubim; the Virgin Mary,* fragments from the *Altarpiece of St. Nicholas of Tolentino.* 1501. Oil on panel. 112 × 115 cm. (both fragments together). Naples, Galleria Nazionale di Capodimonte.

These two fragments from the upper part of the altarpiece, showing God and the Virgin Mary holding crowns over the head of St. Nicholas, have often been attributed to Evangelista da Pian di Meleto who is mentioned with Raphael in the contract for the commission. But the fullness and freedom of the forms of the two main figures argue against such a hypothesis. It is more likely that Evangelista merely collaborated on certain parts of the cherubim, the architectural decoration and the application of the gold.

6/7 *Angel holding an inscription,* fragment from the *Altarpiece of St. Nicholas of Tolentino.* 1501. Oil on panel. 57 × 35.8 cm. Paris, Musée du Louvre.

The recent discovery of this picture by Sylvie Béguin has enabled us to form a much clearer idea of Raphael's earliest documented work. It was acquired by the Louvre in 1981. An essential contribution to our knowledge of the young painter, it demonstrates his mastery of the rendering of volumes in space. The photograph reproduced here shows the work undergoing restoration (during March 1983). The overpainting that had altered its appearance has been removed; the missing parts of the original painting have yet to be retouched.

to his master's uncomplicated art a slight awkwardness, both overly sweet and contrived, in his half-length Virgins and rather lifeless and repetitive altarpieces. Santi would appear to have met at Urbino some of the greatest artists of the *Quattrocento*: in 1469 Piero della Francesca, who had come to the city to paint an altarpiece commissioned by the Confraternity of the Corpus Domini, probably stayed at his house; in 1467 and 1468 he may have come into contact with Uccello; and he may also have known Perugino — in 1488 they were both working in Fano, a town close to Urbino. He joined the brilliant ducal court of the Montefeltro family later in that year at the time of the marriage of the young Duke Guidobaldo to Elizabetta Gonzaga, sister of Francesco II Duke of Mantua. Santi became the Duchess' painter and produced a somewhat graceless series of *Muses* (now in Florence at the Galleria Corsini) for the Ducal Palace. Since 1483 Evangelista da Pian di Meleto had been Santi's assistant (*garzone*).

Giovanni and his first wife Magia, the daughter of an Urbino merchant, had one surviving child Raphael who was probably born on Friday the 28th of March 1483. Another son, perhaps the eldest, and a daughter were also born to the couple but lived for a tragically short time. In 1485 Giovanni Santi's father died, together with one of his sons, Raphael's brother; in October 1491 Giovanni's mother died, followed by his wife Magia and small daughter. At that time Raphael was only eight years old. In May 1492 the painter was married again to Bernardina, the daughter of a goldsmith, whom Passavant described as a selfish and shrewish woman. The following year Santi returned to Urbino in poor health from Mantua where he had been summoned to paint a portrait of the Duchess, Isabella d'Este. He died during the summer of 1494 when Raphael was eleven.

There followed a long period of legal wrangling among his heirs; Bartolomeo, Giovanni's brother and Raphael, who was placed under his uncle's guardianship, were made residuary legatees. Soon afterwards a dispute arose between Bartolomeo, on the one hand, and on the other, Bernardina, her daughter Elisabetta, and her father the goldsmith who was also an executor. It was not until 1500 after a succession of lawsuits that matters were settled. And so Raphael's childhood years were filled with grief and mourning, followed by unpleasant and petty legal quarrels and difficulties, all of which must have made them far from happy.

As a child Raphael probably learned the rudiments of painting in his father's studio. The extent to which his mature style was influenced by this early training is not easy to judge. However, Santi was a lively if mediocre painter, and his most ambitious works contain echoes of the art of Melozzo as well as that of Piero which may well have left a lasting impression on the young Raphael. Two altarpieces of 1489, the *Buffi Virgin* (Urbino, Galleria Nazionale delle Marche) and the *Virgin with Saints* (Monastery of Montefiorentino), notable for their use of antique architecture bathed in a strong, clear light and the slightly crude appearance of their large, overcrowded figure groups, find a response in Raphael's first altarpieces. And the angel musicians of the Montefiorentino altarpiece look forward to those in Raphael's Oddi *Coronation of the Virgin*.

Relying perhaps too closely on Vasari who cites only Perugino as the young Raphael's master, historians have for a long time confined Raphael's formative period to his apprenticeship with Perugia's leading painter. Vasari states that he assimilated Perugino's style to the point where it is difficult to distinguish between the two artists' works and so Raphael was seen as asserting his own artistic personality by gently freeing himself from Peruginesque models. They searched for the boy-genius' earliest brushstrokes in Perugino's most accomplished and gracious works, paintings which are almost too Peruginesque and possess a sweetness that could only have come from Raphael. This was the wrong approach. Claims have been made, for example, that Raphael's hand can be detected in some of the frescoed figures in the Audience Chamber of the Collegio del Cambio at Perugia (c.1497–1500) but the sections in question, and in particular the fresco depicting *The Eternal Father with Prophets and Sibyls* which stands out from the rest in the purity and skill of its execution, are most probably those which Perugino painted himself, with no help whatsoever from his assistants.

The case of the Fano predella is more difficult. The polyptych in the Church of Santa Maria Nuova at Fano, painted by Perugino, bears the date 1497 on its central section. The predella, almost three meters in length, illustrates on one panel five scenes from the *Life of the Virgin* which an old tradition attributes, with certain other areas in the altarpiece itself, to the young Raphael. Roberto Longhi has drawn attention to the *Birth of the Virgin*, the first of the predella's small scenes, where the wonderfully deft grouping of the tiny figures and the tender emotional atmosphere which seems to bind and surround them, do indeed have a Raphaelesque quality. However, without entirely excluding the possibility that the thirteen- or fourteen-year-old Raphael collaborated in the predella, it seems preferable to continue to view it as one of Perugino's masterpieces; the figure types, their shape and appearance, are completely in his style. Moreover, a pen sketch of the composition, in the Uffizi, is much more likely to be the work of Perugino than Raphael.

The Fano predella, of all Perugino's works, is perhaps the one from which his young pupil learned most; the grouping of the figures within the architecture is recalled, not exactly but fairly closely, in the Oddi altarpiece. Other sections of Perugino's finest paintings have occasionally been attributed to Raphael but it would surely be rather ridiculous to take away from this artist the very masterpieces which represent the peak of his achievement and give them to the younger man. As the *Altarpiece of St. Nicholas* clearly demonstrates, what distinguishes the work of the young Raphael from that of his master is precisely the absence of the sweet langor, the soft indolence of his figures. Raphael's works are far sharper, almost aggressive in quality; the figures more realistic, reacting convincingly to the central event. All in all it would seem that any attempt to reconstruct Raphael's work before he was seventeen is not very fruitful and it is better to simply accept the fragments of the *Altarpiece of St. Nicholas* and its preparatory drawings as his earliest works.

When did Raphael travel to Perugia to work with Perugino? The precise date is uncertain but it was probably very early in 1494 or 1495, and it is even possible that Santi, an admirer of Perugino, took his son there before he died. Vasari, who makes no mention of the early deaths of Raphael's parents, imagines a scene in which father introduces son to Perugino — and this, together with the many later romantic representations of the supposed event, is not perhaps as far fetched as one might imagine. On the other hand Perugino moved frequently from place to place and the young Raphael would have had to follow him to Florence as early as 1495. In fact, the very earliest of Raphael's works seem to reveal some acquaintance with Florentine drawings and paintings. And even if Raphael passed the main part of his "Umbrian period" in Perugia, his first works reveal a sophistication and breadth of visual knowledge which could only have come from travel. It is at least certain that he was in Città di Castello (a city to which he seems to have been particularly attached, painting several of his earliest altarpieces for its churches) in December 1500; and in Siena where

he was involved in the decoration of the Piccolomini Library, probably in 1502. He must have returned to Urbino from time to time to oversee his father's workshop, a task he may have shared with Evangelista da Pian di Meleto. It is difficult to estimate the length of time he spent with Perugino; however, it is significant that in the contract for the *Altarpiece of St. Nicholas*, drawn up in December 1500, he is already considered a master (*Magister*) in his own right.

Raphael's style of painting in 1500–1501, with the almost brutal strength and liveliness of its well-placed and balanced figures, its vivid color contrasts and elaborate use of decoration — that is, everything that seems least Peruginesque in the *Altarpiece of St. Nicholas* — is difficult to analyze. His confident use of space perhaps owes something to the paintings of Giovanni Santi, with their rather clumsy attempts to suggest solidity and depth. Whether Timoteo Viti (1467–1525) also influenced the young Raphael or was himself influenced by him is difficult to say. He was a native of Urbino who trained in Bologna in the workshop of Francesco Francia and back in Urbino in about 1495 completed the series of *Muses* at the Ducal

8 *Study of two soldiers for the Resurrection of Christ.* About 1500. Metal-point, heightened with white, on grey paper. 32 × 22 cm. Oxford, Ashmolean Museum.

9 *Study of a soldier and an angel for the Resurrection of Christ.* Metal-point, heightened with white, on grey paper. 32.7 × 23.6 cm. Oxford, Ashmolean Museum.

There is no doubt that the two studies in the first drawing and one of those in the second were used for the Sao Paulo *Resurrection*. Their attribution to Raphael is unquestioned. The light but decisive touch is still very close to that of Perugino. The kneeling angel in the second drawing, who holds an object difficult to identify (a chalice ?), may be a preparatory drawing for an unrealized project or a lost work.

10 Raphael (?). *The Resurrection of Christ.* Oil on panel. 52 × 44 cm. Sao Paulo, Museu de Arte.

The attribution to Raphael of this picture, which was once in the collection of Lord Kinnaird in London, remains disputed. It resembles Perugino, but even more strongly Pinturicchio, especially in the vivid coloring and precious character of the details.

16

Palace left unfinished by Santi at the time of his death. Perhaps he imparted to Raphael's work something of Francia's graceful, sculptural quality. However, the strength and vigor of Raphael's forms must owe far more to Luca Signorelli, almost forty years his senior. Signorelli's *Martyrdom of St. Sebastian* in the Church of San Domenico at Città di Castello, probably painted in 1498 and today in the Pinacoteca Communale, was admired by the young painter; there is in the Ashmolean Museum at Oxford a rough sketch by Raphael of one of the archers in the foreground of the painting in which he improves upon the man's awkward stance. Another sketch, on the same sheet, can be linked with the banner in the *Creation of Eve* which dates it almost certainly to about 1500.

This provides fascinating proof of Raphael's interest in Signorelli's crudely constructed athletic figures, their violently twisted bodies bathed in a harsh light, which are far removed from Perugino's more ideal treatment of the human form. Raphael's taste for bright color and elaborate decoration suggests a knowledge of Bernardino Pinturicchio, thirty years his senior, a pupil and assistant of Perugino. Pinturicchio's work may have inspired the vivid colors of the altarpiece with its glittering gold highlights and the rather over-insistent detailing of the antique architectural reliefs — the overall effect must have resembled a magnificent playing card. Moreover, Konrad Oberhuber has rightly remarked that the figure types of the Virgin, with her robe drawn over her head, and especially the *Angel* in Brescia, with its delicate face and full mouth, are close to those of Pinturicchio.

So it would seem that Signorelli and Pinturicchio were, with Perugino, the painters who most impressed the young Raphael and whom he set himself to emulate. But he was, of course, far more than the sum of his influences; there is a strength, a bright freshness about the two *Angels* in the Louvre and in Brescia — a quality which Raphael's paintings were never to lose, as lively as the wind which gently ruffles the beard and hair of God the Father and lifts the angels' tresses. The *St. Nicholas of Tolentino* already begins to demonstrate the special qualities of Raphael's art — its delicate elegance, and, above all, its deft placing of forms in space. His colors are bright and clear, with occasional soft shades of gray and orange and those touches of white of which he was to become so fond and which recur, often set against black, throughout his work. An examination of the paintings of his "Umbrian period" will show how he developed and strengthened these qualities.

Raphael painted another work for Città di Castello at about the same time as the *Altarpiece of St. Nicholas of Tolentino*. This was a processional banner having, on one side, a painting of the *Holy Trinity adored by St. Sebastian and St. Roch* and on the other, *The Creation of Eve*. Commissioned by the Confraternity of Santa Trinita, the banner was an *ex voto*, an offering of thanks for the departure of the plague which had ravaged the city probably from 1499 to 1500. And so there is every reason to date it around 1500 rather than, as Roberto Longhi has argued, 1503–1504; this would make it Raphael's very first work — still earlier perhaps than the *St. Nicholas*.

Unfortunately, it is today in very poor condition. Its two sides, now separated, are in the Pinacoteca Communale at Città di Castello and have lost much of their original paint surface. The little that remains, however, contains, like the *Altarpiece of St. Nicholas*, elements of Santi's style as well as revealing the influence of Perugino, Signorelli and Pinturicchio.

The Resurrection of Christ, a small painting in the Museum at Sao Paulo, has excited much critical speculation as to whether or not it is by Raphael. The two schools of thought have equally distinguished supporters. The attribution is apparently supported by two drawings in the Ashmolean Museum in Oxford which are certainly by Raphael; each shows two young men, preliminary studies for the four soldiers in the painting with raised arms who surround the sarcophagus. *The Resurrection* at Sao Paulo is, despite superficial similarities between particular figures, strikingly unPeruginesque when compared with Perugino's own treatment of the subject. Painted in 1499–1500 for the Church of San Francesco al Prato at Perugia and today in the Vatican Museum, it is not clear whether this dates from before or after the small Sao Paulo panel. The perfect symmetry of Perugino's figures is broken by the subtle changes in the positioning and spatial relationships of the four soldiers and by the landscape stretching away into the distance — a landscape in which the approaching holy women, far from being mere figures picked out on a backcloth, share the same space as those in the foreground. The sense of animation, the historical correctness of the details especially of costume, the overall charm of the painting, are all close to Pinturicchio's work while the highly wrought gold detail on the sarcophagus, with its precious marbles and gilded dolphins, recalls Florentine models. The angels in their elaborately draped robes, very different from those of Perugino, more simply attired, may also echo Pinturicchio's ornate manner and look back to slightly earlier Florentine models, such as those of Verocchio which had become diffused in the work of Perugino; Pinturicchio, however, remained attached to them as can be seen for example in the angel framing the *Virgin and Child* in a lunette in the Palazzo dei Priori at Siena (1486). Nevertheless, the *Resurrection* would appear to have more to teach Pinturicchio than to learn from him. The deftness and delicacy shown in the positioning of the four soldiers leaves Pinturicchio's mannequin-like figures far behind; no other contemporary painter except perhaps Signorelli could match it. The painting can be viewed as a synthesis, a small jewel containing, in essence, all the most attractive qualities that later fifteenth century painting could offer to a young artist.

11 *Virgin and Child with St. Jerome and St. Francis.* About 1501. Oil on panel. 34 × 29 cm. Berlin, Staatliche Museen, Gemäldegalerie.

Commentators have always pointed out the close relationship between this little picture, with its unusually tight composition, and the work of Pinturicchio. It seems to be Raphael's earliest surviving Madonna.

19

12 *St. Sebastian*. About 1501. Oil on panel. 43 × 34 cm. Bergamo, Accademia Carrara.

The facial type and the trace of preciousness and melancholy about the features show the clear influence of Perugino, yet the sense of structure is already Raphael's.

The *Madonna with St. Jerome and St. Francis* (Berlin-Dahlem, Gemäldegalerie) may have been painted in 1501 which would make it contemporary with the *Altarpiece of St. Nicholas* and so perhaps the first certain work by Raphael to have survived intact. The small painting, very crowded in composition, looks back to the Sienese artists of the *Quattrocento*; its almost square format and richly glowing pictorial surface make it rather icon-like in appearance. Of all Raphael's paintings, it is the one in which there is the least attempt to give a sense of three-dimensionality. This delicate, elaborately ornamented art, with the gold glints of the small knots of embroidery on the Virgin's robe and the cushion on which the Infant Christ sits, and of the haloes, the stippling, the star at the Virgin's shoulder, is very close to and shares a sense of quiet piety with the work of Pinturicchio. Pinturicchio is also recalled in the dark veil framing the Virgin's face and the slightly contrived, contorted grace of the Infant Jesus; this is a far from timid work, confidently executed and designed to please.

The *Saint Sebastian* in the Accademia Carrara at Bergamo, so Peruginesque at first glance, reveals on further analysis the distance that exists between Raphael and his master from his very earliest paintings. Perugino painted many such studies of young men and women, their heads tilted, viewed full-face. However, several subtle differences — a firmer chin, a more finely modeled mouth, the very well structured nose whose bridge appears to join the arch of the eyebrow, a greater sense of volume — show this painting to be far removed from him.

The highly embroidered robe, the pattern on the shirt like notes of music, the slashed velvet of the jerkin decorated with knots and palmettes of gold, point to a love of ornamentation which comes from Pinturicchio but the saint's neck-chain, clearly copied from a real example, so variously and convincingly do its links catch the light, is close to northern painting and has no equivalent in the work of Perugino or Pinturicchio. The saint grasps the fragile arrow of his martyrdom like a sceptre; it is a marvelous image, a *tour de force*. The subtle treatment of the head, slightly tilted away from the spectator, is close in style to the *Madonna with St. Jerome and St. Francis* in spite of the difference in scale and like that painting, striking in its icon-like character and lack of three-dimensionality, it can be dated a little later in the same year, 1501.

The *"Solly" Madonna*, also at Berlin-Dahlem, has clear links with Perugino's works. The design is very close to his half-length *Madonnas* of that period, those for example in the Ford Collection at Detroit or that in the National Gallery in Washington usually dated around

Moreover, its draftsmanship and brilliant use of space are quite without precedent among Umbrian painters.

Who, then, was the artist of this exquisite painting? Close as it is to their work, it would seem to have been neither Pinturicchio nor Timoteo Viti. Was it really the young Raphael? As bright and jewel-like as an illuminated miniature, its style seems somehow less robust than that of his first known works and fits uneasily into the pattern of his early development. Perhaps it should be dated still earlier than the *Altarpiece of St. Nicholas*, and simply accepted as an exceptional masterpiece painted by a fifteen-year-old. Perhaps the artist was a pupil of Raphael, long since forgotten, to whom he "lent" his designs, as he did Pinturicchio for the frescoes in Siena. In any case the *Resurrection* at Sao Paulo, despite the many problems it poses, is too closely associated with Raphael to be excluded completely from his *oeuvre*.

13 *Solly Madonna*. 1501 or 1502. Oil on panel. 52 × 38 cm. Berlin, Staatliche Museen, Gemäldegalerie.

The austere simplification of the clothing emphasizes the robust power in the forms of the figures, which seem on the point of disrupting the conventional Peruginesque grouping. The picture was part of the Solly collection which was bought in 1821 and helped form the basis of the Berlin Museum.

14 *The Virgin and Child with a Book (Norton Simon Madonna).* 1503 or 1504. Oil on wood. 39 x 28 cm. Pasadena, California, Norton Simon Museum of Art.

The book constitutes the center of the painting. In its subtle rhythms it seems to be of a later date than the *Solly Madonna.*

15   *Study for the Virgin and Child with a Book.* 1503 or 1504. Metal-point on light grey paper. 25.8 × 19.1 cm. London, British Museum.

A study for the Virgin's head made from a female model wearing a veil. The lines of the drawing model the rounded forms with great gentleness yet remain lively and energetic.

16   *Study for The Virgin and Child with a Book.* 1503-1504. Metal-point on light grey paper. 25 × 17.5 cm. Lille, Musée des Beaux-Arts.

This life study from a male model in contemporary dress establishes the pose of the the Virgin. The face, however, does seem to have been drawn from a female model, probably the same one who posed for the head in the British Museum. There is a detailed study for the hand holding the book in the lower part of the sheet. The collar is a later addition.

17   *Study for The Virgin and Child with a Book.* Pen and ink. 11.6 × 13.2 cm. Oxford, Ashmolean Museum.

Compositional sketch differing only slightly from the final design. On the right is a rapid sketch for the landscape in the painting. Further landscape sketches are on the verso.

18 *Departure of Enea Silvio Piccolomini for the Council of Basle.* 1503? Black chalk, pen and ink, wash, heightened with white. 70.5 × 41.5 cm. Florence, Uffizi.

This "little cartoon" is the compositional sketch for the first of a set of fresco decorations executed by Pinturicchio in the Piccolomini Library at Siena Cathedral. The grouping of the masses, so well organized in the third dimension, and the flowing rhythms of the composition are rendered dry and stiff in the final fresco. A similar cartoon by Raphael for *The Meeting of Frederick III and Eleanor of Aragon* in the same series is in an American private collection.

1500–1501. Raphael takes the pose of Christ almost literally from these paintings or others like them, and the position of the head, turned to the side and angled backwards, returns constantly in Perugino's paintings of about 1493–1500. However, Perugino's slightly banal striving after gracefulness becomes, with Raphael, a desire to paint in as life-like a manner as possible. The extended right leg of the Infant Jesus seeks his Mother's cradling touch; his hands firmly grasp the bird and the cord which holds him prisoner; above all, his gaze, lifted on high, is not an attempt of a kind often made by Perugino to express a mystic and dreamy ecstasy but simply the child's wish to see what is in the little book which the Virgin is holding at an angle slightly too high for him and which she herself with lowered eyes is reading. Compared with a Perugino Virgin, the *"Solly" Madonna* handles shape and form more deftly. The arm holding the book which is foreshortened marks a new preoccupation with the third dimension, in bringing both hand and book into the foreground. The robustness of the tautly drawn forms, full of life, belongs unmistakeably to Raphael; the body of the Infant Jesus, firm and strongly built, is that of a little Hercules. Nevertheless, the Berlin painting is of an almost austere simplicity. There is no use of ornament apart from the border of the Virgin's robe and the color contrasts are stark with the sharp silhouette of the Virgin outlined against the blue of the sky which throws into relief the dark hooded robe which frames her face — a very unPeruginesque effect, of which the young Raphael was to make constant use. The robe is quite simple and plain, its folds hugging the outlines of the body. The Virgin faces the spectator with an air of great strength and calm. And so the "sweetness" of which this painting — often judged one of Raphael's least original works — has been accused is dispelled on close examination. It is in any case primarily a consequence of our approaching it as a near-Perugino, and to view it with half-closed eyes serves only to confirm this impression. In fact, the true case is quite different. The *"Solly" Madonna* is a Perugino at first glance but it is a Raphael disguised as a Perugino — an easily penetrable disguise. It might be compared with Rubens' very early works, so close to those of his master Otto Venius that they might be mistaken for his if there were not also present a particular quality of life and freedom.

The *"Solly" Madonna* may be dated at the end of 1501 or in 1502 shortly before the *Oddi Altarpiece.* The athletic appearance of the almost geometrically placed bodies, the generous, supple folds of dark drapery, even the child's type of face, so different from that of the angels in the *Altarpiece of St. Nicholas* — all these qualities look forward to the *Vatican Altarpiece* and have far less in common with such more obviously picturesque works as the *Madonna with St. Jerome and St. Francis* and the *Altarpiece of St. Nicholas.*

Almost unknown before its purchase in 1972 by the Norton Simon Museum in Pasadena, California, the *Madonna and Child with a Book,* also known as the *Norton Simon Madonna,* is certainly close in the positioning of its figures to the *"Solly" Madonna* in which the gazes and gestures of Mother and Child are also directed towards

19 *Four horsemen and a man running.* About 1503? Pen and ink. 27.2 x 40 cm. Florence, Uffizi.

This vigorous drawing, with its dashing arabesques, has been related to the fresco of *The Departure of Enea Silvio Piccolomini for Basle*, in Siena. The horseman on the left is very close to the one on the left of Raphael's cartoon for the fresco, which is also in the Uffizi.

and centered on a book; also, there is an almost oppressive sense of power and authority. However, the slight stiffness of the Berlin picture has here disappeared and the design is fully and convincingly related to the book at its center. Happily, several preparatory drawings for the Pasadena *Madonna* have survived, providing valuable information about the painter's working methods. One, now in Lille, shows a young male model in the pose of the Madonna; another, in Oxford, is divided in two with pen sketches of the overall design of the composition and details of the landscape; a third, in silverpoint in the British Museum, is an exquisitely restrained, modest study of the Virgin's head. This painting may confidently be dated after the *"Solly" Madonna* — at the end of 1503 or the beginning of 1504.

The frescoes in the Piccolomini Library at Siena are a particularly complex and interesting example of collaboration between two painters. And they pose the question at the beginning of Raphael's career as to what constitutes "originality" in matters of artistic creation — a question that will be asked as keenly but in different terms when we come to his very last paintings.

Cardinal Francesco Piccolomini Todeschini who was to become Pope Pius III in 1503 decided in about 1492 to build a library adjoining Siena Cathedral in memory of his uncle, Enea Silvio Piccolomini, Pope Pius II from 1458 to 1464. The contract to decorate the library walls with frescoes was signed by Bernardino di Betto di Biagio, known as Pinturicchio, who had been summoned to Siena by Cardinal Francesco at the end of June 1502. In particular, the painter undertook to portray scenes from the life of the Cardinal's illustrious ancestor. He began with the vault which he decorated with grotesques. In spring 1503 work on the ten wall frescoes had not yet begun. In the autumn of that year Cardinal Francesco was elected Pope but he reigned for only a few days, dying almost immediately in September or October. After his death work on the library was suspended until 1504 when a new contract was drawn up; in any event, Pinturicchio did not paint the ten frescoes until 1505–1507.

Vasari is the first to speak in his biographies of Raphael and Pinturicchio of the part played by the former in the decoration of the library at Siena. He comments that, as he writes, a cartoon by Raphael for one of the paintings is on display in Siena and that he himself possesses some of Raphael's original designs. The collaboration between the two painters has been doubted or even flatly denied and Vasari has been accused of unfairness towards Pinturicchio. Erwin Panofsky, however, clearly established in 1951 that Raphael provided Pinturicchio with the finished drawings or "modelli" for two of the frescoes, and other designs for a third. One of the two "modelli" in an American private collection shows the *Meeting of Frederick III and Eleanor of Portugal*; the other, in the Uffizi, the *Departure of Enea Silvio Piccolomini to the Council of Basle*. Less elaborate drawings, containing studies of various figures or of horsemen, are to be found in Oxford, the Uffizi and the Louvre.

Konrad Oberhuber recently argued that all of the frescoes, or at least eight of them, were painted after Raphael's designs, claiming that their handling of space is far beyond anything of which Pinturicchio was capable. This cannot be denied. Oberhuber thinks that Raphael worked on this project in two bursts, in 1502 and 1503, and that the two remaining "modelli" belong to each of these two stages. Stylistically, the two drawings seem closest to the *Oddi Altarpiece*. The first, now privately owned, is very neatly and carefully executed and has certain Peruginesque qualities, with its solidly constructed draped figures, their rounded heads looking back to those of the great *Coronation of the Virgin*. The second, now in the Uffizi, is, as Oberhuber states, of a later date and freer in execution, evoking in a striking manner the predella panels of the *Oddi Altarpiece* — almost certainly painted last of all, with their more slender, animated figures. The closeness of this second drawing to the left-hand section of the *Adoration of the Magi* is revelatory in this respect, with the horses and riders so alike in their poses and a similar courtly, slightly dandified quality.

If Oberhuber is right, and there is reason to believe that he is, the paintings in Siena provide an extraordinary example of the nineteen- or twenty-year-old Raphael's attempts at spatial composition. The difficulty lies in deciphering Raphael's designs behind Pinturicchio's frescoes. A comparison of the two surviving "modelli" with the finished paintings is disturbing. We have only to compare

the drawing and fresco showing Enea Silvio's departure for Basle — the lively, dancing motion of the pike-carrier at the right restraining his horse in the Uffizi drawing appears heavy, cramped and less animated in the fresco's corresponding figure — and here his gesture appears meaningless. The painting is altogether harder, more dry, and the variations or elaborations which the painter allows himself are all inclined towards anecdote and excessive detail; here a large hat, there a dog, flowers, grander clothes, the inevitable trees — a whole architecture of anecdote. Nothing remains of the drawings' gentle, rhythmic sense of movement, the soft modulations, the carefully judged tensions. Pinturicchio presents us with something else — an elaborate, and rather over-brash, strip cartoon. And so it is no easy matter to find Raphael in the library at Siena. We can only notice here and there groups or single figures whose pose is stronger, more supple and free than the rest, and who appear more than mere starched costumes; perhaps it was Raphael who so conceived them.

Large altarpieces were the most ambitious works attempted by the young Raphael, and the study of them should give us the key to his art, his sources and his development as a painter. After the *Altarpiece of St. Nicholas*, firmly dated 1500–1501, dating becomes difficult, and no one is in agreement over the chronological sequence of surviving works until 1504, at the end of Raphael's "Umbrian period." This is the date inscribed on the glorious *Marriage of the Virgin* (Milan, Brera). These problems of chronology perhaps seem of little importance, and historians may be accused of splitting hairs, but it is surely important to chart the progress of a painter at a time when his style is evolving. If the same doubts and disputes surrounded works of the young Picasso, for example, whose dates had been lost, scholars would move heaven and earth to resolve them. Raphael's early works reveal a good deal, and in arranging them chronologically it is important neither to abandon preconceived ideas nor to dismiss the notion that, particularly where such a young artist is concerned, the evidence does not necessarily point to a linear progression. The three altarpieces to be discussed, each of which retains all or a part of its predella, are in the National Gallery, London, a *Christ on the Cross with Saints*, known as the *Mond Crucifixion* after its last owner; in the Vatican Museum, a *Coronation of the Virgin*, often called the *Oddi Altarpiece* after the family who commissioned it; and finally, in the Metropolitan Museum, New York, *Madonna Enthroned with Saints*, commonly known as the *Colonna Altarpiece* after

20 *Group of four standing soldiers*. About 1502. Metal-point on grey prepared paper. 21.3 x 22.3 cm. Oxford, Ashmolean Museum.

Three of the figures in this drawing, so full of life in its graceful lines, recur in a different grouping in one of Pinturicchio's frescoes in the Piccolomini Library in Siena, that of *Enea Silvio Piccolomini receiving the poet's crown from Frederick III*. It is difficult to tell whether Pinturicchio might have used sketches like this directly, or whether Raphael would have made a small, detailed cartoon, now lost, of the same type as the two that have survived.

the Roman family who owned it in the eighteenth century. All three are of a similar size, a little less than three meters high.

The *Mond Crucifixion* in the National Gallery, London, shows Christ on the Cross with St. Jerome and St. Mary Magdalen kneeling at either side. Behind the two saints and a little distance away are the Virgin and St. John; above them, two angels holding chalices collect the blood trickling from Christ's wounds. The altarpiece was painted for the Gavari family chapel in the Church of San Domenico at Città di Castello where Vasari saw it. Of all Raphael's works it is perhaps the most Peruginesque. Vasari writes, "If his name was not written upon it, no one would believe it to be by Raphael but rather by Pietro." The painting is indeed signed; it is Raphael's earliest known signature. The Peruginesque quality of its composition with its perfect symmetry is immediately apparent, and the positioning of the four saints precisely recalls that of the figures painted by Perugino, perhaps between 1502 and 1504, to flank a sculpted Crucifix in the Church of San Francesco al Monte at Perugia. The closeness of the figures to those of Perugino is striking. St. Jerome, in particular, is very like the St. Jerome of the *Tezi Altarpiece* (1500), painted by Perugino for the Church of Sant' Agostino at Perugia (Perugia, Galleria Nazionale). The curlicues formed in the sky by the angels' girdles recall the scrolls in the *Ascension* in the Church of San Pietro in Perugia (c.1496, Musée de Lyon), and the Magdalen's robe cascades over the ground

like those in the *Adoration of the Shepherds* in the Cambio at Perugia (c.1500). And even the body of the crucified Christ with its elongated proportions and delicate musculature has a prototype in an earlier Perugino, the triptych formerly in the Church of San Domenico at San Gimignano and today in the National Gallery at Washington, known as the *Galitzine Triptych* (c.1482); other examples were to be found in Umbria.

Compared with Perugino's paintings, however, Raphael's light is brighter, his outlines more clean, his colors more vividly contrasted. Perugino's motifs seem somehow out of their element. The angels who appear to be balanced in flight upon little clouds are also borrowed from Perugino, but Raphael endows them with a delicately supple quality which those of his master who occasionally appear to be bouncing feebly upon balloons, completely lack. The *Mond Crucifixion* manages to avoid being over-schematic, a charge which might be laid against it because of its symmetry, through the beautiful fan-like effect created by the dead Christ's arched arms. Against the blue of a porcelain sky are set the dancing shapes of the angels' robes, their wings and the curved flourishes of their girdles. The altar, still in place, in the Gavari Chapel in the Church of San Domenico in Città di Castello, bears the date 1503; this may be the date of the completion of the chapel with the *Crucifixion* dating from the previous year. 1502 would seem to fit better with the overall design and the vivid use of color in the London painting.

The *Coronation of the Virgin*, today in the Vatican Museum, commissioned by Alessandra di Simone degli Oddi for the Church of San Francesco in Perugia, was almost certainly painted during 1503 when the Oddi family were living in the city. The composition of the altarpiece with its upper and lower regions clearly separated but linked by the upward gaze of the Apostles, comes from Perugino, as do many of the physical types. The work probably derives from Pinturicchio its slightly squat figures and its brilliant and varied use of color. However, this composition discards the symmetry of earlier altarpieces. Raphael includes, placed at an oblique angle on a neutral, smooth ground, the massive quadrangular shape, simply ornamented, of the sarcophagus. Its front corner, one side of which is in shadow and the other bathed in light, forms a vertical line which as the eye travels upwards is on an axis with the figure of the Virgin. The composition is thus subtly off center, and the disciple on the right leans towards the Virgin, abandoning the position which he

21 *The Penitent St. Jerome.* About 1502? Pen and ink. 24.4. x 20.3 cm. Oxford, Ashmolean Museum.

A small picture by Raphael of this subject, now lost, was mentioned in the 16th century as being in a collection in Padua. The drawing, which lost its attribution to Raphael but was rehabilitated by Sylvia Ferino, shows an urban setting of such precision that it has been identified as a district of Perugia. The delicate face, tense and fervent, recalls the Florentine facial types seen in the works of Leonardo and Lorenzo di Credi. There is a related *Head of an Old Man,* very Leonardesque in handling, in Lille. The verso of the Oxford drawing shows landscape studies connected with the *Colonna Altarpiece.*

22 *Christ on the Cross with the Virgin, St. Jerome, St. Mary Magdalene and St. John* (the Mond Altarpiece). About 1502. Oil on panel. 280.7 × 165 cm. London, National Gallery.

Painted for the church of San Domenico in Città di Castello, this altarpiece passed through a number of collections, including that of Cardinal Fesch, before entering the National Gallery in 1924 as part of the Mond Collection. The composition and figure types are closer than anywhere else in Raphael's work to those of Perugino. The colors are very vivid and boldly contrasted.

should, according to Perugino's rules of symmetry, have held at the extreme right. This design gives the painting a new sense of freshness and life. The weighty conception of the figures is also new and striking. The young apostle standing to the right, for example, so Peruginesque at first glance in his stance and backward tilted head, is solidly three-dimensional. His feet are set firmly on the ground and the hem of his robe, its decorative neck-band, and his belt are portrayed with a convincing use of perspective. The light falling from above catches the arm and leg on the right and throws into shadow the other side of his body, the illuminated area set off by a dark robe, the silhouette in shadow sharply drawn against the clear bright sarcophagus; and the figure's own shadow, thrown across the ground and the sarcophagus, gives it a still greater air of solidity.

23 *Coronation of the Virgin (Oddi Altarpiece)*. 1503. Oil on panel, transferred to canvas. 267 × 163 cm. Vatican Museum.

Commissioned by Allessandra di Simone degli Oddi for her family chapel in the church of San Francesco in Perugia. The panel was removed by French troops in 1797 and put on show in the Louvre until 1815. It was during that time that the work was transferred onto canvas. At twenty, Raphael leaves his early models Perugino and Pinturicchio behind him to produce his first masterpiece, impressive both for its power and its coherence as a composition.

24 *Study of an angel for the Oddi Altarpiece*. 1503. Metal-point, heightened with white, on pale grey prepared paper. 18.9 x 12.6. cm. Oxford, Ashmolean Museum.

This study of a young man in contemporary dress playing a kind of small rebeck was used, with some variations, for one of the angels in the upper part of the Coronation of the Virgin, in the background on the right. The other half of the sheet, which was long ago cut up, is also at Oxford; it is a study for the angel playing a tambourine on the extreme left.

In contrast, the figure of St. John to the right of the middle section of the *Mond Crucifixion* is an almost flat silhouette, poorly integrated into its space; the difference in technique is so great that we can only conclude that the two paintings are of different dates. Moreover, the colors in the *Coronation* are very unlike those of the London painting which are rather crude. The *Oddi Altarpiece* is striking in its inclusion of unusual shades of orange, pale greens, slate greys, and in the prominence given to beige tones like that of the sarcophagus or that almost pale yellow of the robe worn by the saint on the left. Luminous touches of white are used for the tunics or the wings of some of the angels, the robes of some of the apostles; they have the effect of softening the other colors while emphasizing their beauty — an effect which Raphael was frequently to evoke.

For the first time in this painting Raphael achieves a sense of balance. With any other artist, this would be attributed to maturity but Raphael was only twenty years old. He displays a strong pictorial sense; the variety of facial types among the apostles, the psychological subtlety of their expressions, look forward to the works of his Roman period and the two small cherubs on either side of the sacred group are very close to those in the *Sistine Madonna*.

Finally, after the *Mond Crucifixion* and the *Oddi Altarpiece*, we come to the *Madonna Enthroned with Saints*, known as the *Colonna Altarpiece* (Metropolitan Museum, New York). Perhaps it should have been the first of the three to be discussed. Its place in the chronology of Raphael's works has been hotly disputed. Traditionally considered to be a painting begun in 1503 or 1504 before Raphael's departure for Florence and finished at the end of 1505 when he returned to Perugia, Konrad Oberhuber has recently dated it 1501–1502 immediately after the *Altarpiece of St. Nicholas*. Painted for the monastery Church of Sant' Antonio at Perugia, the altarpiece contains, like the already discussed polyptych of the *Ascension* by Perugino painted for the Church of San Pietro at Perugia, and today for the most part in the Museum at Lyon (1496), a lunette which is separated from the main painting but part of the whole *ensemble* depicting *God the Father* in the sky flanked by two angels.

The unusual square format of the central panel which gives the composition weight and stability and also its slightly compressed air was adopted by Giovanni Santi for comparable subjects — for example, the altarpieces of Gradara, Montefiorentino and Fano. And this suggests that the work was painted or at least conceived at an early date. The comparable *Madonnas Enthroned with Saints* by Perugino, those of 1493 in the Kunsthistorisches Museum in Vienna and in the Uffizi, that of 1494 in Sant' Agostino at Cremona or, closest of all, that painted in 1495–1496 for the Chapel of the Palazzo Publico at Perugia and today in the Vatican Museum, are all squarish in format but slightly higher and have a quite different appearance in that Perugino places the line of the horizon distinctly lower than it is in the *Colonna Altarpiece*. This method of raising the spectator's eye is characteristic of those altarpieces, already discussed, of Giovanni Santi who handles perspective clumsily, and especially of Pinturicchio who can in this way devote more space

to the elaborate description of the landscape which he loves. The links between the painting in the Metropolitan Museum and the works of Pinturicchio have been most convincingly analyzed by Oberhuber. He discusses the clothes worn by the Virgin and by Christ, the elaborate decoration of the central section with the lavish patterning of the cloth of honor and the steps to the throne, the glinting, stippled pattern of the Virgin's robe which evokes Vuillard, the brilliant use of color, all of which seem to be direct echoes of Pinturicchio's enchanting, highly finished art — for example, the central panel of his altarpiece depicting the *Madonna and Child with the Young St. John*, today in the Galleria Nazionale at Perugia and originally painted for the Church of Santa Maria dei Fossi in that town (1495). In comparing the two paintings, it is at once apparent that Raphael's use of decorative motifs has an impeccable strength derived from Perugino; it is tempered by the authority of line and architecture. Pinturicchio would not have been able to resist scattering one or two books or pieces of fruit here and there. The recent restoration work carried out on the altarpiece in New York has brought its non-Peruginesque side to the fore in revealing color contrasts of reds, greens and luminous yellows and sharp outlines. In removing the marbling on the white steps of the throne, a later "embellishment," it has uncovered the original purity of the forms, reminiscent of Piero della Francesca. The umbrella-like canopy which protects the principal group plays an essential part in the painting's spatial unity, lifting up the composition in the top section and emphasizing its perfectly square proportions.

As Oberhuber explains, the painting, like the *Altarpiece of St. Nicholas*, also reveals the influence of Luca Signorelli. Large and rather mannered, the animated figures of the two saints in the middle ground, deliberately contrasted in pose, are reminiscent — particularly in the case of St. Catherine in profile to the left — of many of Signorelli's female figures. His violent style, with dark colors harshly contrasted and strongly etched contours, is not unlike Raphael's at this time. The *Altarpiece of Saint Onofrio*, today in the Museo del Duomo at Perugia, had been in a chapel in the Cathedral since 1484 and must have been studied there by the young Raphael. Its forms are well constructed, bathed in a clear light, and the bishop saint reading a book (on the right) is close to the figure of St. Paul in the New York painting. The works of Signorelli also contain solid figures in heavily-draped robes comparable with the apostles in the *Colonna Altarpiece*; there is no need, as has so often been done, to invoke the influence of Fra Bartolomeo. The contained strength of St. Peter and St. Paul, their sad almost tragic air, is perhaps derived from Signorelli. The starkness of the shadows, particularly that of St. Paul thrown onto the steps, is closer to the work of Signorelli than to that of either Perugino or Pinturicchio.

All these elements suggest that the altarpiece was painted at a very early date, probably in 1502; it may even have been begun in the previous year. A drawing in the Ashmolean Museum at Oxford, published by Sylvia Ferino as by Raphael, contains pen studies for the right hand section of the landscape behind the figure of St. Paul. It would indeed seem to date from very early in his career and so strengthens Oberhuber's argument.

On examining the main section of the altarpiece, however, one cannot fail to be struck by its difference from the lunette; Konrad Oberhuber rightly comments on the latter's at once more developed and more Peruginesque style and concludes that it was painted after the main panel. The two angels, strong yet gentle, move easily in space, without the slightly jerky, constrained air of the two saints below. Could they have been painted before those of the *Coronation of the Virgin* in the Vatican, forceful and independent, yet striking the same pose and before those very delicate angels in the London *Crucifixion*? Surely the divergence in style points to a different dating. The *Coronation* and its predella, which will be discussed later, were probably painted at the end of 1504 or the beginning of 1505. The main composition, mostly painted in 1501–1502, was perhaps finished at this later date; certain sections, notably on the left hand side — part of the robes of St. Peter and St. Catherine and their hands in particular, perhaps also some part of St. Paul, the feet of the two saints and the figures of the two children, Christ and St. John — may have been left unfinished and completed then. A study of hands is revealing in this respect: the plump, supple hands of St. Catherine and the powerful ones of St. Peter, firmly grasping his book, are so very different from those, far less well-structured, of the *Mond Crucifixion* and those, finely described and variously shaped, but with less assurance, of the *Oddi Coronation* that they cannot have been painted at an earlier date. They are close to the strong, capable hands, well modeled in light and shade of the *Terranuova Madonna*, one of the first works of Raphael's Florentine period. There is an element of paradox in the conclusion that the lunette was painted at a later date than the main composition in that the former is commonly and rightly judged more Peruginesque and therefore, wrongly, less "advanced" and the later more highly developed, according to the often repeated theory that it reveals the influence of Fra Bartolomeo and so must date from Raphael's Florentine period. Nevertheless, the idea that the *Colonna Altarpiece* was painted at two separate times has often been advanced on different grounds, first by Cavalcaselle and later by Longhi; according to this view the work was begun in 1503, shortly before Raphael's departure for Florence, and finished in 1505.

A sense of unity is maintained in the altarpiece by the echoing yellows, greens and reds of the robes and drapery and the blue of the sky which has faded almost to white at the horizon but deepens at the top of the main painting to the Wedgwood shade of the lunette; this gradual deepening lightens the figures and gives life to the whole design, even if the half-length figure of God the Father at the top seems to have been conceived without due attention to the proportions of the Virgin's throne beneath Him — a fact which may suggest that the lunette was originally part of an independent design.

The predellas of the three altarpieces — the London *Crucifixion*, the Vatican *Coronation of the Virgin* and the New York *Madonna with Saints* — should be considered separately as a group. These small paintings, of different sizes but all on the same scale, presented a perfect opportunity for the painter to experiment, whether portraying his figures in the open air or in an architectural setting. The tiny, animated figures of the predellas participating in a narrative are quite different from the posed static figures on a far grander scale of their principal paintings; in these small works are revealed the beginnings of the "history-painter" which Raphael was to become.

There are only two surviving panels of the predella of the *Mond Altarpiece*; originally there were probably three. These are *St. Jerome reviving three youths* (Lisbon Museum), and *St. Jerome punishing the heretic Sabinianus*, (North Carolina Museum of Art, Raleigh). The bright colors of the clothes reflect those of the main painting. The light, graceful proportions of the figures who seem hardly to touch the ground also recall those of the sacred characters in the *Crucifixion* and the highly decorated section, identical in both small paintings with trees intricately silhouetted against a clear sky, echoes the graceful patterns made by the angels' girdles. All the evidence would seem to point to an early date for these small works, probably the end of 1502; the slightly timid, awkward stances of the figures, their marionette-like gestures, their appearance of being spread out in space. In the Lisbon panel, the figures on the left are very Peruginesque with their large shoulders and bizarre hairstyles and are reminiscent of the frescoes in the Cambio at Perugia. In the Raleigh panel the executioner with his sword who spins around with the same movement as the *Great St. Michael* of 1518, and the soldiers fleeing to the left are all twisted elongated shapes. And it is worth noting that the movement of the soldier with the shield, seen from behind, is very close although in reverse to that of the horseman at the extreme right of the *Departure for Basle*, painted by Pinturicchio for the Piccolomini Library at Siena after a drawing by Raphael.

These features confirm a dating of 1502 for the Mond altarpiece. The paintings at Lisbon and Raleigh thus become the earliest small-scale works securely attributed to Raphael; with their use of detail both fearsome and miraculous, the scenes contain that mixture of violence and innocent wonderment found in stories told by children, and puppet shows.

26/27 *Virgin Mary Enthroned with the Christ Child and the Infant St. John surrounded by four Saints; God the Father between two angels* (the Colonna Altarpiece). 1502, then 1504? Oil on panel. 169.5 × 169 cm. and 65 × 171.5 cm. New York, Metropolitan Museum.

The four saints around the central group are St. Peter and St. Paul with St. Catherine and St. Margaret (or St. Cecilia) behind them. The altarpiece was commissioned by the nuns of the Convent of Sant'Antonio in Perugia, who according to Vasari insisted that the Christ Child be shown dressed. The two main panels were sold by the nuns in 1677 and became part of the Colonna Collection in Rome. They were bequeathed to the Metropolitan Museum by Pierpont Morgan who acquired them in 1901.

34

28 *St. Jerome raising three corpses from the dead,* predella panel from the *Mond Altarpiece.* About 1502. Oil on panel. 23 × 41 cm. Lisbon, Museu de Arte Antiga.

29 *St. Jerome punishing the heretic Sabinianus,* predella panel from the *Mond Altarpiece.* About 1502. Oil on panel. 23 × 41 cm. Raleigh, North Carolina Museum of Art.

The panels in Lisbon and Raleigh representing miracles of St. Jerome are all that remains of the *Mond Crucifixion's* predella. The first consideration here was clearly narrative and picturesque detail. The luminous colors are close to those used in the main panel.

In the predella scenes of the *Oddi Altarpiece*, the only ones that are today displayed with their principal painting, the atmosphere seems very different although it is true that their subjects, the *Annunciation*, the *Adoration of the Shepherds and the Magi* and the *Presentation in the Temple*, lend themselves to calmer and more solemn settings. Raphael is strongly influenced here by the predella of Perugino's *Fano Altarpiece* — a work in which he played no part. He adopts, very successfully, Perugino's skillful method of arranging his figures in architectural settings opening onto bright landscapes. And yet he transforms Perugino's slightly jerky line into a softer more supple one in a well-considered three-dimensional design enhanced by a strong, clear handling of light. There may be a faint echo here, not in any vague atmosphere of tender religiosity but in the deftness of the placing of the figures in space, and the bright light in which they are bathed, of the predella of the triptych painted by Fra Angelico for the Chapel of St. Nicholas in the Church of San Domenico in Perugia.

The young Raphael must have studied the *Episodes from the Life of St. Nicholas* which it depicts, with their sharp-edged architecture and roundly-formed figures. The delicate half-light of the *Death of St. Nicholas* (Perugia, Galleria Nazionale) is particularly memorable, its combination of strength and deep feeling worthy of Piero della Francesca. The larger figures in the *Coronation of the Virgin* as well as those of its predella with the new freedom of their brightly-lit robes may be influenced by the simply and gracefully clothed figures of Fra Angelico's triptych — in particular, the Virgin at the center.

The figures of the Oddi predella are convincingly grouped within a carefully designed architectural space and have an extremely lifelike air of movement. In the *Adoration of the Shepherds and the Magi* the two horsemen seen from behind (on the left) demonstrate how far Raphael's draftmanship has progressed; firmly placed and yet supple they are captured in a moment of fine balance, one with his staff and the other his pike. The bright, gay colors interspersed like

those of the *Coronation* with softer shades and whites create an overall golden tonality. This is an ideal world, at once noble and sweet, but it contains a freshness, vivacity and even a sense of humor and fun that are lacking in Perugino's works, in which the solemn atmosphere can occasionally verge on the tedious. At the edge of this panel Raphael includes a horse that looks out at us with an almost human eye while elsewhere he adorns the head of one of the Magi's *entourage* with an improbably elaborate hat.

The three sections of the predella of the *Colonna Altarpiece* are now dispersed. The central panel of attenuated proportions depicting *The Road to Calvary* is in the National Gallery in London; it was originally flanked by the *Agony in the Garden* (Metropolitan Museum, New York) and the *Pietà* (Isabella Stewart Gardner Museum, Boston) — these last two being far narrower in width. The composition of the altarpiece's main panel probably accounts for these differences in format. The section in London repeats the pattern of elongated rectangles on the steps leading to the Virgin's throne while the smaller panels correspond with the upright figures of St. Peter and St. Paul.

The three paintings are striking, in comparison with the predellas of the *Crucifixion* and the *Coronation of the Virgin*, in the plainer, heavier single figures who occupy a greater part of their surface, and in the tighter more compact figure groups. The proportions of these figures are fairly short, often stocky. The slightly bland faces of the earlier predellas with their child-like, inscrutable air, smiling and sulky at the same time, give way to a more varied range of expression. Thus the face of the executioner who leans forward as he drags Christ along and turns towards Him and those of the Virgin and the other standing figures of the *Pietà* respond to the drama they are involved in. The handling of space is also original; the *Agony in the Garden* and the *Pietà* reveal a new and complex organization of landscape with small hills surrounding the foreground in which the sacred drama is enacted. The soft

30 *Annunciation,* (predella of the *Oddi Altarpiece*). Oil on panel, transferred to the same canvas. 1503. 27 × 50 cm. Vatican Museum.

The predella of the *Oddi Altarpiece* suffered the same fate as the main composition. The scenes are derived from those Perugino painted on the predella of the altarpiece of the church at Fano. But the integration of the figures in space and the delicate rhythms that link them together point to an altogether more serious approach.

31 *Study for The Adoration of the Magi from the Oddi Altarpiece.* 1503? Pen and ink. 27.2 × 42 cm. Stockholm, National Gallery.

This careful, delicate drawing belonged to the French painter Jacques Stella in the 17th century and was part of the Crozat and Tessin collections in the 18th. It differs only in details from the final composition.

32 *The Adoration of the Magi* (predella of the *Oddi Altarpiece*). Oil on panel, transferred to the same canvas. 1503. 27 × 50 cm. Vatican Museum.

draperies, unlike those of the Mond and Oddi predellas, have many intricate folds treated in a more linear fashion. The trees are very delicately drawn, with feathery foliage outlined against a bright sky — quite unlike the earlier schematic shapes. All these features make it impossible to date the Colonna predella in 1502; it must have been painted at the end of 1504 or in 1505. In the case of these small paintings, the chronological development can only be the one already outlined; the early, frail, grasshopper-like figures gradually find an equilibrium, acquire a three-dimensional structure.

The study, in relation to the work of the young Raphael, of Umbrian drawings of the last years of the *Quattrocento* and the early 1500's, brilliantly undertaken by Sylvia Ferino, will perhaps enable us to approach the problem of the painter's development from a new angle. It clearly reveals the young artist's fundamental debt to Perugino; his earliest sketches for the *Altarpiece of St. Nicholas* are very close in spirit to those of his master while revealing characteristics which are already distinctly his own. There is about them a very subtle, delicate quality, with no heavy emphasis of line which makes the forms appear to tremble in the light. The pen strokes, which are repeated until Raphael achieves the exact effect he desires, seem almost to vibrate. And as we look at the drawings, we can see Perugino's linear, schematic approach gradually being abandoned; his graceful network of lines, which give only the feeblest sense of a third dimension, are transformed in Raphael's desire to convey an impression of volume, of solid, clearly lit forms well integrated in space. In 1500 or thereabouts, it seems that artists such as Lo Spagna and Viti discovered new possibilities, a new freedom in drawing from the life in which the animated forms are

33 *Study for The Presentation in the Temple* from the *Oddi Altarpiece.* 1503. Pen and ink. 20 × 20 cm. Oxford, Ashmolean Museum.

The figures are arranged systematically around the ballustraded altar. The rapid, decisive strokes of the pen here tend to disrupt the simple form of the draperies, making them move with the figures and come alive in the light. The rhythm of the figures looks forward to that of the central group in the *Sposalizio* which was painted the following year.

34 *The Presentation in the Temple* (predella of the *Oddi Altarpiece*). Oil on panel, transferred to the same canvas. 1503. 27 × 50 cm. Vatican Museum.

enveloped in light. Raphael immediately seized upon these new developments with an astonishingly acute grasp of spatial coherence. His figures are never purely graphic; far from being mere silhouettes, they confidently occupy their own space. This marked, in fact, the beginning of modern techniques of drawing.

The sheer life and vivacity which the figures in Raphael's paintings communicate has its origins in the drawings from life which preceded them. Several of those for the *Coronation of the Virgin* in the *Oddi Altarpiece* have been preserved; they show young studio models posing as angels or studies of heads for the Apostles. And this painstaking copying from life ensures that each angel-musician or Apostle has its own particular stance, firmness of conception and solidity of form. Such constant study of human models, a practice followed by Raphael throughout his career, was the very foundation of his art.

Raphael's activity as a portraitist was always to play an important part in his life. It is, however, one of the areas where questions of attribution and dating are extremely difficult. It is particularly necessary to establish how — in what manner and circumstances — he began to paint portraits; but in the case of his Umbrian works this is especially problematic. Let us take as examples two bust-length portraits, both showing middle-aged men wearing hats, set against a landscape background.

The *Portrait of a Man* in the collection of the Prince of Liechtenstein at Vaduz, which is relatively unknown, may be the earliest of Raphael's surviving portraits. It has a slightly stiff, constrained air, lacking the sense of amplitude and the vigor of later works. A landscape occupies a large part of the background, rather as it does in the *Norton Simon Madonna* where there is the same contrast between a somber foreground and a very bright background. The facial type is strikingly close to that of the most elderly figures in the *Marriage of the Virgin* in Milan. But it is still more interesting to notice the close resemblance between this rather stiff subject and certain portraits by Memlinc, who died in 1494, where three-quarter length subjects are shown in front of a landscape and a bright sky. The well-structured, slender face, the narrow jaw, the body's rather cramped appearance, evoke such paintings as the *Man Holding a Medal* at Antwerp, often identified as an Italian, or the *Young Man*

35   *Road to Calvary.* 1504? Oil on panel. 24 × 85 cm. London, National Gallery.

36 *The Agony in the Garden.* 1504? Oil on panel. 24 × 29 cm. New York, Metropolitan Museum.

37 *Pietà.* 1504? Oil on panel. 24 × 28 cm. Boston, Isabella Stewart Gardner Museum.

These three panels from the predella of the *Colonna Altarpiece* have had a different history from the two main sections. The nuns sold them, a short while before the latter works, to Queen Christina of Sweden. They were subsequently in the Orléans collection in Paris and were split up when this was sold in London in 1792. The predella also featured two small panels showing St. Anthony and another saint which are now in the Dulwich College Picture Gallery in London.

38 *Portrait of a Man.* 1503 or 1504. Oil on panel. 55 × 45 cm. Vaduz, collection of the Prince of Liechtenstein.

The attribution of this work to Raphael has not always been accepted, and some have suggested that it might be the work of Francesco Francia. Nevertheless, it seems likely that it is in fact Raphael's earliest surviving portrait, dating from about the same time as the *Virgin and Child with a Book* in the Norton Simon Museum, the landscape element of which is particularly close. The positioning of the group, the facial type and the expression prompt comparison with Netherlandish portraits of the 15th century, notably those of Memlinc.

Its closeness in style to the *Norton Simon Madonna* and the *Marriage of the Virgin* suggests a date of late 1503 or perhaps 1504.

Another *Portrait of a Man*, in the Galleria Borghese in Rome, more confined within its picture space but less formal in appearance, appears more advanced in technique and may have been painted towards the middle of 1504, shortly before Raphael's departure for Florence. It is one of his most Peruginesque works, close in spirit to his master's portrait of *Francesco delle Opere* of 1494 in the Uffizi. The head is placed very slightly off center to the right, and neck, jaw and chin are finely modeled. Perugino possesses a similar delicacy of touch, but his work is less energetic and lacking in

40   *Portrait of a Young Boy holding an Apple.* About 1504. 47 × 35 cm. Florence, Uffizi.

Possibly a portrait of Francesco Maria della Rovere, adopted son of Duke Guidobaldo da Montefeltro, then age fourteen. Note the child-like proportions of the figure, the rather large head and short arms. Its prominent placing of the arm in front and the emphasis on clothes and textures anticipate all Raphael's subsequent portraiture.

39   *Portrait of a Man.* About 1504. Oil on panel. 45 × 31 cm. Rome, Galleria Borghese.

A picture sometimes attributed to Perugino, but the audacity of the positioning in relation to the frame and the powerful structure of the face seem to point to Raphael, about the time of the *Sposalizio*.

at Prayer, perhaps Benedetto Portinari, in the Uffizi dated 1487 which originally hung in the Hospital of Santa Maria Nuova in Florence and was certainly there soon after it was painted, or another painting which had been in Florence for a long time, a *Young Man* in the Corsini collection. The format of the painting places it firmly in the Umbrian tradition of portraits by Perugino, Pinturicchio or Lo Spagna but the intelligence, the subtlety of feeling expressed in the slightly sunken face must owe something to the work of Memlinc or other northern painters as well as Perugino.

volume. Raphael thrusts his subject almost abruptly upon us, without including so much as an arm or a shoulder to create a sense of distance; he confidently stamps the plain, somber surface of his painting with the strikingly simple garment which takes up the whole bottom half of the panel, and the stark outline, against a bright sky, of the asymmetrical hat. The effect is uncomplicated, yet the whole personality of the man is vividly present.

The *Portrait of a Young Man* in the Uffizi may well have been painted, like that in the Galleria Borghese, just before Raphael left for Florence. On a smaller scale than those previously discussed, yet at the same time more ambitious, its subject is almost certainly someone of high rank — perhaps Francesco Maria delle Rovere, at the age of 14 or thereabouts. His expression like those of the preceding portraits at once reserved and firm recalls, as does the precise treatment of the rich fur and the sumptuous materials of his dress, the great Flemish portraitists but this work is quite original in its pose. The placing of the hands in the foreground, and especially the forward tilt of the shoulder and the position of the left arm, were to become a constant feature of Raphael's portraits. This particular painting's slightly cramped, compressed air asks only to be opened out on a larger scale.

In studying Raphael's drawings, we learn still more about his methods as a portraitist. He reveals an ability to seize upon the essential characteristics of a face and to achieve a synthesis, to create in a portrait a recognizable type. He conveys at one and the same time his subject's most individual, and most universal, traits. Several of his earliest surviving drawings reveal a natural inclination towards portraiture. A charcoal drawing in the British Museum, which has on the reverse anatomical studies in pen, may possibly be his first self-portrait, at the age of about fifteen, in around 1498; the solemn, still childish face is drawn with firmness and confidence, a delicacy of line and a sure grasp of volume which recall such Florentine artists as Ghirlandaio or Lorenzo di Credi. Another well-known sheet in the Ashmolean Museum at Oxford shows the face of a young boy who can hardly be more than sixteen years old and might, judging by his narrow shoulders, be still younger. This is how we should like to imagine the young Raphael at the time of his apprenticeship to Perugino, and indeed the drawing is generally considered to be a self-portrait; 1504, however, the date usually proposed on the basis of its confident execution and firmness of line, would make the sitter far too young to be Raphael himself. This is undoubtedly a portrait, Florentine in its delicacy; the head is slightly raised and the expression pensive, slightly distant yet full of charm. It is a perfect image of adolescence for those who believe it to be a happy time in which drawing from nature is joined with the desire to express ideal beauty. Another *Head of a Young Boy* in the Museum at Lille, very probably of an earlier date since it is close in style to the preparatory drawings for the *Oddi Altarpiece* of 1503, is strikingly different in character — more psychologically concise, with the charm of a porcelain doll but displaying a remarkably sure

41   *Head of a young boy (Self-portrait?).* About 1499-1500? Black chalk. 31.4 x 19 cm. London, British Museum.

This may be one of the earliest drawings we have from Raphael's hand, showing us the features of the young artist himself. The direct gaze and the serious, attentive expression would seem to confirm that this is a self-portrait. The anatomical studies on the verso may be a little later in date.

grasp of volume. It appears, although obviously drawn from a model, less like a portrait than the Oxford drawing, rather a figure study for a large painting.

Raphael reached the highest point of his "Umbrian" period in a painting which is at the same time a summation of all that had gone before and a new point of departure, one of the most impor-

42 *Head of a young boy.* About 1503. Black chalk heightened with white, on prepared paper. 21.1 × 18.6 cm. Lille, Musée des Beaux-Arts.

At once solid and graceful, this head drawn from life is very close to those of the angels in the upper part of the *Oddi Altarpiece,* especially the one on the left playing a tambourine, and would seem to have been executed at about the same time.

tant statements of his work as a whole: the *Marriage of the Virgin,* known simply in Italy and elsewhere as *Il Sposalizio.* Today in the Brera at Milan, it was painted in 1504 for a church in Città di Castello. The panel, rather smaller than the four altarpieces that preceded it, was made for the Albizzini chapel dedicated to St. Joseph in the church of San Francesco. The tall symmetrical composition shows the High Priest uniting the Virgin Mary and Joseph in a large paved area in front of a temple. Behind Mary are five companions and behind Joseph the five suitors whose rods have not flowered. Two paintings by Perugino make use of a similar setting and are always cited as prototypes: the fresco of the *Presentation of the Keys to Saint Peter* in the Sistine Chapel in the Vatican (1482), and *The Marriage of the Virgin* (Museum at Caen) which Perugino had just completed in 1504 for Perugia Cathedral. There can be no doubt that Raphael was influenced by Perugino while at the same time intending to rival him. Perugino arranges his figures as seen from the side in a simple frieze-like composition with no sense

of depth. The heavy symmetry of the temple's architecture is echoed in the grouping of the figures; the two seen from the back at the left and at the right like a decorative motif frame a static and symmetrical central group with the High Priest in the middle, standing upright with his legs apart, motionless as a stele. In Raphael's painting, however, the Virgin and her companions, Joseph and the suitors, form two clearly separated groups in an empty foreground, linked by the High Priest who joins the hands of the betrothed couple.

This empty space in the forefront of the painting which sets apart the five principal figures arranged in a semicircle is at first glance of no apparent significance; but in fact it presages Raphael's later more ambitious compositions. It also leads us into the skillful perspective of the tiled pavement which sweeps the eye towards the horizon. The High Priest is placed exactly in the center as he is in Perugino's painting. The conical shape of his heavy dark robe, extended by his pointed hat, and placed in perspective by the elliptical line of its hem is geometrically located within a triangle formed by the receding lines of the pavement which has the effect of firmly situating it in this space. However, the figure's stance tilts the chest and the head to the right and forward like the pendulum of a metronome and brings a welcome sense of human disorder to these geometric forms.

Many features of the painting recall Perugino. Several of the facial types and the fine lines which follow the edges of the robes and culminate in the elaborate embroidery on the Priest's dress, form the axis of the composition. The Virgin's body is gently arched backwards while her neck and head bend forwards, forming a soft S-shape; her delicate and tender silhouette, her fine features and tightly-closed lips, her strong column-like neck, gently caressed by her hair and veil, already belong to the world of the Madonnas of Raphael's Florentine period while her plump companions are still sisters of Perugino's saints. The feet of the principal figures rest lightly on the ground, those of the Virgin and her husband appearing to perform a courtly dance, as a gentle spring breeze seems to blow through the whole composition, balancing the forms to the right and left. But such sweetness should not blind us to the impeccable ordering of space and the placing of the figures within it. The young suitor in front of Joseph who breaks his rod on his knee is perhaps Raphael's most ambitious attempt to date to represent the human figure in the third dimension. The culmination of many drawings of models in closely fitting hose, the weight of his body, firmly balanced on one foot, is given three-dimensionality by

43 *Head of a young boy.* About 1504. Black chalk heightened with white. 38.1 × 26.1 cm. Oxford, Ashmolean Museum.

The drawing bears an old inscription (17th-century ?) identifying it as a self-portrait. This explains its extraordinary celebrity. It shows a boy of thirteen or fourteen years; however, if we accept the generally agreed and reasonable dating to the end of the "Umbrian period," this identification becomes impossible.

44/45 *The Marriage of the Virgin,* called *The Sposalizio.* 1504. Oil on panel. 170 x 117 cm. Milan, Pinacoteca di Brera.

Signed and dated on the central temple, the picture was commissioned by the Albizzini family for the chapel of San Giuseppe in the Church of San Francesco in Città di Castello, where it remained until 1798. After passing through several collections, it came a short time later to the Accademia di Belle Arti in Milan. It is the first perfect realization of the harmonious world of Raphael's paintings, in which figures breathe easily, fully integrated in space and related one to another in the most dignified manner.

Raphael's skillful draftsmanship. He is firmly rooted to the ground by a strong shadow thrown diagonally and, set apart from the principal group, seems to apply himself to his task with the enthusiasm of a young cyclist.

But if the painting possesses a unique character among the world's greatest works of art it is due to the circular temple which dominates the composition both physically and spiritually. Raphael, drawing on the experience gained from the Oddi predella, created in *Il Sposalizio* the most exquisite balance between human and architectural forms. The graceful arch formed by the bodies of Mary and Joseph as they bend towards one another echoes the shape of the panel itself as well as that of the cupola of the *tempietto*. A reminder of Piero della Francesca, but a more tender and ethereal Piero, with softer colors! *Il Sposalizio* recalls the most famous of those architectural views usually known as "ideal cities," showing an imaginary town of antiquity in a symmetrical composition with a circular temple in the center. At one time attributed to Piero, this was by the end of the 16th century in the Ducal Palace at Urbino (and is still there today); there is no reason to think that it was not already there at the beginning of the century when the young Raphael could have seen it. In the Milan painting the ideal city, now inhabited, is not simply a magnificent theatrical backdrop.

"Raphael Urbinas:" the prominence given to the signature on the temple in the center of *Il Sposalizio* emphasizes the importance of Raphael's native town. He always included Urbino in his signature, so stressing the significance of the links forged during his formative years with the town itself and with the court of the Montefeltro family which were never to be broken. This signature also reflects his desire to keep alive the reputation of his father's workshop. It is rash to speculate about the extent to which the young

Raphael was influenced by the paintings he could have seen in Urbino; however, it should not be forgotten that in the town's churches he could probably have studied two of Piero della Francesca's greatest religious works, the *Flagellation* and the *Brera Altarpiece*, and that in the Ducal Palace were Piero's double-sided portraits of *Federigo da Montefeltro* and *Battista Sforza* (Uffizi) as well as the series of *Illustrious Men* painted by Joos van Gent and Berruguete (Ducal Palace and the Louvre). This may have been the source of his fondness on the one hand for sharply defined, well-lit forms and on the other for strongly characterized figures and for that precise description of texture found in Flemish paintings. The court of the Montefeltro appears to have been one of the most pleasant, untroubled and cultivated in Italy at that time; Baldassare Castiglione and Cardinal Bibbiena were among the courtiers.

Guidobaldo da Montefeltro who in 1482 at the age of 10 had succeeded his father Federigo and married Elisabetta Gonzaga, adopted as his heir Francesco Maria delle Rovere, the son of his sister Giovanna and Giovanni delle Rovere. In 1508 on Guidobaldo's death Francesco became Duke at the age of 18. There are portraits in the Uffizi, bust-length and full face, of Guidobaldo and Elisabetta. Their attribution has been much discussed but they may be early works by Raphael painted about 1502, and consequently provide the clearest evidence of his connection with the Duke and Duchess well before his departure from Urbino. It is possible that such highly finished small works as the diptych of the *Dream of a Knight*, divided between London and Chantilly, and the small *St. George* and *St. Michael* in the Louvre, were painted for the Duke at a later date. It was probably in this highly sophisticated and harmonious atmosphere that Raphael developed that "natural inclination towards happiness" noted by Focillon. Throughout his career he was to remain a court painter and a contented man.

II.   Florence 1504–1508: Perfection of technique

In September 1504 Raphael obtained a letter of recommendation from Giovanna, sister of Duke Guidobaldo, whose husband Giovanni delle Rovere, brother of Pope Julius II, was at that time Prefect of Rome. It was addressed to Pier Antonio Soderini, *Gonfaloniere* of Florence. It is usually thought that Raphael left for Tuscany in the autumn of 1504 but it is possible that commissions in Umbria and in the Marches delayed his departure. The details of the young Raphael's travels are little known but he certainly traveled more frequently than has usually been supposed.

Florence was a town in which power was all important; even the artists were fiercely competitive. Florentine art with its courtly, decorative and costumed narratives, was the complete opposite of Umbria's sweet, unworldly and static art. In Florence every possible variation on the representation of the human figure was to be found — the body in action, the relationship of one body with others grouped together or in violent conflict, as well as the characterization of faces. In this exploration, anatomy provided a language. Raphael had much to look at and much work to do. His art developed a new sense of freedom. The drawings of this period show that he studied anatomy with the intention of becoming as skilled as any Florentine in the depiction of movement. Even if there is an element of myth in the idea of a new "virility" in Raphael's art as a consequence of his stay in Florence — since he had almost certainly been there before — it cannot be denied that he developed new powers of artistic expression. Florence was the city of *disegno*, of draftsmanship. Raphael's drawings make use of every possible technique: silverpoint, charcoal and pen as well as sanguine (red chalk) and wash. On some sheets side by side or one on top of the other are lines drawn in more than one of these; and, a very Florentine characteristic, each technique was employed for a specific task, expressing its own innate character from the most impetuous or relaxed to the most precise. In this respect it was Raphael's study of the drawings of Fra Bartolomeo and Michelangelo which was influential. More important still was his contact with Leonardo da Vinci; the two painters undoubtedly knew each other in Florence and may even have been friends. Certain of Raphael's Florentine drawings reveal his fascination with Leonardo: a beautiful pen drawing at Windsor is a copy of his *Leda*, now lost and known only through copies; a sketch tucked into the corner of a sheet of studies at Oxford shows the crush of horsemen in the *Battle of Anghiari*. Indeed, Raphael's admiration for Leonardo is a constant theme of his work right up until his death.

The altarpiece of the *Virgin and Child with St. John the Baptist and St. Nicholas* (National Gallery in London), was commissioned by Bernardo Ansidei for his family chapel, dedicated to St. Nicholas, in the Church of San Fiorenzo dei Serviti in Perugia. Hence its usual name, the *Ansidei Altarpiece*. The date 1505 can just be made out on the edge of the Madonna's cloak. It is difficult to know whether it was painted in Florence and finished in Perugia or entirely painted in Perugia. In any case one cannot fail to be struck by its Umbrian character; the large panel has the same overall design inspired by Perugino as the *Altarpiece of St. Nicholas* with a monumental arch echoing the semi-circular top of the panel, opening on to a landscape, and also the arrangement of the holy figures used by Perugino in his Madonnas with Saints and previously employed by Raphael in the *Colonna Altarpiece*. In the *Ansidei Altarpiece* the simplicity of the composition is particularly effective. The arch of the *Altarpiece of St. Nicholas* has been stripped of its detail and the Virgin's throne in the *Colonna Altarpiece*, an amalgam of different architectural styles, has become a simpler, more credible structure. It seems that at this moment, the beginning of his Florentine period when he had mastered new techniques, Raphael took stock and for the last time painted a work in the Umbrian manner. It can be thought of as a farewell to Perugino. The comparison with the *Colonna Altarpiece* is instructive and emphasizes the verticality of the composition of the London painting; the surface is divided into three equal, clearly differentiated parts, the central band including the pedestal, throne and dais. The figure of St. Nicholas (on the right) once again suggests Signorelli in its modeling in light and shadow; however, the distribution of the whites and the quiet authority of his pose make one think above all of Piero della Francesca. The use of half-tones and of reflections in the hands which hold the book and in the face reveal for the first time Raphael's study of Leonardo. St. John the Baptist (on the left) looks at his magnificent crystal cross and at the same time points at Christ, so associating the Cross with the Child. There is nothing vague in his upward gaze, and the three other sacred figures are similarly preoccupied — St. Nicholas in reading, the Virgin in pointing out the text of the book to the Child whom she seems lightly to push towards it and the Child in looking at the book. St. John's apparent debt to Perugino is deceptive; the foreshortening of the face, the knowledge of anatomy

47 *The Virgin and Child On the Throne and St. Nicholas of Tolentino.* About 1503. Pen and ink, with touches of black chalk and metal-point. 23.3 × 15.4 cm. Frankfurt, Städelsches Institut.

Study for an altarpiece, which was probably never realized, of the same type as the *Ansidei Madonna.* It seems to date from just before the London picture. Showing remarkable assurance and solidity, a real sense of weight about the figures, a vigorous and authoritative touch, this drawing seems to invite comparison with the Louvre's *Virgin and Child with St. Sebastian and St. Roch.* The latter is less generous, starker in its broken rhythms, and must date from a year or two earlier.

46 *Leda and the Swan,* after Leonardo da Vinci. About 1505? Pen and ink with touches of black chalk. 30.8 × 19.2 cm. Windsor, Royal Library.

It is difficult to say with certainty whether this eloquent testimony to Raphael's admiration for Leonardo was drawn from a lost cartoon for the *Leda* which was once in Florence, or from a lost drawing. Unlike extant drawings by Leonardo and copies of the painting executed later and now missing, which show Leda with lowered eyes, the young woman in this drawing is looking at the spectator.

48 *Virgin and Child Enthroned with St. John the Baptist and St. Nicholas of Bari* (the Ansidei Madonna). 1505. 209 × 148 cm. London, National Gallery.

Commissioned for the Ansidei Chapel in the church of San Fiorenzo dei Serviti in Perugia, this picture was in English collections in the 18th and 19th centuries and entered the National Gallery in 1885. It represents a perfect assimilation of the Umbrian style of Perugino and Signorelli. The simple, vigorous design of the architecture, the sense of three-dimensional form and the clear light make it quite different from the more decorative *Colonna Altarpiece.*

49 *The Preaching of St. John the Baptist.* 1505. Oil on panel. 26 × 53.3 cm. (London, National Gallery).

The only extant section of the predella of the *Ansidei Madonna.* The other two, according to old descriptions, showed *The Marriage of the Virgin* and *A Miracle of St. Nicholas of Bari.* The groups of figures, each one precisely characterized, are carefully organized. The most complex, that opposite the preacher, is a marvel of clarity, coherence and the elegant interplay of lines.

50 *Christ's blessing.* About 1505. Oil on panel. 30 × 25 cm. Brescia, Pinacoteca Tosio Martinengo.

Although the delicacy of the forms still recalls the Umbrian period, the firmly articulated draftsmanship and careful modeling are Leonardesque, which suggests a dating for the work — close to the *Ansidei Madonna* — of around the beginning of the Florentine period.

51 *Sheet of studies for the Trinity in San Severo, Perugia.* 1505. Metal-point on prepared paper. 21.1 x 27.4 cm. Oxford, Ashmolean Museum.

Detailed studies of heads and hands, which are sometimes difficult to identify because of the poor condition of the fresco. The drawing is something of a homage to Leonardo da Vinci; the profile of an old man on the left is strongly Leonardesque, and the sketch in the upper left corner is based on the central group of figures in *The Battle of Anghiari.*

evident in the well-muscled arms and legs, bear witness to a new spirit in Raphael's art.

Only one of the predella panels of the *Ansidei Altarpiece* survives. This predella panel was purchased recently by the National Gallery. It is on display in the National Gallery, London, with the principal painting. The *Preaching of St. John the Baptist* contains figures which display an ease in their grouping and in the complexity of their poses and variety of type not previously encountered in works of this kind. This can be taken perhaps as evidence of a later dating than the predella of the *Colonna Altarpiece* — end of 1505 or 1506.

Also on a small scale is the *Christ Blessing* (Tosio-Martinengo Museum at Brescia), which probably dates from around 1505 as does the *Ansidei Altarpiece*. The freedom of handling and the supple, rounded forms of the nude figures are similar to those in the London

painting, in the fresco at Perugia and the *Terranuova Madonna* which will be considered shortly. It is also possible to detect in the air of melancholy sweetness and the slightly bitter expression of the face something of Memling's *Christ as Man of Sorrows*.

The fresco, unfortunately poorly preserved and in part destroyed, from the church of the monastery of San Severo at Perugia, provides clear proof that Raphael was in the town during his Florentine period. The *Glorification of the Holy Trinity*, painted inside a pointed arch, shows in the center, Christ Blessing, with directly above Him on the axis of the composition, the dove of the Holy Spirit and God the Father flanked by two angels. On a slightly lower level are six saints, arranged in two groups which form a semi-circle.

This is a work of the greatest importance, the earliest fresco by Raphael to survive, and since it is in Perugia the spectator is im-

52 *The Holy Trinity*. 1505. Fresco. Base 389 cm. Perugia, church of the monastery of San Severo.

The figures of God the Father and the angel on the right have completely disappeared. The saints on either side of Christ are identified by inscriptions. The six saints in the lower section were painted by Perugino in 1521. The Raphael fresco has usually been dated to 1507-8 but there is actually no reason to doubt the date that appears on the work itself, that of 1505. This was the time at which Raphael was most under the influence of Fra Bartolomeo.

mediately struck by the differences between it and Perugino's murals. After the death of his pupil Perugino completed the work in 1521 by the addition in the lower section of six rather solemn saints, standing three on either side of the central niche. Unfortunately, Perugino did not understand the perspective effect intended by Raphael just below the feet of the seated saints. Perugino places his six figures in front of a low wall with perspective lines suggesting a new horizon lower down so that the simple monumental effect intended by Raphael is diminished and distorted.

The date of the San Severo fresco has been much discussed. Raphael's name and the date 1505 inscribed at the bottom. It has usually been felt that this date does not fit in with the evolution of the artist's style, and instead a date of 1507-08 has been proposed, just before Raphael left for Rome. Konrad Oberhuber has rightly challenged this view and argued that the contemporary inscription containing the date is authentic. In fact, the elongated figure canon, the "olive-shaped" heads like the loose-fitting and voluminous draperies, relate the fresco to the *Ansidei Altarpiece* and the *Christ Blessing*. It seems that it is surely paradoxical that it is in Perugia and that it is one of the first truly Florentine works by Raphael who had applied himself conscientiously to the study of Fra Bartolomeo and of Leonardo. The influence of Leonardo can be detected in certain details, the almost feminine head of the left hand angel, for ex-

ample, and the sinuous curve of its pose. Raphael's study of Fra Bartolomeo is essential to the evolution of this work and has often been noted. The San Severo fresco recalls the upper part of the great *Last Judgement* fresco, painted shortly before at the Monastery of San Marco, in the disposition of the groups of saints, especially the two heavily-draped figures at the sides. The comparison of the Perugia fresco and this one, with its full gracefully folded draperies and pale colors, is most telling.

From Fra Bartolomeo the young Raphael received confirmation of his generous, supple sense of volume; from Leonardo he learned the construction of coherent figure groups and the means of linking them — and especially, a sense of freedom and mastery in draftsmanship, an ability to convey movement coupled with the subtle expression of emotion. The impact of Raphael's familiarity with Leonardo's work and perhaps with the master himself can be discerned in one work after another in the art of his Florentine period.

Two small gems of courtly art, formerly comprising a diptych which for many years was in the Borghese collection in Rome, the *Dream of a Knight* and *The Three Graces*, are today separated; the former is in the National Gallery in London, the latter in the Musée Condé at Chantilly. The iconography of the London panel, long debated, has been identified by Panofsky and André Chastel. It almost certainly represents the *Dream of Scipio Africanus*. The literary source for this subject is to be found in a classical poem by Silius Italicus which was well-known in sixteenth-century Florence. Scipio, like Hercules at the Crossroads, had to choose between the hard road of virtue and the easier, more seductive path of love and pleasure. The *Three Graces* on the facing panel who carry the golden apples of the garden of the Hesperides, symbols of immortality, represent the reward of the virtuous man. The recipient of this "exhortatio ad juvenem" could have been the young Scipio di Tommaso Borghese, born in 1493. The laurel beneath which Scipio sleeps and the golden balls held by the Graces make one think also of the Medici family, perhaps Giuliano, in exile at the court of Urbino.

53 *The Dream of a Knight*. 1504 or 1505. Oil on panel. 17 × 17 cm. London, National Gallery.

54 *The Three Graces*. 1504 or 1505. Oil on panel. 17 × 17 cm. Chantilly, Musée Condé.

These two pictures of the same, perfectly square dimensions form a pair, perhaps a diptych. They were still together in 1650 when they were recorded in the Borghese collection in Rome. The London panel shows the young man who must choose between the difficult path of virtue and the easier path of love and pleasure. The Chantilly panel seems to represent immortality, the virtuous man's reward. The National Gallery in London also has the small preparatory cartoon for *The Dream of a Knight*.

If the ornate character of the *Dream of a Knight* still contains reminiscences of Pinturicchio and Perugino, the faces, in both wings of the diptych, with their variations on the theme of lowered eyes and their half-smiling sweetness, already show the influence of Leonardo. The crowded, dense composition of the *Dream of a Knight*, its bright colors, the profusion of pretty fairy-tale details as if to delight a child, make us think of illuminated miniatures; the emblematic character of the two small panels, embossed and precious, symmetrically arranged, recalls the work of contemporary medalists. In fact, medals from this period do survive, showing as Raphael did the famous antique group of the *Three Graces*, known in many versions — notably, a Hellenistic one in a fragmentary state in the Piccolomini Library in Siena which Raphael certainly saw when he made his drawings for Pinturicchio, for he made a

sketch of it, a copy of which is in the Accademia at Venice. The original of this drawing certainly served for the layout of the composition of the Chantilly painting which is in one sense a restoration of the Antique; our first sight of a Raphael who was at the same time painter and archaeologist. The balance of the curves which link the three figures who echo one another gives the almost androgynous, curious small bodies of the Graces, robust and firm, scarcely out of infancy, an air of moving gently from side to side, like the quiet rhythm of a pendulum.

The two paintings were long considered Raphael's earliest works, painted about 1500-01. Now, however, they are usually placed in 1504 or 1505 at the very beginning of the Florentine period. There is a striking closeness in style between these two works and the predella of the *Colonna Altarpiece*, especially the New York and

56 *St. George and the Dragon.* 1505. Pen and ink with touches of black chalk. 26.6 × 26.7 cm. Florence, Uffizi.

Cartoon for the *Small St. George* in the Louvre, pricked through for transfer. The drawing is at the same time precise and full of impetuous energy.

55 *St. Michael trampling on the Devil,* also known as *The Small St. Michael.* 1505. Oil on panel. 29.5 × 25.5 cm. Paris, Musée du Louvre.

Traditionally paired with the *St. George,* the picture shares the same provenance, having been in the collections of Mazarin and Louis XIV. The identical size of the two works, their similar subjects and the precious, courtly manner in which they are both painted suggests that they were executed for the same patron, perhaps Guidobaldo da Montefeltro. The work is known as *The Small St. Michael* to distinguish it from the large picture of the same subject painted by Raphael in 1518 and now also in the Louvre.

57 *St. George and the Dragon,* also known as *The Small St. George.* 1505. Oil on panel. 29.5 × 25.5 cm. Paris, Musée du Louvre.

The pendant to the *Small St. Michael,* this work is sometimes confused with the picture of a similar size now in Washington. The rearing white horse relates to classical prototypes such as the horses on the Quirinal in Rome, but seems to be based on lively pen-and-ink studies made somewhat earlier, at the time of the Piccolomini Library project.

58 *St. George and the Dragon.* 1506 or 1507? Pen and ink with touches of black chalk. 26.2 × 21.3. Florence.

Cartoon for the Washington *St. George*, also pricked through for transfer. The more flowing, controlled lines of this work, and the supple rounded forms are symptomatic of the difference in date from the cartoon for the Louvre *St. George*.

59 *St. George and the Dragon.* 1506 or 1507. Oil on panel. 29 × 21 cm. Washington, National Gallery.

On his left leg the saint wears the Order of the Garter, an allusion to the decoration conferred by Henry VII of England upon Guidobaldo da Montefeltro. It has been suggested that the work may have been brought to England by Baldassare Castiglione in July 1506. In the 17th century it belonged to Mazarin; in the 18th it was bought by Catherine II and entered the Hermitage; and in 1937 it was sold by the Soviet government to Andrew Mellon who bequeathed it to the National Gallery in Washington. Clearly indebted to Leonardo in the drawing of the dragon and the saint's face, the work must date from shortly after the *St. George* in the Louvre.

60 *The Theological Virtues: Hope, Charity, Faith* (predella of the *Baglione Altarpiece*). 1507. Oil on panel. 16 x 44 cm. (each section) Vatican Museum.

The predella of the *Baglione Altarpiece* has the same history as the principal scene, *The Deposition,* but entered the Vatican Museum in 1815 on returning from Paris. The use of grisaille that imitates sculpture is in the tradition of similar work by Mantegna. The figures of angels and putti are among Raphael's freshest and most touching representations of childhood. The medallions demonstrate his liking and his aptitude for organizing compositions to fit a circular format.

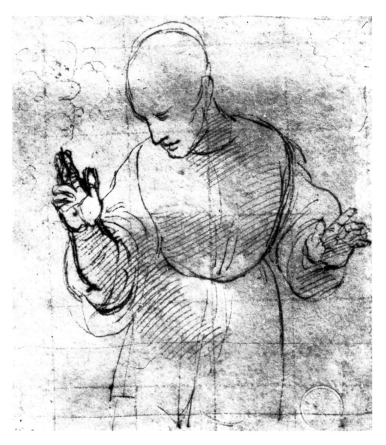

61 *Study of a man, for the Baglioni Altarpiece.* 1507. 11.3 x 10.2 cm. Pen and ink. Lille, Musée des Beaux-Arts.

Preparatory study for God the Father in the *Baglioni Altarpiece.* The panel to which it relates was painted from Raphael's drawings by Domenico Alfani and is the only part of the altarpiece still in Perugia, in the Galleria Nazionale. In its simplification this sketch from the life anticipates the boldest drawings of Flaxman or Ingres.

Boston panels. The shortish figures, with their forceful heads, the overall heaviness of touch, the appearance of the draperies, the types and expressions of the faces, are similar in both paintings if allowance is made for the finer technique which is a consequence of the smaller scale of the diptych. The complex and allusive pose of the young, sleeping Scipio reveals a stage in the representation of foreshortening similar to that of the sleeping apostle in *Agony in the Garden* in New York. The slight distortion, bordering on clum-

siness, of the *profil perdu* of the central Grace in the Chantilly panel, is a stylistic trait similar to that employed in the face of Christ in the New York panel; and the delicate head of *Virtue* in the London panel recalls that of St. John in the Boston *Pietà*.

Slightly larger, yet of a similar courtly type, the *St. Michael* and the *St. George* (both in the Louvre), must have been painted shortly after the London and Chantilly panels, very probably in 1505; like those pictures, they may have been painted for the ducal court at Urbino, possessing the same air of fantasy and gentleness, conveyed with a fine but not minutely detailed touch with a marvelously thick and rich application of paint. The *St. Michael* is particularly close to them in the short proportions of its figure. It clearly demonstrates how, after the first small-scale works painted by Raphael, his figures have progressively developed weight and structure, now filling their space and having their own equilibrium.

A comparison of the *St. Michael* and the figure of the executioner in the *Miracle of St. Jerome* at Raleigh, part of the predella of the *Mond Crucifixion*, is revealing in that the poses are virtually identical. Yet the latter scarcely possesses any weight; he is like a skater with his supple elongated silhouette. The archangel of the Louvre, on the other hand, pushes down with all his broad-backed adolescent force on the monster suffocating beneath him; and the twisted body, one leg outstretched behind, the arms and wings all with a solidly three-dimensional quality, balances on the leg which serves as a pivot. The group formed by the saint and the writhing demon is isolated, set apart, like a signpost in a bare landscape, as empty as a deserted stage-set. The infernal region populated with figures inspired by the *Divine Comedy* is unique in Raphael's work of this period in its air of fantasy without much spatial coherence and with nightmarish animals surrounding the balletic figure of St. Michael. The search for a somber and dramatic atmosphere is new for the artist. He uses an unusual range of colors, almost sulphurous, variations on the tones of copper and slate.

It is possible, as Konrad Oberhuber believes, that the small *St. George*, also in the Louvre and hung together with the *St. Michael* for a very long time, was painted at a later date; it is more probable, however, that it dates from about the same time, around 1505. The influence of Leonardo is more evident in the former, above all in the skillful drawing of the horse, also inspired by the Antique, and in the care with which the lively movement of the figures is con-

veyed. Other elements reveal Raphael's study of small Flemish panels; for example, the reflection of the horse's head in the warrior's helmet, or the trees with fine vertical trunks and leafy branches fanned-out like a bouquet of a type that can be found in all Florentine landscapes. It was Memlinc who loved to place such trees, in order to create *coulisses* on the hillsides of the tender and luminous landscapes which provide a background to his religious scenes. The small, lively silhouette of St. George remains entirely "Gothic": his black armor, shiny as a scarab, is outlined against the vermilion of the saddle, an effect which still recalls Pinturicchio. The *St. George* in the Louvre may have been commissioned by Guidobaldo da Montefeltro for Henry VII of England who had presented him with the Order of the Garter of which St. George is the patron saint; indeed the painting appears to have been in the British royal collection since the middle of the 16th century.

Another *St. George and the Dragon*, of similar size and in the National Gallery in Washington, has often been confused with the one in the Louvre. In the Washington panel the saint wears the Order of the Garter with the first word of the motto clearly legible, and the horse's trappings bear Raphael's signature. It is reasonable to suppose that this was a diplomatic gift sent by the Duke of Urbino to the King of England, and that it was carried there in July 1506 when Baldassare Castiglione led a mission which had originally been planned for February of the preceding year to the English court.

The *St. George* in Washington must for stylistic reasons be fairly close in date to the Louvre painting. It is obvious at first glance that Raphael has here conveyed the third dimension entirely successfully with the bodies of rider and horse effective in their sense of movement and tension, and well-integrated into the landscape. The assimilation of Leonardo's art can be seen in the overall coherence of the composition, more successful than in the Louvre *St. George*, which almost seems in comparison a pretty, mechanical toy. The helmeted head of the Washington saint, bereft of parade plumes, is of an entirely Leonardesque type, as is the dragon, one of the most elaborate (and credible) fantasy animals ever painted whose twisting movement possesses an almost Chinese elegance. The difference between the two *St. Georges* is evident if we look at one simple detail, the cloak which billows out behind him. In the Louvre painting it is treated in an entirely two-dimensional, linear fashion

whereas in the Washington picture it occupies its space convincingly with a real sense of volume. And these features are perhaps even more striking in the cartoons for the two paintings, both in the Uffizi.

It is entirely logical to propose for the Washington picture a date in the first months of 1506, just before Castiglione's embassy to the English court. But one could ask whether the picture should not in fact be dated a year later, at a time of greater maturity. In many ways it resembles the Borghese *Deposition* painted in 1507, although it is true that it is a different type of painting and on a quite different scale. They display a similar diagonal division of space, the same treatment of vegetation in the foreground, studied painstakingly from nature, lightly and deftly described, which closely resembles Leonardo's nature studies as well as those of Memlinc.

62 *Lamentation over the Dead Christ, a study for the Borghese Deposition.* 1507. Pen and ink. 17.9 × 20.6 cm. Oxford, Ashmolean Museum.

A first idea for the composition, showing the Virgin, the holy women and the disciples weeping over Christ's body. A pen and ink study for the right side of the design is in the British Museum and a highly finished study for the whole is in the Louvre.

63/64 *The Entombment of Christ,* also known as the *Borghese Deposition (The Baglione Altarpiece).* 1507. 184 × 176 cm. Rome, Galleria Borghese.

This signed and dated work remained until 1608 in the church of San Francesco al Prato in Perugia for which it was painted. It was then sent to Pope Paul V who gave it to his nephew Scipione Borghese. In 1807 it was bought with the rest of the Borghese collection by Napoleon. It was restored to the Papal States after Waterloo. The complexity of the work is reflected in the large number of preparatory drawings. This was the most ambitious project of Raphael's Florentine period.

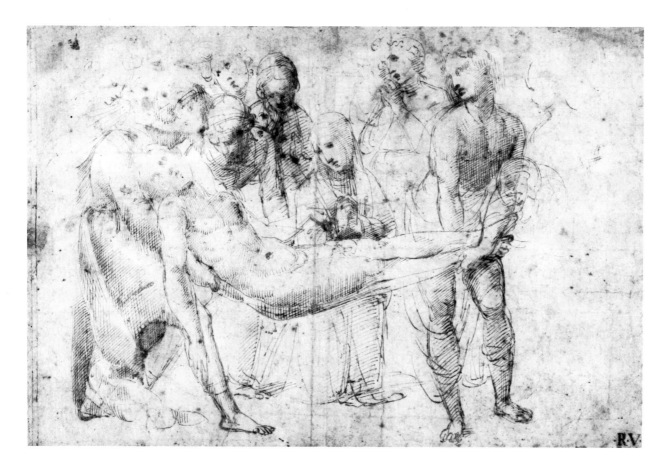

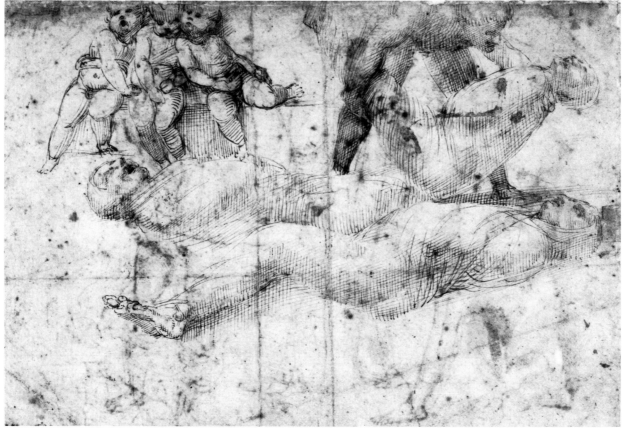

66

The face of the rescued princess (on the right) is much like that of the Magdalen in the *Deposition* and that of *Faith* in the altarpiece's predella. It would be necessary, however, in accepting such a dating, to abandon the idea that this was the painting carried to London by Castiglione.

The large *Entombment*, signed and dated 1507, in the Galleria Borghese in Rome, is the most ambitious work painted by Raphael in Florence. It is often called the Borghese *Deposition* because it has been in the collection of that Roman family since the beginning of the eighteenth century, or the *Baglioni Altarpiece*, after the man who commissioned it. It was painted for Atalanta Baglioni in memory of his son Grifone, murdered in 1500, for the Baglioni chapel in the church of San Francesco in Perugia. A lunette showing *God the Father surrounded by Angels* was painted by Domenico Alfani following drawings by Raphael. The surviving section is in the Galleria Nazionale at Perugia. The predella, today in the Vatican Museum, shows three grisaille medallions representing the *Theological Virtues*, framed by small angels. The *Entombment* had without doubt a long and complex evolution. There are numerous preparatory drawings which enable us to follow the process of its creation more closely than that of any other painting by Raphael. The subject was first to be the *Lamentation*. Several drawings survive of individual details and of the whole composition showing the figure group of the Virgin and the Holy Women seated and on their knees supporting the dead body of Christ, surrounded by standing figures. The most complete drawings, notably those in Oxford and in the Louvre, show a composition very close to that of the *Lamentation* (Florence, Pitti) painted in 1495 by Perugino for the Florentine convent of Santa Chiara. Raphael later made changes in the design, showing Christ's disciples carrying His body to the tomb. Another splendid series of drawings, in pen like their predecessors, progress as far as the design of the final painted composition, marking the different stages of its evolution. One of them, in the British Museum, shows a sweetness, tenderness and sense of coherence in the grouping of the figures. The short adolescent proportions recall the Colonna predella and have disappeared in the more tightly composed and ambitious final painting.

The *Borghese Deposition* is so well-known that we are too apt to see its figures as a fixed, static group whereas in fact it represents

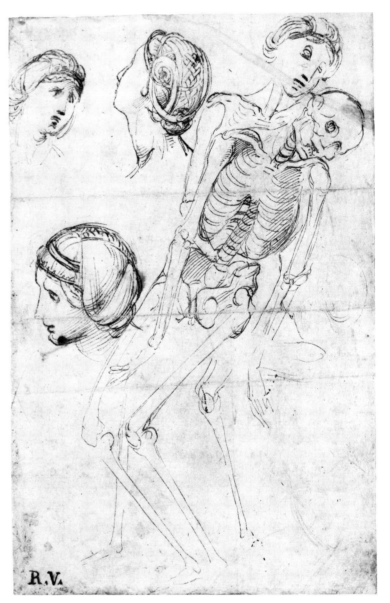

65   *Study for the Borghese Deposition.* 1507. Pen and ink. 20.7 × 31.3 cm. London, British Museum.

66   *Sheet of studies: dead bodies in shrouds and three young children.* 1507. Pen and ink, 20.7 x 31.3 cm. London, British Museum.

This exceptional drawing comes from the verso of the study for *The Borghese Deposition* reproduced on page 67, and it shares the same cross-hatching technique. The studies, conveying a great emotional intensity, show corpses wrapped in shrouds. They may have been drawn from nature in a cemetery, since one of them shows a man lifting up one of the bodies.

67   *Study for the Borghese Deposition.* 1507. Pen and ink with light touches of black chalk. 30.7 x 20.2 cm. London, British Museum.

This surprising study, which shows the figures represented as skeletons, demonstrates how conscientiously Raphael studied anatomy in Florence. The drawing is a study for the figures of the Virgin and the holy woman who supports her from behind in the *Borghese Deposition*. The woman kneeling in front of them in the painting is merely hinted at in a light tracing of lines. The three isolated heads seem to be studies for the heads of the holy women who, in the finished work, surround and comfort the Virgin.

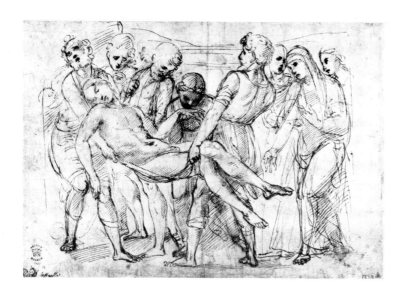

68   *Study for the Borghese Deposition.* 1507. Pen and ink. 23 × 31.9 cm. London, British Museum.

69   *Study for the Borghese Deposition.* 1507. Pen and ink with touches of black chalk, squared up in red chalk and pen and ink. 28.9 × 29.8 cm. Florence, Uffizi.

These three drawings give an idea of how the design developed. The group becomes more complex, agitated and dramatic. The stiffness, full of emotion, seen in the first British Museum drawing gives way in the second to a sweet, almost tender balance of forms. The composition of the Uffizi study is very close to the one adopted in the painting itself.

Raphael's first real attempt to express movement. The painting would appear very different, and far more moving, less of a stylistic exercise, if we were to view it as a group of figures in motion, possessed of a lively dynamism. The principal group moves vigorously towards the left in order to place the body of Christ in the tomb whose entrance can be seen in the rock at the extreme left. The young man in the center steps forward, the upper part of his body bent backwards in order to balance the weight of his burden, while behind him Mary Magdalen, holding Christ's hand, is also moving forward. The two men on the left climb the steps carved in the rock with considerable difficulty, heaving the body upwards. This movement to the left is contrasted with that of the group of women in the background, turning as if carried along by the current of a river. The backward arch of the foreground figure supporting Christ's legs, the oblique line of his outstretched arm in the center of the painting, links together the two groups. This violent and audacious work which is difficult for a modern audience to respond to is the first picture by Raphael to show so clearly the artist's new command of anatomy. This can be seen in the rendering of the body of the young man in the center, especially his bare neck and arm and of that of Christ, with its delicate and precise modeling of the chest muscles and collar bone, and the accurate description of the shoulders and trailing arm. There is probably an echo here of the young painter's admiration for Michelangelo's cartoon of the *Battle of Cascina* (1505/06); and, as has often been noted, the Virgin in Michelangelo's *Doni Tondo* (1505, Uffizi) must have suggested the pose of the Holy Woman on the right who kneels, her body twisted backwards, as she supports Christ's Mother.

The painting is a *tour de force*. Within its square format there are clearly drawn diagonals, the movements of the figures repeating, opposing and crossing one another. But the composition of the picture with its self-consciously learned references takes on a deeply human and religious significance given the circumstances of its commission. The group formed by the two bearers who support the sagging body of Christ was inspired in the first place by an engraving of Mantegna and the pose of Christ's body by an antique sarcophagus showing the *Funeral Rites of Meleager*. The painting has not always found critical favor, formed as it is of two separate groups which are linked in a somewhat artificial manner; in fact, in both actual and emotional terms, the subject is this break, this final separation of the Mother, pushed into the background, and the Son pulled towards the left and upwards. The image was appropriate for the mother of a murdered son. The contrast between and separation of Christ and the Virgin, their faces turned aside with eyes closed, mouths half-open and arms trailing, is in fact the painting's theme. Surrounding each of them are suffering faces, supporting and consoling arms, consumed with grief and rendered helpless by the tragic fact of Christ's death.

On close inspection the *Entombment* can be seen to be painted with quick decisive brushstrokes. The area of landscape, for example, where three figures are standing beneath trees which are reflected in the river, is treated with surprising freedom, using only the tip of the brush. The colors revealed by a recent restoration are startling in their clarity; there are bright vermilions, yellow-greens, slate blues and the soft pink of Christ's loincloth which does not distract the eye from the sinuous curve of His lifeless body.

The painting may represent a revival of the formulae used by Fra Angelico in two great interpretations of this subject in a similar format, both today in Florence at the Museo di San Marco: the *Lamentation*, painted for the Confraternity of Santa Maria della Croce al Tempio, and the *Deposition*, formerly in Santa Trinita. Among the possible sources Signorelli's *Deposition*, painted in 1502 for the church of Santa Margharita in Cortona and today in the

70   *The Lady with a Unicorn.* About 1505. Oil on panel. 65 x 51 cm. Rome, Borghese Gallery.

When this painting was restored in 1935 and layers of paint were stripped away, so too were a cloak on the young woman's shoulders, a wheel and a palm, all of which had led to her being identified as St. Catherine. Then the unicorn, a symbol of chastity, made its reappearance. Unfortunately, the surface of the painting has suffered some damage. The composition of the picture and the placing of the figure in a loggia opening out onto a landscape were inspired by the *Mona Lisa.*

71 *Portrait of Agnolo Doni.* 1505 or 1506. Oil on panel. 63 × 45 cm. Florence, Pitti Palace.

This work and its pendant remained in the possession of the Doni family, in Florence, then Avignon, until it was bought in 1826 by the Grand Duke Leopold II. Agnolo Doni was one of the greatest connoisseurs of art of his time and owned the *Doni Tondo* by Michelangelo which is also now in the Uffizi and may well be contemporary with the Raphael portraits.

72 *Portrait of Maddalena Doni.* 1505 or 1506. Oil on panel. 63 × 45 cm. Florence, Pitti Palace.

Maddalena Strozzi married Agnolo Doni in 1503. More insistently sculptural, tenser in expression and clearly influenced by Leonardo da Vinci's portraits, this may have been the first of the two works to be executed.

73 *Portrait of a woman,* also known as *"La Donna Gravida."* About 1507. Oil on panel. 66 × 52 cm. Florence, Pitti Palace.

The mystery of the sitter's identity has never been solved. The simplification of volumes, the subtleties in the treatment of the light and shade, together with the contented expression, point to a date towards the end of the Florentine period.

74 *Portrait of a Woman,* also known as *La Muta.* About 1507. Oil on panel. 64 × 48 cm. Urbino, Galleria Nazionale delle Marche.

The attribution to Raphael of this masterpiece, formerly in Florence at the Pitti Palace then the Uffizi, has long been in question, and some have suggested it may be by Perugino. The model is unknown, although she has occasionally been identified as Elisabetta Gonzaga or Giovanna della Rovere. The tense, nervous forms, the slight modeling and the reserved, almost mournful expression have rightly been compared with the portraits of Van der Weyden.

town's Diocesan Museum, should be included. It is difficult to imagine that at one time or another Raphael, in traveling from Perugia to Florence, did not stop at Cortona to admire the most recent work by a painter to whom he owed so much.

As with the portraits of his extreme youth, it is preferable to consider those of Raphael's Florentine period together in order to appreciate both the originality of the young painter and his development. The *Portrait of a Young Man* in the Museum at Budapest, usually dated 1504, is too far removed in style from the portraits in Vaduz and in Rome to have been painted at that date. A dating of around 1505 in Florence is more likely. The landscape, the contrast between the vermilion of the clothes and the bright, clear blue of the sky, recall such small-scale Florentine paintings as the *Dream of a Knight* diptych or the *Small St. George.* Oberhuber, however, suggests an even later date, 1508, which the confident handling and the air of joyful well-being would support despite a design which at that time would seem almost archaic.

The chronological sequence of the five far more famous and important half-length portraits painted by Raphael in Florence is open to argument; but they were executed in quick succession between 1505 and 1507. The first is perhaps the *Lady with a Unicorn* in the Galleria Borghese in Rome, fascinating in its limpid quality and its startling immediacy and also in its inclusion of the fabulous animal, a symbol of chastity, which the lady carries beneath her arm and which transforms her into a legendary princess. The loggia of *La Gioconda* opens onto an extensive landscape, lacking in mystery. The three-quarter length format with the arms gently relaxed in a simple pose which draws attention to the slightly tilted face whose gaze, arrestingly turned to one side, fixes the spectator, is borrowed from Leonardo's *Ginevra de' Benci* and the *Mona Lisa*. The nearer shoulder is almost deliberately underemphasized in order to stress the long line from neck to arm, an effect which Raphael was to repeat with many subtle variations throughout his career as a portrait painter. A pen drawing in the Louvre, clearly inspired by *La Gioconda* and very close in style to the *Lady with a Unicorn* may be a study for another contemporary portrait, never painted or perhaps lost.

Close in composition, the *Portrait of Maddalena Doni* in the Uffizi with its pendant of her husband *Agnolo Doni*, displays stylistic similarities with the *Lady with a Unicorn*. Less attractive than its companion in its almost overpowering forcefulness and its subject's rather sullen expression, *Maddalena Doni* is in purely formal terms finer, as smooth and plain as a highly polished pebble. The strongly graphic treatment of the black bands on her dress, the border of her shawl, the necklace from which her jewel hangs, the eyelet-work of her bodice, the tree silhouetted against the sky, gives life to the rounded forms and places them firmly in space. The hands, superbly drawn from nature and effectively modeled in half-tones, are prominently displayed in the foreground. They were much admired by Ingres who made a painted study of them which is today in the Musée Bonnat at Bayonne. The treatment of the face, subtly shaped by light, shadow and reflection, reveals Raphael's new admiration for Leonardo; here, as with the *Lady with a Unicorn*, one is reminded of the *Mona Lisa*.

The portrait of her husband *Agnolo Doni* is more relaxed and informal in composition without the linear elements of his wife's portrait and may have been painted at a slightly later date. The positioning of the arms, with elbows bent, recalls in a far freer, less constrained manner that of the *Young Man with an Apple* in the Uffizi. His clothes are in contrasting colors of red and black, his black beret outlined sharply against the sky. Compared with many portraits of young Florentines from the early years of the Cinquecento, *Agnolo Doni*, with his attractive, kindly but slightly weary face, stands out in his robust good health, elegant but far from romantic.

Of a later date, both probably painted in 1507, are two female portraits of unknown sitters, similar in their half-length format and shown in three-quarter profile against a dark background. They are Raphael's greatest achievement as a portraitist before his Roman masterpieces. Both are recognizable as human types and are generally called by their Italian names, *La Gravida* or the Pregnant Woman (Florence, Uffizi) and *La Muta* or the Dumb Woman (Urbino, Galleria Nazionale delle Marche).

La Gravida, compared with the *Maddalena Doni* to which it is so close in its handling of large, heavy forms, has a distinctly calm, contemplative air. Its design is even simpler and more authoritative, with the elbow, forearm and hand gently curved and resting on the lower edge of the painting. The whole figure, detached from and yet not contrasting harshly with the semi-dark background, is bathed in white light which gently models its forms. Some elements in the very simple costume — the wide black band of its neckline, the gold chain around the neck — help to define the volumes, which possess the smoothness and solidity of ivory billiard balls. Beneath its apparent naturalism, no painting is more carefully contrived. The woman's short, almost peasant-like hands rest on her pregnant stomach with a confident, protective gesture: it is a warm, generous and modest painting with a significance that goes beyond itself to state a more universal truth.

Compared with *La Gravida*, *La Muta* is more tense and nervous in mood. Its mysterious (and irreplaceable) title endows it with a poetic quality so that it becomes a kind of allegory of the inexpressible, a timeless image of the power of art. Once again the pose echoes that of *La Gioconda*; but the gentle forward tilt of the body, the erect head express an intense concentration. The pose of the hands, one resting upon the other, is enlivened by the outstretched index finger of one and the gracefully arched little finger of the other — a pose which François Clouet was to use in his portrait of *Elizabeth of Austria* in the Louvre. The almost grief-stricken seriousness of the face with its narrow jaw, lingers unforgettably in the mind. The rich colors, red, green and white, are close to those of the *Borghese Deposition*. The portrait has justly been compared with those of Van der Weyden in its sharpness of form combined with a characteristically Flemish attention to detail, particularly effective in the treatment of the plaited gold chain carrying a small cross (and the trembling shadow thrown by it on to the bare throat), of the rings and the fine embroidery on the white linen.

Among the Madonnas painted by Raphael between 1504 and 1508 are some of the most famous works in the history of painting. They show many subtle variations on the theme of maternal love in which Christendom or, in an even wider context, popular sentiment has recognized a definitive image of the Virgin Mary and through her of maternity. In addition, they provide powerful proof of the influence on Raphael of some of the most impressive images ever painted of Mary and her Son by Leonardo da Vinci. Raphael's Florentine Madonnas were painted in homage to Leonardo whom he seems to have very quickly identified as his true master and followed from this moment on.

The delightful bird-like *Conestabile Madonna* in the Hermitage at Leningrad is the earliest of Raphael's many circular Madonna and Child compositions. The head of the Virgin, just emerging from her blue cloak, is bent over to read the small book which the Child leans towards, but above all to echo the rounded edge of the tondo. The child's body is delicately arched in order to follow the same curve. The slightly static air of the fragile, almost timid forms, has prompted the suggestion that the painting was executed in Umbria but Roberto Longhi's idea that it should be dated at the end of 1505 when Raphael settled in Florence is perhaps more convincing. The delicate face with its carefully arranged bands of smooth hair and the plump, lively body of the Child already evoke Leonardo da Vinci.

The *Terranuova Madonna* (Berlin-Dahlem, Picture Gallery), which almost certainly dates from 1505, is Raphael's first ambitious circular composition. The Florentine enthusiasm for works in a circular format in painting as much as in sculpture is well known and the Berlin picture can be compared with various Florentine *tondi* from the end of the Quattrocento — for example, the similar *Madonna and Child with the Infant St. John* by Piero di Cosimo in the Museum at Strasbourg probably painted a few years earlier. Like Piero di Cosimo, Raphael accords a prominent place to landscape but the spatial relationships are quite different. Piero shows the two children in the foreground on a parapet which Raphael places behind the Virgin, forming a horizontal which divides the painting in two, giving it a reassuring stability and isolating the figure group. The comparison with Piero di Cosimo, among Florentine artists, is instructive, for he defined his forms powerfully in lights and shadows and in a manner quite different from Botticelli's linear technique. Like Piero, Raphael introduced "northern" elements into his paintings — objects, or landscapes, treated in a painstakingly realistic style. Raphael, however, integrated these elements within a unified composition with an unerring confidence, guided by a striving towards an ideal beauty which Piero di Cosimo did not achieve nor indeed aim at. Rather he was in search of the exotic, of arcane mysteries. The *Terranuova Madonna*, with its ample forms convincingly placed within the circular format and gracefully linked as if in movement, suggests above all Leonardo da Vinci in the pyramidal composition as well as in the new, more tender and emotionally responsive relationship between the figures. The delicate shadows on the body of Christ and on the face of the Virgin, as well as those which steal across the landscape — with the rocks of the *St. Anne* on the right — are all Leonardesque in inspiration.

The famous *Madonna del Granduca* in the Palazzo Pitti in Florence and, stylistically very close to it, the small *Cowper Madonna* in the National Gallery at Washington, should follow the *Terranuova Madonna* in date and could have been painted in 1505–06. The apparent Leonardesque quality of the *Madonna del Granduca* is somewhat misleading. A preparatory drawing for the painting (Uffizi) shows that Raphael had at first planned a circular composition and a landscape background which was in fact painted, creating an effect similar to that of the small *Cowper Madonna*. Before this landscape was sadly hidden by black overpainting, the silhouette of the Madonna and Child, far easier to make out in front of a bright

75 *Conestabile Madonna.* 1504. Oil on panel, transferred to canvas. 18 cm. diameter. Leningrad, Hermitage.

The picture was acquired from the Conestabile family in Perugia by Tsar Alexander II in 1870 and entered the Hermitage in 1880. Shortly afterwards it was transferred from panel to canvas, which revealed that an early stage of the composition the Christ Child was holding an apple and a pomegranate rather than a book. Longhi has suggested a dating at the end of 1504, when Raphael was first establishing himself in Florence.

sky, would have possessed a gentle sense of movement rather than its present distressingly static quality. It is this black background which has had the effect of obscuring the forms in a misty *sfumato*, giving it its present appearance of an over-sweet religious icon, something between Carlo Dolci (who actually owned it at one time) and Henner. Although in this way it has come to be regarded as Raphael's worst painting — or at least the most difficult to appreciate — the *Madonna del Granduca* is still striking in the remarkable coherence of its vertical composition, seen in the elongated oval of the Virgin's face, her slender shoulder and over-long arms and the feet of the Child, one dangling beneath the other. The painting marks a moment of dreamy inspiration in the artist's work, tinged with a kind of Peruginesque nostalgia. The small *Cowper Madonna* in Washington is very similar in feeling but livelier.

Three Madonnas, among the most popular and widely reproduced, mark the highest point of Raphael's Florentine achieve-

76　*The Terranuova Madonna.* 1505. Oil on panel. 86 cm diameter. Berlin, Staatliche Museen, Gemäldegalerie.

Until its acquisition by the Berlin Museum in 1854, this work belonged to the Dukes ,of Terranuova in Genoa and Naples. The composition has greater breadth than the preparatory drawing in Lille, already revealing the influence of Leonardo in the integration of the group of Virgin, Child and St. John. The child saint on the right has not been positively identified.

ment. Each shows the Virgin seated in a meadow, with the infant Christ standing, leaning against her and, kneeling or standing in front of Him, the infant St. John.

The *Belvedere Madonna* (Kunsthistorisches Museum, Vienna), named after the Viennese castle where it hung for many years, is clearly dated 1506 on the embroidered neckline of the Virgin's robe and was almost certainly painted in Florence for Taddeo Taddei. The grouping of the figures in a pyramidal composition reveals the influence of Leonardo which for the first time can be felt in the overall design and not just in individual details; in particular, Raphael was impressed by the *St. Anne*, the cartoon for which was at that time to be seen in Florence. The outline of the Virgin's robe and the position of her arms, supporting the Child, are very close to the *St. Anne* in the Louvre painted by Leonardo (shortly afterwards). The face with its lowered eyes is similar, if we imagine it raised a little, to that of the *Leda*, now lost but copied by Raphael in a drawing today at Windsor; and also to the face in a red chalk drawing of a head, said to be that of St. Anne, again in the Royal

78   *The Granduca Madonna*. 1505 or 1506. Oil on panel. 84 × 55 cm. Florence, Pitti Palace.

Having belonged to the Florentine painter Carlo Dolci in the 17th century, the picture was acquired in 1799 by the Grand Duke Ferdinand of Tuscany — hence the name under which it has become popular. The black background is a repainting that weakens and distorts the design. It was added to cover up a landscape, perhaps because it had been damaged, or because someone thought the work would be better without it.

77   *Study for the Granduca Madonna*. 1505 or 1506. Black chalk. 21.3 × 18.4. Florence, Uffizi.

The oval, nearly circular format and the suggestions of landscape are different from the composition in the Uffizi Museum. There is already an indication in the lower left corner of a rectangular framing. Here everything is more dynamic than in the final picture, thanks to the varied accents, sprightly then soft, forceful then light, of the black chalk.

79   *The Small Cowper Madonna*. About 1505. Oil on panel. 58 × 43 cm. Washington, National Gallery.

Called by this name to distinguish it from another Raphael also from Lord Cowper's collection and also in Washington, the work originally came from a private collection in Urbino. It is stylistically close to the *Granduca Madonna*.

80 *The Belvedere Madonna.* 1506. Oil on panel. 118 × 88 cm. Vienna, Kunsthistorisches Museum.

Signed and dated along the neckline of the Virgin's dress, this work was almost certainly painted for Taddeo Taddei. It belonged to Ferdinand of Austria in the 17th century and remained in the Austrian Imperial collection during the 18th century. It is sometimes called the *Belvedere Madonna,* after the palace in Vienna in which it was kept. It represents the complete mastery of Leonardo's pictorial language. Note the pyramidal compostion, the sculptural and psychological integration of the figures and the limpid quality of the light.

81 *Sheet of Studies for The Madonna of the Meadow. (The Belvedere Madonna.)* 1506. Pen and ink. 24.5 × 36.2 cm. Vienna, Albertina.

Collection. There is sadness in the mysterious half-smile and dim light which steals softly over the forms. The face is perhaps the most marvelously effective of all attempts to imitate Leonardo. The misty landscape, with the soft band of sunlit haze over a lake which stretches across the entire painting on a level with the Virgin's shoulders, strikes the same note of gentle melancholy.

Probably painted in the same year, the *Madonna with a Goldfinch* (Uffizi) has had a checkered history. As early as 1547 it was badly damaged in the collapse of a house in Florence belonging to the Nasi family who had commissioned it. Subsequently it has, like the *Madonna del Granduca,* the *Madonna della Sedia* and the *Sistine Madonna,* been turned into a kind of icon by the zeal of religious enthusiasts.

Its subject, like that of the Vienna *Madonna,* is Christ's Passion, represented by the goldfinch which St. John holds out to the Infant Jesus. The figure group echoes that of the *Belvedere Madonna,* though it is more compact. The lozenge-shaped arrangement, with the Infant Christ balanced between the Virgin's knees, has been compared to Michelangelo's *Bruges Madonna,* sculpted in Florence between 1501 and 1504, which remained in the city until 1506. The trees in the *Madonna with a Goldfinch,* strongly linear in design, in contrast with the softly modeled, tender central group, assume a greater prominence here than in any other painting by Raphael.

The *Madonna Jardinière* (Louvre) at first appears less Leonardesque than the two discussed above. Those in Vienna and Florence have the dreamy faces, the distant yet sweet expressions of Leonardo's Madonnas, and their landscapes recede into a haze whereas that of the Louvre painting is more naturalistic and *gemütlich.* It is not surprising that this picture, with the *Colonna Madonna* in Berlin and the *Borghese Deposition* in Rome, calls to mind, more readily than any of Raphael's other paintings, the work of the German Nazarenes. The peaceful blending of idyllic countryside and an image of radiant maternal love explains the painting's popularity and the name by which it is familiarly known, the *Belle Jardinière*. It is more lively and natural than the paintings in Vienna and Florence in the gently affectionate relationship between the three figures and in the absence of mystic symbolism, such as Christ's caressing of the goldfinch in the Florence painting or His taking of the cross from St. John in the Vienna picture. (Such symbolism has often been dismissed by those unwilling to make the effort to decipher it as mere "prettiness").

It may be that here Christ is shown stretching out his arm to reach the book in His mother's lap, a gesture which can be interpreted symbolically; but it is in fact more likely that He is simply trying to climb onto her knees. The figures' "stretched" poses echo each other and balance the group as a whole. After the plump, slightly timid Christ Child of the *Belvedere Madonna*, the well-rounded, firm, shell-like curves of the Child in the *Belle Jardinière* are striking. The influence of Leonardo, although it may not be immediately apparent, is crucial. The blue robe of the Virgin is very similar to that worn by her in the *St. Anne* in the Louvre which also reveals just

83 *Study for The Belvedere Madonna.* 1506. Red chalk. 22.4 × 15.4 cm. New York, Metropolitan Museum.

The Albertina studies show Raphael's first idea for the composition with the Virgin's arms describing a broad, dynamic movement, which in the other studies comes to rest. The Oxford drawing shows an extraordinary assurance in the simplification of forms and a subtlety of chiaroscuro that recalls Leonardo. It cannot have been executed long before the New York study, in which the variations in the strength of the line create the most sensual inflexions, and the poses are very close to those of the final painting.

·R·V·

82 *Study for the Belvedere Madonna.* 1506. Brown wash over metal-point with touches of red chalk. 21.9 × 18 cm. Oxford, Ashmolean Museum.

84 *The Belvedere Madonna.* Detail of illustration 80.

80

85/86 *Virgin and Child with the Infant St. John,* also known as *La Belle Jardinière.* 1507. 122 × 80 cm. Paris, Musée du Louvre.

Signed and dated on the hem of the Virgin's garment, the picture is generally identified as the Madonna Raphael painted for the Sienese Filippo Sergardi, and would have been bought in Siena for François I. It is impossible to tell from an examination of the work whether Vasari is correct in his assertion that it was left incomplete at the artist's departure from Florence and that a blue drapery was finished off by Ridolfo Ghirlandaio.

87 *Study for La Belle Jardinière*. 1507. Pen and ink, squared up in red chalk. 30 × 20.5 cm. Paris, Musée du Louvre.

The full, rounded forms of the Virgin suggest the use of a female model. The two children seem to be playing at her knee and she is looking at the young Baptist, crowned with leaves, who is holding the lamb up against him. Another compositional drawing in Chantilly is closer to the final painting.

88 *The Cardellino Madonna*. About 1506. Oil on panel. 107 × 77 cm. Florence, Musée des Offices.

The work was painted for Lorenzo Nardi and suffered damage when the house belonging to the Nardi family was destroyed in 1547. It later belonged to Cardinal Carlo de' Medici and entered the Uffizi in 1666. It is difficult to tell whether or not it predates the *Belvedere Madonna* but the way the clear light brings out the flesh tints, recalling the *Granduca Madonna,* and the appearance of the trees, so like those in the portrait of *Maddalena Doni,* suggest a rather early date, probably 1506.

one of her feet in the center — further evidence that Raphael had studied the cartoon in Florence. The *Belle Jardinière* is almost a simplified version of Leonardo's painting, an earlier stage as it were of its evolution; and it is significant that in the large preparatory drawing, now in the Louvre, Raphael shows the Infant St. John cradling his lamb. This sheet, carefully squared up for transfer, shows that the design of the painting may originally have been very like that of the Madonnas in Vienna and Florence: a dialogue between the two children with the Virgin's gaze directed at them both — a very similar grouping though in reverse to that of the *Belvedere Madonna*. At this point it seems Raphael looked again at Leonardo's *St. Anne*, as can be seen in the new design of the Virgin's robe, already used in the Vienna painting, but especially in the tender exchange of glances between Christ and His Mother.

The painting is arched at the top, unlike those of Vienna and Florence which are rectangular. This is the only occasion on which Raphael gave an easel painting the shape chosen for most of his large-scale church altarpieces, from the *Altarpiece of St. Nicholas* to the *Madonna di Foligno*. Its shape gives it a unique air of majesty and grandeur, an effect which is heightened by the placing of the horizon slightly lower than in the other two paintings. This gives the Virgin's upper body and shoulders, turned a little to her right, a new strength and emphasis. The *Belle Jardinière* is more comfortable, simple and natural in her pose than the Madonnas of Vienna and Florence, and has a more compelling presence. It is an enchanting picture in every detail — the Virgin's intricate hairstyle, covered by a light veil, her charming red bodice, slashed at the neck, the black border of which describes a marvelously graceful curve. And all these details appear entirely natural, bathed in a Tuscan light. The Virgin looks almost like a young girl dressed for a fete. It is impossible not to be moved by the engaging simplicity of the image.

The *Belle Jardinière* is dated 1507, the same year as the *Borghese Deposition*, which may have been painted earlier as it displays a slightly less coherent sense of form. In this year Raphael also seems to have painted several of his other Florentine Madonnas, but another group of paintings, which probably date from 1506, should be considered first, in particular a *Holy Family* in the Hermitage at Leningrad, usually known as the *Holy Family with the Young St. Joseph*; it appears to have been painted after the *Madonna del Granduca* and before the *Belvedere Madonna*. It has the former's static and dreamy qualities and the latter's gentle melancholy. The influence of Leonardo can clearly be seen in the fine, tormented face of Joseph but is less evident elsewhere. The painting seems imbued with a kind of Umbrian nostalgia. Two small *Madonnas*, now lost and known only through old copies, also date from 1506. These are the *Madonna with a Carnation* and the *Madonna with a Rose*, each showing the Infant Christ sitting on a cushion on His mother's knees, grasping a flower taken from her bouquet. The influence of Leonardo was clearly present — for the former, his *Benois Madonna* (Hermitage) was the source of inspiration, and for the latter his *Madonna with a Carnation* in the Alte Pinakothek at Munich.

89 *The Holy Family with the young St. Joseph.* About 1506. Oil on panel. 122 x 80 cm. Leningrad, Hermitage.

This painting, which found its way through several Parisian collections in the 17th and 18th centuries, ended up in the possession of Crozat, Baron of Thiers. From there it passed into the collection of Catherine II of Russia, with the rest of the Crozat paintings, in 1771. The picture has been restored several times and its authenticity sometimes unfairly put in doubt. The figure of St. Joseph on the left is very close to Leonardo da Vinci.

90 *The Orleans Madonna.* About 1507. Oil on panel. 29 × 21 cm. Chantilly, Musée Condé.

In Paris during the 18th century in the Crozat and Orleans collections, then in London collections, the picture was acquired in 1869 by the Duke of Aumale, who bequeathed it with the rest of his collection to the Institut de France to form the Musée Condé. The unusual still life in the background recalls Northern painting. The fine, tapering forms indicate a probable date of 1507.

91 *The Holy Family under a Palm Tree.* About 1507. Oil on panel, transferred to canvas. 101.4 cm diameter. Edinburgh, National Gallery of Scotland, on loan from the Duke of Sutherland.

Having been in several Parisian collections, the work came into the Orléans collection; its subsequent provenance is the same as that of the *Bridgewater Madonna.* A preparatory drawing in metal-point at the Louvre shows many variations in the poses of the Virgin and Child; on the same sheet is a very Leonardesque study for the head of a clean-shaven St. Joseph.

92 *The Canigiani Holy Family.* About 1507. Oil on panel. 131 × 107 cm. Munich, Alte Pinakothek.

The most complex and ambitious variation on the theme of the Madonna and Child or Holy Family in a landscape painted by Raphael during his Florentine period. It was seen by Vasari in the possession of Domenico Canigiani's heirs in Florence; it passed into the collection of the Medici family and was given by Cosimo III de' Medici to the Elector Palatine on the occasion of the latter's marriage to his daughter. The composition originally included groups of angels in the clouds to either side of the upper part of the work, but these were painted out, probably at the end of the 18th century.

93 *The Colonna Madonna.* About 1507. Oil on panel. 77 × 56 cm. Berlin, Staatliche Museen, Gemäldegalerie.

This picture was in the Salviati collection in Florence and the Colonna collection in Rome before entering the Berlin Museum in 1827. It is often considered to have been partly painted by an assistant, but is in fact completely by Raphael, though perhaps unfinished. It dates from about the same time as the *Canigiani Holy Family* — the figures of the Christ Child are particularly close — and was probably painted towards the end of 1507.

94 *The Bridgewater Madonna.* About 1507. Oil on panel, transferred to canvas. 81 × 56 cm. Edinburgh, National Gallery of Scotland, on loan from the Duke of Sutherland.

The picture may have been in France since the 16th century. There are certainly a number of French copies and versions of that period. It was later in the Seignelay and Orléans collections in Paris and was bought at the sale of the latter by the Earl of Ellesmere for Bridgewater House in London from whom it passed by family descent to the Dukes of Sutherland. The powerful, animated forms of the Christ Child show the influence of Michelangelo's *Taddei Tondo.* X-rays have revealed that there was originally a window in the right background.

The realistic note struck by the wooden, indoor shutters of the *Madonna with a Rose* recurs still more strikingly in the beautiful little *Orleans Madonna* in the Musée Condé at Chantilly which shows shelves in the background upon which are displayed in the Flemish fashion various pots and vessels. The fluid, slender forms, the sense of movement, the influence of Leonardo (here more completely assimilated with, once again, the robe taken from his *St. Anne*), all point to a slightly later dating, probably 1507, judging by the painting's closeness in style to the *Borghese Deposition.*

The Holy Family Beneath a Palm Tree, in the collection of the Duke of Sutherland and on loan to the National Gallery of Scotland, is unusual in its circular shape and bipartite composition, with St. Joseph and the Virgin shown in profile, face to face and the precariously balanced Child bridging the gap between them. A fence on the right once again creates a relaxed, pastoral atmosphere, and the plants dotted about the ground remind us of those in the *Borghese Deposition.*

Later in the same year, 1507, perhaps after the *Deposition*, Raphael painted the *Holy Family with St. Elisabeth and the Infant St. John*, in the Alte Pinakothek at Munich. It is known as the *Canigiani*

96 *Sheet of studies with several Madonna and Child groups.* About 1507. Pen and ink over red chalk. 25.4 × 18.4 cm. London, British Museum.

Full of life and nervous spontaneity, this sheet shows a number of poses for Madonnas. The one on the right relates directly to the *Colonna Madonna,* although the overall movement of the body is different and the arm with the book is missing. The central sketch is for the *Bridgewater Madonna,* the basic lines of which seem to have been established.

95 *Study for The Virgin and Child.* About 1507. Metal-point, pen and ink, on pinkish-beige prepared paper. 25.6 x 18.4 cm. Vienna, Albertina.

The verso of this drawing bears further studies of Madonnas comparable to those in the British Museum — it may even be a section cut from the same sheet. There is a striking similarity with *The Bridgewater Madonna.*

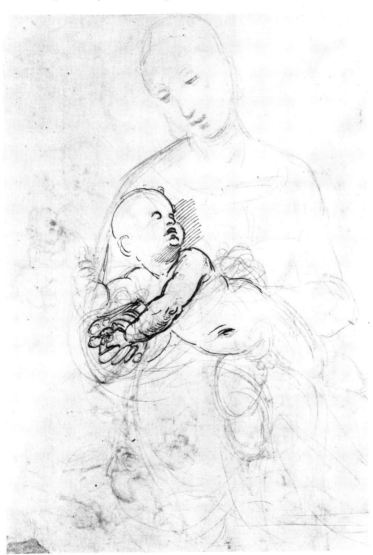

Holy Family after the Florentine family who once owned it. The original painting included groups of small angels in the clouds on either side of the upper section; today these are obscured by over-painting but could be revealed once more by restoration. They would have had the effect of completing the diagonals in the composition created by the poses of the bodies of the Virgin and St. Elizabeth. The pyramidal design and the naturalness of the figures with their wide, twisting movements which fill the picture space reveal how completely Raphael had by now assimilated Leonardo's style. The exchange of affectionate glances leads the eye from one figure to another, and the lively, fluid lines join and fuse together in a way which subtly balances the composition. Joseph, the central protective figure, adopts the pose of a gondolier pushing on his oar.

The *Colonna Madonna*, at Berlin-Dahlem, has a vigorous animated quality which is similar to that of the *Canigiani Holy Family*, and probably dates from the same time. The painting's jerky, slightly contorted, almost mannered style of execution has often prompted the idea that Raphael had a collaborator. This is too facile an answer to the problems it poses; the slender, almost spiky forms,

91

98 *The Virgin and Child with the Infant St. John the Baptist.* 1508. Pen and ink with touches of black chalk. 28.5 x 19.1 cm. Florence, Uffizi.

Cartoon, pricked through for transfer, for the *Esterhazy Madonna.* The grouping of the figures, the facial types and the draftsmanship are especially close to Leonardo da Vinci.

97 *The Holy Family with a Lamb.* 1507. Oil on panel. 29 × 21 cm. Madrid, Prado.

Signed and dated along the neckline of the Virgin's dress, the picture must have been painted at the end of 1507. The full, animated forms look forward already to the works of the Roman period. Yet again, homage is being paid to the work of Leonardo da Vinci, especially the *St. Anne.* The cartoon survives in a badly damaged state at the Ashmolean Museum in Oxford.

99 *The Esterhazy Madonna.* About 1508. Oil on panel. 28.5 × 21.5 cm. Budapest, Museum of Fine Arts.

A work given by Pope Clement XI to the Empress Elizabeth of Austria, then by her to Prince Kaunitz; it next passed into the possession of the Esterhazy family. Painted delicately but rapidly, it seems unfinished. It is yet another variation on a theme of Leonardo da Vinci and must date from the very end of the Florentine period.

100 *The Tempi Madonna.* About 1508. Oil on panel. 75 × 51 cm. Munich, Alte Pinakothek.

Owned in the 17th century by the Tempi family in Florence, the picture was bought in 1829 by Ludwig I of Bavaria. Contemporary with the *Niccolini-Cowper Madonna* and the *Baldacchino Madonna,* like them it shows a sense of monumentality combined with the observation of momentary, spontaneous actions expressive of domestic happiness.

101 *The Niccolini-Cowper Madonna,* also known as *The Large Cowper Madonna.* 1508. Oil on panel. 68 × 46 cm. Washington, National Gallery.

This painting, which is signed and dated along the neckline of the Virgin's dress, was in the Niccolini collection in Florence, then in that of Lord Cowper. The animation of the figures, their expressions of holiness and vivacity, and the freedom of the brushwork used to achieve new vibrant effects, are reminiscent of the Baldacchino Madonna with which it is contemporary.

102/103 *Virgin and Child with Saints and Angels,* also known as *The Baldacchino Madonna.*
About 1507-8. Oil on panel. 277 × 224 cm. Florence, Pitti Palace.

The saints represented are St. Peter and St. Bruno on the left, St. James on the
right and St. Augustine in the foreground. This great altarpiece, commissioned by
the Dei family for the church of Santo Spirito in Florence, was left unfinished on
Raphael's departure for Rome. At the end of the 16th century it was in the cathedral
at Pescia; it was sold in 1697 to Ferdinando de' Medici, who had it restored and
finished by Niccolo and Agostino Cassana. The architectural background seems to
have been added and not to have been part of Raphael's intention, as do the two
angels in the upper part of the composition.

like those of the *Orleans Madonna*, are part of Raphael's attempt at this particular time — probably still in 1507 — to convey movement in a manner he was to develop and perfect in the *Bridgewater Madonna*, the *Niccolini-Cowper Madonna* and the *Tempi Madonna*. The *Colonna Madonna* would seem to have been an experimental painting which makes it particularly interesting. It is impossible to know whether Raphael considered it to be unsuccessful and so left it in a half-finished state, almost transparent, but striking in its draftsmanship. Its charm is of a somewhat Germanic type in the manner of Cornelius; the ultimate resting place of a painting is not always a matter of pure chance or without consequence.

The *Bridgewater Madonna*, like the *Holy Family Beneath a Palm Tree* lent by the Duke of Sutherland to the National Gallery of Scotland, displays the same qualities as the *Colonna Madonna*, but with fuller forms treated in a sculptural manner which, especially in the pose of the Child, recalls Michelangelo. The composition reveals a knowledge of Leonardo's two lost paintings of the *Madonna and Child*, one sometimes known as the *Madonna with the Drink*; it survives in a painting attributed to Giampetrino in the Galleria Borghese in Rome. The other, known as the *Madonna of the Yarnwinder*, is preserved in several copies. Raphael brings the two figures close to the spectator. A robust Child posed obliquely across the Virgin's lap and almost independent of her, has a rather sad air and seems anxious to escape His mother's grasp, but the Child remains trapped, like a little swimmer between her gently caressing hands. The influence of Leonardo must have been still more obvious before the overpainting at a later date of an arch on the right, opening onto a landscape. The rather slight, tense appearance of the Virgin suggests that this work also dates from 1507.

The exquisite small painting of the *Holy Family with a Lamb*, which bears the date 1507 and is now in the Prado at Madrid, was probably painted at the end of that year. The fleshy figures and the plump face of the Virgin, the softness of the draperies and the relaxed pose of Joseph are very close in style to the last of Raphael's Florentine works and look forward to those of his Roman period. The influence of Leonardo's *St. Anne* is particularly strong, especially in the figure of the Child astride the lamb. The slightly contrived appearance of instability is also very Leonardesque; it can be seen in the sliding movement, like a wave which dips towards the lower left hand corner, which is held in check by Joseph's prominently placed staff — an important feature of the painting's design — and by the position of Christ's body and His gaze directed up at Joseph. This small, highly finished panel which resembles a Flemish primitive is the last of Raphael's works to show the influence of Memlinc. It can be seen in the arrangement of the landscape with its Nordic architecture and in the appearance of the lamb which is very close to that in the *St. John the Baptist* at Munich. It is known that in 1535 Pietro Bembo had in his collection at Padua a diptych by Memlinc similar to Raphael's painting.

Another very small painting, showing the *Madonna and Child with the Infant St. John* (Budapest Museum) probably dates from 1508;

it is known as the *Esterhazy Madonna* after the Hungarian family who owned it. This marvelous, small-scale *"Virgin of the Rocks,"* here seen in the bright light of summer, seems to have been intended as a deliberate homage to Leonardo. The Virgin's body is twisted to the side, recreating the pose of *Leda*. The extraordinary preparatory pen drawing, now in the Uffizi, is still more Leonardesque with its higher horizon which has the effect of tilting the figures forward, and its vigorous draftsmanship.

Two half-length paintings of the *Madonna and Child*, more cramped in design than those previously discussed, were painted in 1508 shortly before Raphael's departure for Rome, and represent the culmination of his Florentine variations on this theme. The *Niccolini-Cowper Madonna*, in the National Gallery in Washington, is striking in comparison with the *Colonna Madonna* because of its powerful monumental design and freshness of natural expressions and gestures. Although the painting has faded, it is clear that the technique has a new liveliness. The *Tempi Madonna* in the Alte Pinakothek at Munich, still simpler in design, has a similarly vigorous air. The impression of movement is brilliantly conveyed. The Virgin seems to be walking slowly forwards, hugging the Child protectively to her. The grouping of the figures looks back to Florentine treatments of the subject, such as those by Botticelli and his studio, but Oberhuber has noted the importance for this painting of the sculpture of Donatello which Raphael seems to have studied enthusiastically at this time. It is a long way from the rather sleepy monumentality of the *Madonna del Granduca*.

These two paintings mark a significant stage in the evolution of Raphael's Madonna and Child compositions. The strongly linear outlines of the figures in the *Borghese Deposition* and the *Belle Jardinière* have here lost their rigidity in favor of a richer pictorial sense which is more closely based on the study of nature. At the same time Raphael's technique has become softer and more varied, sometimes more delicate; the light is more diffuse, playing freely upon the forms. Raphael's art has fully matured.

A large altarpiece, the *Madonna del Baldacchino* (Florence, Pitti Palace), is the last of the series of Florentine Madonnas similar in composition and artistic aim begun by the *Ansidei Altarpiece*. The painting, commissioned for the Dei family chapel in the Church of Santo Spirito, remained unfinished when Raphael left for Rome in 1508, and was subsequently completed and altered by others, particularly in the upper section. It shows the new style of the

104 *St. Bruno, study for the Madonna del Baldacchino.* About 1508. Pen and ink bistre wash, white body color and black chalk. 21.7 x 13.2 cm. Florence, Uffizi.

A beautiful, lively sketch, freely worked over with the wash. The technique of combining pen and ink with wash, which Raphael puts to good use at the beginning of the Roman period in his sketches for the *Disputa*, is also seen in a contemporary sketch of a *Madonna and Child* also relating to the *Madonna del Baldacchino* and now in the Louvre.

105 *St. Catherine.* Cartoon for the London picture. Black chalk with touches of body color on greyish paper (several sheets attached together). Pricked through for transfer. 58.7 × 43.6 cm. Paris, Musée du Louvre.

Washington and Munich Madonnas applied to an ambitious, large-scale composition. It is organized on a spacious scale, the figures unified by a strong fall of light and further linked by the direct exchange of glances. St. Augustine, on the right, looks benevolently out at the spectator and stretches out his hand towards the Virgin and Child. The Child, apparently eager to play like the two little angels in the foreground who are examining a scroll, has the cheerful self-confidence of his counterpart in the *Niccolini-Cowper Madonna.* The forms are rounded and full, the draperies loose and richly varied in the intricate patterns made by their folds. It is a painting whose relaxed and happy mood seems more vulnerable to the least hint of tension than any other of Raphael's works. It would appear that at the end of his stay in Florence, there is in his paintings a feeling of liberation, which displays itself in a certain liveliness, a simple striving after happiness. And this moment seems to coincide with a new mastery of draftsmanship which can be seen, especially in the case of this altarpiece, in the variety of style and technique found

in the many preparatory drawings (the majority in wash) which testify to this new freedom.

The *St. Catherine* in the National Gallery in London shows, perhaps even more clearly than the Madonnas in the degree to which it reveals a new emotional maturity, the stage which Raphael had reached in the development of his art before his departure for Rome. The twisted rounded shapes gracefully rendered in three dimensions recall the *Borghese Deposition* and especially the *Belle Jardinière* to which the painting is very close in date; it was probably painted at the end of 1507. In the same way, the landscape, treated so pictorially in its effects of humid clear light, is close to those in the paintings in Rome and Paris and the colors, particularly the

106 *St. Catherine.* About 1507. Oil on panel. 71 × 56 cm. London, National Gallery.

The early history of this picture is obscure. It was in Rome in the 18th century and was bought by the National Gallery in 1839. On stylistic grounds it is datable to the same period as the *Borghese Deposition;* it shows the same skillful integration of forms in space as that work, and the same sense of pathos. The cartoon, which survives in the Louvre, is slightly different from the painting itself: the head is held less high and the dramatic effect is perhaps not so powerful.

107   After Raphael. *Christ among the Doctors*. Original about 1507 or 1508? Pen and brown wash, on three sheets glued together. 54 x 41.9 cm. London, British Museum.

This seems to be a faithful copy of a Raphael drawing, either for a picture or a mural decoration, dating from the end of the Florentine period. The original must have been a fascinating document, representing a link in the development of large compositons with architectural settings, between the frescoes in the Piccolomini Library in Siena, such as *The Canonisation of St. Catherine* and *The School of Athens*. The groups of figures, their emotions expressed through forceful movements, clearly recall Leonardo and are close to those of the early drawings for the *Disputà*.

108   *Battle scene with prisoners*. About 1508? Pen and ink, with touches of black chalk. 26.8 x 41.7 cm. Oxford, Ashmolean Museum.

This drawing is the verso of a sheet, the recto of which shows a closely similar subject. It is not a preparatory sketch for the late *Battle of Ostia* but, as is suggested by the similarities with Pollaiuolo, Signorelli and Michelangelo's *Battle of Cascina*, a work of the end of the Florentine or the beginning of the Roman period.

purplish blue sheen on the grey robe which gives the yellows their full warmth, closely resemble those of the *Deposition*. The solid forms which have for the first time achieved a convincing fullness are gently turned like those of a beautiful *amphora*, and arranged in space around the elliptical shape of the wheel which they echo and amplify. The Cabinet des Dessins in the Louvre has the complete cartoon for the *St. Catherine* which shows the head in a slightly different position, tilted less far back. In any event Raphael returned, for the position of the head in the painting itself, to a detailed drawing which can be found on a sheet of studies at Oxford. The mood of the cartoon is warmer, more animated and at the same time more delicate; the slightly *di sotto* viewpoint in the painting gives the forms a more monumental effect. In front of that statuesque silhouette in strong *contrapposto* in which the folds of the drapery closely follow the curves of the body, one cannot fail to think of antique sculpture, and to ask — as in the case of the *Baglioni* predella — which classical marbles Raphael would have seen in Florence. His mastery of technique enabled him to achieve a new heightening of emotion in this painting. The pathos which informs the pose of the saint has a direct and simple force; it can be seen in the eyes raised to Heaven, the swelling of the chest, the way in which the landscape is unified with the stormy sky and the divine burst of golden rays which lights up St. Catherine's ecstatic face. In a more ambitious work like the *Borghese Deposition*, such strength of emotion is not always achieved, having been to some extent sacrificed to the elaboration of the composition. But it does contain something of this intensity of feeling.

1507 marks an end of one phase of Raphael's career — or alternatively the beginning of another. His mastery of technical skills, some far more difficult than others and acquired through the most intense effort, enabled him to depict the human body in all its expressive power and to convey feelings, however rarified. Now the painter could leave for Rome and tread upon a larger stage. He left Florence in 1508 at the age of 25 with only twelve more years in which to paint.

III. Rome 1508–1511: The Fulfillment of Ambitions

The exact date of Raphael's departure for Rome is not known; it probably took place in the last months of 1508. According to Vasari, Raphael left Florence rather abruptly, summoned by the Pope, who was acting on the advice of Bramante. A papal document of January 1509 records a payment to Raphael, probably for the Stanza della Segnatura.

The summons from Julius II, whose family the Della Rovere was related to the Montefeltro of Urbino, was crucial for the development of Raphael's career. The pontiff chose the young painter to decorate his personal apartments in the Vatican. As Vasari says, the support of Bramante, whom Raphael had known in Urbino, and who was in Rome working on the new St. Peter's, was important in this choice.

The powerful personality of Julius II, Pope since 1503, is well known — a man of action, exacting and domineering, he was determined to restore the power of the Church and at the same time reestablish the "imperial" authority of Rome. This "Renaissance" of a strong Rome went together with the gradual weakening of Florence; the departure for Rome of Michelangelo in 1503 and of Raphael five years later were part of this process. The extent of Julius' ambition can be seen in the beginning of the work on the new St. Peter's, an undertaking entrusted in its early stages to Bramante. Raphael was — like Bramante and like Michelangelo who had just begun his frescoes on the vault of the Sistine Chapel — to glorify both Julius II and the city of Rome.

The fresco decoration of the three rooms or *stanze* in the Vatican was Raphael's grandest and most ambitious undertaking. The three rib-vaulted rooms, each about ten meters by eight, are known in order of their decoration as the Stanza della Segnatura, the Stanza d'Eliodoro, and the Stanza dell'Incendio. This vast undertaking occupied Raphael from the end of 1508, the moment of his arrival in Rome, until his death in 1520 when he had just begun the decoration of a fourth room, the Sala di Constantino, which was painted by his pupils. It is known that Julius II had decided to occupy this suite of rooms in which there were frescoes by Piero della Francesca, Signorelli and Bartolomeo della Gatta. An equally heterogeneous group of painters including Sodoma, Peruzzi, Bramantino, Jacopo Ripanda, Signorelli, Lorenzo Lotto and Perugino himself, had been given the task of their redecoration but Julius very quickly recognized Raphael's talent and entrusted the whole enterprise to him.

Raphael began with the central room in Julius II's apartments, the Pope's private library. This was called the Stanza della Segnatura because it was here that the sessions of the Signatura Gratiae, the Papal Court of Justice, were held. However, its function as a library is confirmed by the bases for cabinets which stand to a height of about six feet, made by Fra Giovanni da Verona, the best known marquetry designer of the day, which were probably intended to support cupboards for books. Imagine rich, warm *boiserie* contrasting with the pallor of the frescoes. One can get an idea of the original appearance of the rooms from a *trompe l'oeil* painted in fresco beneath the grisailles on the *Parnassus* wall. At the time of Pope Paul III the cabinet bases were replaced by imitation bas-reliefs which have an effect quite different to, indeed the complete opposite of, that intended by Raphael. The original function of the room as a library can be seen from one fresco to another in the inclusion of books, writing-tablets, rolled-up papers and cartouches which are carried by the writers and the sacred figures who are often shown speaking or writing, or which lie on the ground, or are held by putti and angels in such a way that the spectator can read them. They all proclaim the necessity of the written word through which knowledge, religion, law and poetry are diffused. The program seems to have been planned, at least in general terms, by Julius II himself. It depends on one central idea, the essential unity of Graeco-Roman antiquity and Christian spirituality. The four frescoes each show one of the four aspects of humanist culture — philosophy, theology, law and poetry, all inspired by their ideal of the true, the good or the beautiful. The truth is shown in two manifestations: revealed truth, in the theology of the *Dispute of the Holy Sacrament*, and rational truth in the philosophy of the *School of Athens*. Good is represented by the *Virtues* who appear above the scenes of *Trebonianus Handing the Pandects to Justinian*, an illustration of civil law, and *Gregory IX Promulgating his Decretals*, an illustration of canon law. The beautiful is represented by poetry, illustrated by *Parnassus*.

Raphael has given human form to these abstract ideas. Each of the four great frescoes is in the first place a remarkable figure composition in which the convincing characterization of each participant, every one passionately involved in the action, is of the greatest importance. They include a series of portraits like earlier *uomini illustri* but the subjects are all shown in action, linked by the search for a common ideal. It is for this reason that the Stanza della Segnatura is so moving an image of the aspirations of the human spirit, the most complete expression of the great optimism of the Renaissance and its faith in Man.

It has usually been thought that Raphael began his great undertaking by painting the vault. This had just been painted, and had probably been completed, by Giovanni Antonio Bazzi, known as Sodoma. A little older than Raphael, Sodoma came from Verceil where he had been a pupil of Spanzotti. At this time he had just finished his work at Monte Oliveto Maggiore near Siena where he had completed the frescoes in the cloister that had been begun by Signorelli. Sodoma had divided the vault of the Stanza della Segnatura into distinct areas separated by bands of decoration — a central octagon, four large circular compartments and four rectangular compartments, while the remaining ones which were much smaller had trapezoidal or triangular shapes. All these, compartments as well as bands of decoration, were placed on a background of imitation gilded mosaic and the shapes of the compartments were firmly outlined by moulded frames which remained empty. Raphael retained this layout, including the central octagon where this time, outlined against the sky in an illusionistic manner, putti support the papal arms. He redesigned the eight principal compartments, retaining the background of gilded mosaic. Casting aside this background and Raphael's power of abstraction, the eight compositions, four circular and four rectangular can be thought of as separate paintings which do not form a ceiling decoration of the type created by Sodoma.

Each of the four medallions shows a seated female figure, seen full face resting on clouds and symmetrically framed by two or four putti holding cartouches bearing large inscriptions, legible at a distance. These young women are allegorical representations of Theology, Philosophy, Poetry and Justice and refer to the subjects of the large frescoes on the walls below them — the *Dispute of the Holy Sacrament*, the *School of Athens*, the *Parnassus* and the *Virtues*. The animated figures seem about to spring from their seats. The background of gold mosaic has the effect of settling them, however, emphasizing the beautiful and vivid outlines and taming the profusion of designs, forms and colors which might otherwise appear overwhelming. In this way the figures acquire the timeless dignity of antique works of art. *Theology*'s veil is blown out by the wind and the angels who frame her dance an unrestrained saltarelle. *Philosophy* is more imperious and commanding in pose, supported by two putti on either side; *Justice*, whose body is vigorously arched, raises her sword with a gentle, sweeping gesture like the conductor of an orchestra, and her smile, with her eyes lowered, is reminiscent of

Leonardo's faces. But it is *Poetry* who presents the most complex and unstable design — the putti seem to tremble and only the arm which holds the closed book on her knee counteracts the restlessness of the curves of the wings, the lyre and the crossed legs. Carefully elaborated echoes of these four figures can be identified in contemporary and slightly later works — the diagonal arm of *Philosophy* in the *Mackintosh Madonna* and the *Galatea*, *Theology*'s hand holding the book in the *Alba Madonna*, the movement of the upper body, head and raised arm of *Justice* in the *Madonna del Loreto*.

The four rectangular compositions, in an almost square format, slightly taller than wide, each show a mostly nude figure group on a smaller scale than the four allegories of the medallions and painted in less contrasting colors. The subjects of these scenes were selected to be viewed in conjunction with the two allegories that frame and dominate them. In this way *Adam and Eve*, the first sinners, are beneath *Justice* and on the other side call for redemption, the province of Theology; the *Judgement of Solomon* clearly refers to *Justice* and to the moral value of wisdom, the purpose of Philosophy; *Urania* or *Astronomy* personifies the power of intelligence, and so Philosophy, and at the same time the harmony of the universal order, which must govern *Poetry*; *Apollo and Marsyas* alludes to Poetry and to the triumph of divine authority, Theology's domain. But this last theme is often interpreted in the manner of the neo-Platonic philosophers as Divine Harmony victorious over Earthly Passions and their banishment from the human soul. All four scenes display a striking ability to organize in a restricted space scenes modeled in depth which only the gold background prevents from "making a hole" in the wall.

This can be seen in a spectacular manner in the *Judgement of Solomon*, a composition which is at one and the same time compact and uncluttered, and whose power presages the paintings of the Stanza d'Eliodoro where the bodies partially conceal one another and where forms are thrust diagonally into depth. *Adam and Eve* is arranged on the principle of a corkscrew, the shape of the serpent wound around the tree. Here and there direct borrowings from antique sculpture give the impression that it was Rome which created the young artist, but we can often still detect reminiscences of Leonardo; in particular, the *contrapposto* of the *Leda* which underlies the quivering body of Eve. This new breadth of style in the development of forms in space and its assimilation by figures of strong and supple posture could well be illustrated by *Uranus* leaning on the globe. It also illustrates Raphael's preference for the perfect shape of the sphere which draws together and unifies, focuses and develops and often dominates his compositions. A further example of this is to be found in the *Judgement of Solomon*. All the figures on the ceiling, supple and muscular, demonstrate this new style of figure painting. They are fuller, freer and more plump, as they were in the Florentine *Tempi Madonna*, *Cowper Madonna* and the *Madonna del Baldacchino*.

The preparatory drawings for the eight compositions show a freedom of line, an ability to change from one technique to another,

109 *Ceiling of the Stanza della Segnatura.* Around 1509. General view. Vatican.

The division of the surface into compartments separated by mouldings with grotesque decoration against a gold background goes back to Sodoma who had painted the whole ceiling including the central octagon with papal arms. Raphael respected the divisions, unifying the eight large compartments, four circular and four rectangular, by using a background of fictive gold mosaic.

a strength in the construction of space and a lively energy in the drawing which all merge together. All outlines have disappeared and the forms are completely opened up, allowing the light to flow through. A pen study at Oxford shows the first brilliant attempt at the figure of *Theology*; a page of sketches of male nudes in the Louvre, drawn as if at random but with a faultless grace and a marvelous lightness of touch, contains five explanatory studies for *Adam*'s pose. A delicate drawing sketched in silverpoint at Oxford shows an early composition with nude figures of *The Judgement of Solomon* before Raphael achieved the organic coherence it has in the fresco by drawing the group closer together.

Other studies, both quickly sketched and carefully drawn, in pen or in red or black chalk, of the isolated figures of *Uranus* and *The Judgement of Solomon* can be found in the Albertina in Vienna. Two drawings in black chalk, a putto in Lille for the Theology and especially a large study for the figure of *Poetry* at the British Museum, both economical and unrestricted in a technique learned from Fra Bartolomeo, show modulations of great delicacy which three centuries later were to influence Prud'hon's most gentle and languid style. The British Museum also possesses a fragment of the cartoon

111   *Study for Theology.* About 1509. Pen and ink. 20.1 × 14.3 cm. Oxford, Ashmolean Museum.

This fiery study for the figure of *Theology* on the ceiling of the Stanza della Segnatura shows a number of variant positions for the left arm which in the fresco holds a book that rests on the knee.

110   *Study for Poetry.* About 1509. Black chalk on prepared paper, squared up. 36 × 22.7 cm. Windsor, Royal Library.

A languorous, sensual preparatory drawing at Windsor shows that Raphael thought at one stage of having the figure half nude; indeed, the first rapid traces of the stylus on the prepared paper, which are still easily visible, describe the model as if entirely nude.

112   *Poetry.* About 1509. 180 cm. diameter. Vatican, Stanza della Segnatura.

One of the four allegorical figures of the ceiling of the Stanza della Segnatura, *Poetry* is placed above the Parnassus. Winged and crowned with laurels, she holds a lyre and a book. The inscriptions carried by the angels are quotations from Virgil's *Aeneid* (Book VI).

113 *The Judgment of Solomon.* About 1509. Fresco. 120 × 105 cm. Vatican, Stanza della Segnatura.

Drawing inspiration from classical sculpture, this scene from the ceiling of the Stanza della Segnatura shows the most extreme concentration of dramatic action, typifying Raphael's mastery of three-dimensional effects.

114 *Study for Astronomy on the ceiling of the Stanza della Segnatura.* 1509. Pen and ink. 23.5 x 40.8 cm. Vienna, Albertina.

On the verso of this impressive study for one of the rectangular compartments of the ceiling of the Stanza della Segnatura — sometimes called *Astronomy* or *Uranus,* sometimes *The First Movement of the Universe* - are red chalk studies for *The Massacre of the Innocents,* which was engraved by Marcantonio Raimondi.

for *Poetry*; the head of the putto on the right is drawn with bold, broad strokes, the locks of hair flowing outwards in spinning curls and the face lined with heavy hatching. These are all that remain of what were probably numerous drawings but they are enough to demonstrate their dazzling authority and unrivalled technique.

The *Disputa*, although it would be more correct to call it The Triumph of the Eucharist or more simply the Triumph of the Church, was the first fresco in the group to be executed in 1509, (probably even before the decoration of the ceiling), or so Vasari would lead us to believe. He also claimed that Julius II was so overcome with admiration before the painting that he had commissioned for the *Stanza della Segnatura* that he dismissed all the other painters, among them Sodoma, so that Raphael could continue the work

alone. This would appear to be borne out in an almost peremptory fashion by the style of the first drawings for the composition which must be early since they are so similar to the last of the Florentine studies.

A fairly large number of these drawings for the *Disputa* has been preserved, and in the case of the Stanza paintings allow us to follow the various stages of Raphael's work. From the outset the symmetrical composition is split into two levels, the terrestrial and the celestial. Three wash drawings show the first conception which contains neither the central altar nor the steps that lead up to it, and in which the celestial figures stand on two different levels. A detailed drawing at Windsor for the left half of the composition sets out this section in a concise and lively way, with the architectural addition of a portico and column at the side to close the composition. A further page in Oxford shows only the celestial section but more clearly, with the characters superimposed on two horizontal levels. The figures are all carefully related to one another but the sense of perspective, with the characters spread out as though on a semi-circular gallery viewed from beneath, an effect that is already suggested in the drawing at Windsor, is not in evidence. Finally, a drawing from the Musée Condé at Chantilly shows the whole group of the Doctors of the Church in the terrestrial part, reusing the group in the drawing at Windsor for the left hand section. The Leonardesque character of this last drawing has, correctly, often been emphasized. Indeed it is strikingly reminiscent of the famous *Adoration of the Magi*, left unfinished by Leonardo in 1482 and today in the Uffizi. This can be seen in the clear and precise juxtaposition of light and shadow and in the almost liquid control of light which gives each group its coherence and psychologically unites the figures. The other drawings, both for the lower part of the composition, indicate that Raphael was not happy with this still disorganized area even though he had already thought out the basic idea for the grouping. Above some steps in the center he placed an altar. In this way he could place the seated Fathers of the Church on the same level as the altar without their appearing overcrowded, positioning the other figures below.

One of these pen drawings at the British Museum, heightened by a light wash, establishes the positions of the draped figures. The idea of the large empty space in the foreground is also to be found here. This is fundamental to the composition since it directs the eye, with its perspective, right up to the altar and its surmounting chalice. The other highly finished pen drawing uses, more or less, the figures in the London drawing. Here they are drawn nude and are clearly studies from life, of an unparalleled precision, strength and elegance. There is also a rhythmic quality in the very clever balancing of the figures, which form animated groups within the picture space. However the artist was still not satisfied with this arrangement and it was to undergo numerous small changes before the final work.

In its completed form the fresco is striking in its symmetry and powerful effect of its perspective. The Eternal Father, Christ, The

Holy Spirit, the monstrance and the altar are placed on a single central axis. The monstrance, the aura that surrounds the dove of the Holy Spirit and that surrounding Christ, form three circles of increasing size. The Holy Spirit as the geometric center of the work and the lines of the architecture — the flagstones, the steps, the structure on the right — converge at the base of the monstrance which is level with the horizon. The host and the altar, isolated in the center behind the paved space above the white steps, thus become, in a most effective manner, the physical and spiritual heart of the composition. There is a natural link with the upper part in spite of the horizontal caesura of the bright sky, arising from the strength of the vertical axis from which the pattern of circles arises, growing like ripples. In this way the overall design of the composition recalls a vast chalice.

It has often been noted that Raphael reused with greater breadth of style the composition in his fresco in the church of San Severo in Perugia for the upper section of the *Disputa* which in turn was based on the composition of the *Last Judgement* fresco by Fra Bartolomeo in the convent of San Marco in Florence. Raphael's St. Peter, whose profile can be seen in the foreground on the left, is almost identical with the St. Peter in the same position in Fra Bartolomeo's fresco. It is possible that there is an echo of another Floren-

tine work in Raphael's painting. The overall organization of the composition recalls the enormous crowds that are to be found in Last Judgement scenes of the Quattrocento, particularly one by Fra Angelico that Raphael must have seen in the church of Santa Maria degli Angeli. The likeness has often been commented upon, and it is indeed striking. They have the same general design Christ is shown in glory, flanked by the Virgin and St. John the Baptist, surrounded by the apostles and the saints seated on their semi-circle of clouds, with an impressive use of linear design in the lower section in the work's axes. In Fra Angelico's work there is the fascinating geometric pattern, like a broken chessboard, of a range of opened tombs; in Raphael's the perspective of the flagstones and the steps.

115   *Study for the Disputà.* 1508 or 1509. Pen and ink with brown wash, heightened with white. 23.2 × 40.5 cm. Chantilly, Musée Condé.

One of the first studies for the lower part of the fresco before the introduction of the central altar. The animated yet coherent grouping of the figures and the fluid play of light and shade are strikingly reminiscent of Leonardo da Vinci's unfinished *Adoration of the Magi* (Uffizi). The figure on the extreme left seems to have been taken directly from Leonardo's composition.

The *Disputa* develops the idea of a chancel of a church under construction of which only the basic structure has been erected, on the right, with the paving, the altar and the steps leading up to it already in position. The celestial vision arranged in the form of a semi-dome creates the ideal apse for the building. The church both as a work of architecture and as a meeting place for believers in Christ thus symbolizes one idea: the true theme of the *Disputa*, the construction of the church, with the inclusion of all the forces brought to bear on this work. The host, situated in the center of the composition between the earth and heaven, represents the mystery of the Eucharist, through which man achieves divine grace. Sitting on a hemicycle of clouds in heaven and surrounding the cross-shaped group of the Trinity, the Virgin, St. John the Baptist and a row of prophets and saints symbolize the Church Triumphant. From left to right, St. Peter, Adam, St. John the Evangelist, David, St.

116 *Study for the Disputà.* 1508 or 1509. Pen and ink, 28 × 41.5 cm. Frankfurt, Städelsches Institut.

A rare insight into Raphael's working method, the drawing shows the figures as nude and represented with the highest degree of anatomical accuracy. The grouping of the figures in the lower left part of the composition was to be altered again in the fresco itself.

117/118 *The Disputà.* 1509. Fresco. Base 770 cm. Vatican, Stanza della Segnatura. ▷

Probably the first fresco Raphael painted in the Vatican, the great success of which made his name and led Julius II to hand over to him the decoration of all the Stanze. With its double register, celestial and terrestial, the two zones linked by the vertical axis on which the Host and the Holy Trinity are aligned; and with its assembly of prophets, saints, theologians, doctors of the Church and faithful, it represents both the structure of the Church and its triumph.

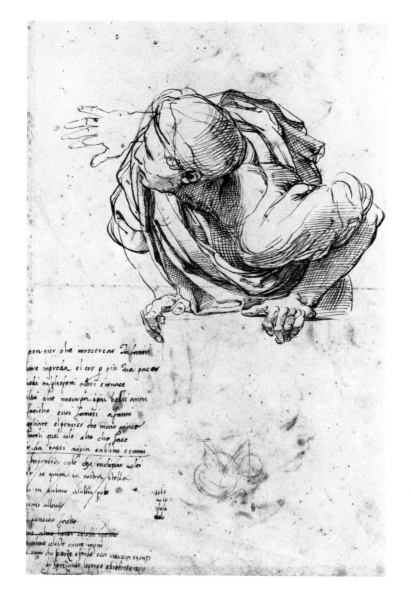

119/120 *Study for the Disputà of a man leaning forward.* 1508 or 1509. Pen and ink. 36 × 23.5 cm. Montpellier, Musée Fabre.

A study for the figure on the extreme right of the fresco who seems to be leaning out over the door of the room. The sonnet *Fello pensier* is by Raphael. There are further detailed studies for the same figure on the verso.

Stephen, Jeremiah, then Judas Maccabeus, St. Lawrence, Moses, St. James Major, Abraham and St. Paul. Doctors of the Church, Popes, theologians and the faithful are assembled on earth. The four Fathers of the Church are seated on either side of the altar: St. Gregory and St. Jerome on the left and St. Ambrose and St. Augustine on the right.

Opposite the *Disputa*, the triumph of truth revealed through divine grace, the *School of Athens*, certainly painted throughout 1510 although it may have been begun towards the end of the preceding year, represents the quest for truth through human reason. In a vast building reminiscent of Roman baths or, perhaps more probably, of some of Bramante's plans for St. Peter's basilica, stand groups of scholars, wise men and philosophers of antiquity. The architecture asserts itself with a power greater than in any other painting by Raphael, through the simple effect of symmetrical perspective. The vigorous linear pattern of the dual-colored paving and the coffering in the vaults emphasizes the effect of this perspective. The line of the horizon is higher than that in the *Disputa* and this allows the inclusion of more figures. They stand on two levels: asymmetrical groups are in the foreground and, at the top of the four steps, small groups are spread out. In the center stand the figures of Aristotle and Plato on whom all the lines of perspective converge. The architecture allows a broad spread of the figures and controls the effect of the lighting; and there was never a more perfect harmony between the human form and the space it occupies than that seen here. Never has human form contributed in this way to expression. The rounded arches of the arcades are amplified and

122/123 *The School of Athens.* 1510. Fresco. Base 770 cm. Vatican, Stanza della ▷
Segnatura.

Philosophers and men of learning from Antiquity dispense their wisdom under a
vast edifice with a centralized perspective probably reflecting Bramante's designs
for St. Peter's. The figures form coherent groups on two different levels connected
by a flight of four steps. The assembly is dominated by Plato and Aristotle in the
center. In the 20th century this has become Raphael's best known work and is considered the epitome of Renaissance humanism. It is placed opposite the *Disputà,* which
represents truth revealed by God, to represent the pursuit of truth through the intellect.

121 *The Disputà.* Detail of illustration 117.

radiate around the central group of the two philosophers, rendering their words and teachings sonorous, almost tangible, and suggesting a long triumphal pathway along which they advance with their disciples in rows on either side. The group does not join up behind them so that the two heads are clearly delineated, standing apart, as in Leonardo's *The Last Supper* where Christ is at the center of the work in front of a bright sky. Once again the influence of Leonardo's masterpiece can be detected everywhere in a number of physical types, in particular those of the old men in the larger groups and in the eloquence of their gestures, with hands that point and summon and explain.

In the left foreground and from left to right the following can be identified: Fra Angelico, Bramante in the foreground leaning on a railing, then Francesco Maria della Rovere, the young blond man who is turning towards Bramante; on the right behind St. Augustin there are St. Thomas Aquinas, Innocent the Third, St. Bonaventure; then Sixtus IV and Dante; in the background is Savonarola. These figures are arranged in order to create a triumphal path along the steps as they watch or point towards Christ or the host with movements in keeping with their characters. The faultless control of space, the perfect distribution of light and shade in harmony of gold, blue and white gives each individual figure included in this hierarchy of color and light, a life of its own. Every body and every face radiates power.

The most varied physical types nevertheless assert Raphael's preference for broad, full and structured faces: these are already

124　*Cartoon for The School of Athens.* 1510. Black and white chalk, body color. 280 × 800 cm. Milan, Pinacoteca Ambrosiana.

This huge drawing, used for the actual execution of the fresco, was in Milan at the beginning of the 17th century in the Borromeo collection. The figure of Heraclitus with the features of Michelangelo, which was inserted into the foreground of the fresco at the last minute, is absent. In many respects, in the play of the chiaroscuro and in certain physical types, the cartoon is strikingly reminiscent of Leonardo da Vinci.

to be found in the works executed towards the end of his stay in Florence. His preoccupation for individualizing faces sometimes leads to surprising deformities, bordering on caricature. Such is the case of the bearded man to the left of Francesco Maria della Rovere, or of the man even further to the left, conversing with Bramante.

Elsewhere a bishop has a profile where the line of the nose and that of the forehead, extended by the miter, form an obtuse angle that appears quite unrealistic. Everywhere the flesh appears supple, almost malleable; it is firm, yet soft and rounded. Even if the faces by Raphael often represent certain types, they never conform to an insipid "ideal beauty". They are beautiful for their youthfulness or for their expressions of wisdom and experience.

The diversity in the techniques and in the execution of the preparatory drawings of details of the *Disputa* reveals the total mastery of a draftsman who seems to have studied and completely assimilated the art of his predecessors. The different studies that have been preserved are evidence of this variety and this breadth of inspiration. A drawing in black chalk for *St. Stephen* in the Uffizi

has the constructive power and resolution of the most beautiful of Fra Bartolomeo's studies; also at the Uffizi is a preparatory drawing for the figure of *Adam*, similar in technique yet clear and concise.

There are also some drawings colored with a bold, fluid wash like the study for *Christ* in Lille with beautiful, traditionally Florentine drapery; pages with charcoal drawings like the one in the Louvre of the delicate studies for *Bramante*; studies in pen, some of which have been quickly sketched, in the manner of Leonardo of which there exists a double-sided example in Lille and others which have been carefully drawn but possess an unequaled expressive power, very Michelangelesque, like the double-sided drawing in Montpellier for the figure leaning forward, supporting himself on the wall on the extreme right of the fresco. One can only marvel at such studies which are so humble and yet so authoritative, created through a deep awareness of living forms.

125 *Study for The School of Athens.* 1510. Silver-point heightened with white on prepared paper. 28.7 × 38.7 cm. Vienna, Albertina.

This careful drawing from live models is for the lower left part of *The School of Athens* where we recognize Pythagoras surrounded by his disciples and perhaps also Parmenides. In the fresco Pythagoras is shown seated closer to the ground in a more closed position. On the right of the drawing "Parmenides" is represented twice, with the model supporting himself by leaning on a stick, then draped, establishing the suppler swinging rhythms the figure exhibits in the fresco itself.

126 *Studies for a statue of Minerva and other statues.* About 1510. Metal-point heightened with white, on pale pink prepared paper. 27.4 x 20.1 cm. Oxford, Ashmolean Museum.

A particularly fine preparatory study for the statue of Minerva in *The School of Athens* in a niche on the right, and for the other statues visible in the architectural perspective.

In the center of the fresco indicated by the convergence of the lines of perspective, Plato, carrying his *Timea*, points towards the sky and converses with Aristotle who holds the *Ethics* and points the palm of his hand towards the floor. Each illustrates in one simple gesture the essence of his philosophy. Many figures can be identified with some certainty. In the foreground starting from the left, there is Zenon with a child, then Epicurus reading; next a seated Pythagoras is writing in a large book with Averroes behind, then perhaps Parmenides and, seated and leaning pensively on his elbow, Heraclitus. Towards the right in the center of a large group is Euclid leaning over to measure a mathematical figure with a pair of compasses; then come Zoroaster and Ptolemy. Behind, on the left, Socrates talks with a group that can be identified as Alcibiades and Xenophon. In the center, lying on the steps, is Diogenes. Just as he does in the *Disputa*, Raphael establishes a relationship between the characters of the past and his contemporaries, giving several of the scholars and philosophers the features of living artists. Leonardo da Vinci's face is used for Plato, Michelangelo's for Heraclitus and Bramante, once again, is given the features of Euclid. Elsewhere other well-known people can be identified — in particular, Francesco Maria della Rovere and on the far right Raphael paints himself, half-hidden by his master Perugino.

Far fewer drawings survive for *The School of Athens* than for the *Disputa* or *Parnassus*. This can only be explained by a major accident in which a number of important pages had perhaps remained joined together and were all destroyed. The drawings that survive are all drawn in charcoal on prepared paper, and are also masterpieces of extraordinary delicacy. They show, in Vienna, Pythagoras and the surrounding group posed by semi-nude models in contemporary costume; at Oxford there is the surprising duo, set in a mandorla, of the two figures climbing the steps, one of whom points towards Diogenes, the other towards Plato and Aristotle, thus ensuring the subtle link between the two levels of the composition; in Frankfurt there is a drawing of Diogenes in a nude study that contains several alterations of detail; in Oxford again, studies for the statue of Minerva in the background together with other statues; and, also in Oxford, the group of mathematicians with Euclid and Ptolemy. There is only one drawing executed in red chalk and this is a plan in Oxford for the bas-relief on the left underneath the statue of Apollo.

Miraculously, the cartoon for all the figures in the fresco exists. This is at the Ambrosiana in Milan. It is a colossal drawing, eight meters in length, and perhaps the most beautiful, or at least the most striking of all the drawings in its remarkable black and white simplicity, and the subtlety and sweetness of the swift, light draftsmanship. In its appearance of a vast grisaille and also in the type and the expression of many of the faces, the cartoon at the Ambrosiana has a positively Leonardo-like charm, much of which is lost in the fresco sacrificed in favor of more fullness and power. One figure is missing in the Milan cartoon: the crucial figure of Heraclitus-Michelangelo, whose imposingly heavy build is to be

127   *Study of two standing male figures and a Medusa's head.* 1510. Silver-point heightened with white on pale pink paper; traces of oxidation. 27.8 × 20 cm. Oxford, Ashmolean Museum.

A delicate study for the two men conversing and pointing to Diogenes on the steps of *The School of Athens*. Contained within an overall almond shape, this group links the two levels of the composition. The screaming head of Medusa is a study for the shield of Minerva, a statue of whom stands in a niche on the right.

128   *School of Athens.* Detail of illustration 122.

seen, foreshortened, in the front of the painting. Technical examination of the fresco has confirmed that the figure was indeed painted later and added last of all, possibly after August 1511 when part of the Sistine ceiling, which influenced the figure of Heraclitus, was unveiled. Thus the enormous space across the foreground of the *School of Athens* was cleverly embellished by this "pensieroso." Without this would not the setting have been too similar to that of the *Disputa* where the composition draws its power from this very space, wide and paved and surmounted by four steps? The addition of Heraclitus is much more than just a filling in of space; it further enhances the effect of the *Disputa*.

The inevitable comparison of the two frescoes is more telling. With the same care for exact symmetry a variety of subtle responses resonate from one wall to the other. The arch of the vault corresponds to the semi-circular halo surrounding Christ. Where one fresco has empty spaces, those of the other are full. In this way the horizontal area crowded with people in the *School* corresponds to

the clear sky in the *Disputa*. The black and white figure of Fra Angelico, to the left in the latter, corresponds to the black and white group of Raphael and Perugino on the right of the *School of Athens*.

It is perhaps worth mentioning something about the painter's insistence on paying homage to Fra Angelico. The influence of his *Last Judgement* in Florence on the *Disputa* has already been discussed. The *School of Athens* reveals this influence even more strongly. The painting that is closest in its conception is to be found in the Vatican itself, in a room close to where Raphael worked, and there can be no doubt that Raphael knew this work well. In his frescoes in the chapel of Nicholas V, Fra Angelico depicts colonnades, recesses and pilasters, reviving all that was finest and most esteemed in antiquity. As in the *School of Athens*, huge white areas of architecture, skillfully spaced, balance the compact groups of figures clothed in bold yet gentle colors. In the fresco of *St. Lawrence Giving Alms to the Poor*, the beggars, arranged in receding perspective on the side of the saint in front of the symmetry of the architecture, already evoke the two groups of disciples that surround Plato and Aristotle in the *School of Athens*. And the *Ordination of St. Lawrence* recalls in its overall arrangement *Gregory IX Approving the Decretals* in the Segnatura. Some of Fra Angelico's figures are very like those of Raphael in their plasticity, their human presence and their capacity to convey conviction with such perfect reserve; take, for example, the characters present at the *Stoning of St. Stephen*, or the group of St. Peter and the kneeling saint in the *Ordination of St. Stephen*.

In the fresco of *Parnassus* dated from the end of 1510 to 1511, Raphael is confronted with a wall surface that is much more complex than that of the *Disputa* or *The School of Athens* where he elegantly "erased" the corner of a doorway by including its lightly-colored frame in the architectural design. Here the opening of a rectangular window in the center of the wall provides an irregular surface area. Moreover it is an area much smaller than that of the two preceding paintings since this is a wall that spans the width of the room, shorter than the length and, in order that the painting should have similar proportions to its predecessors, it is not as tall. The height of the fresco and the distance of the figures from the floor are well in keeping with the subject. An abrupt outcrop of land dominates the empty surface taken up by the window; on this sits Apollo with the nine muses behind encircling him. Next to the carefully constructed

129 *Parnassus*. Detail of illustration 130.

130 *Parnassus*. 1510-11. Fresco. Base 650 cm. Vatican, Stanza della Segnatura. The central window made this a difficult space to decorate. Raphael's solution to the problem was to place two groups of figures to the sides at the foot of a hillock which rises up above the top of the window frame and is occupied by Apollo and the Muses. The decoration of the lower part is completed by two grisailles, one on each side, representing *The Emperor Augustus saving the Aeneid from being burned* and *Alexander the Great having the works of Homer placed in the tomb of Achilles*.

131 *Melpomene. Study for the Parnassus.*
1501-11. Pen and ink. 33 × 21.9 cm. Oxford,
Ashmolean Museum.

An especially fluid and vigorous study showing the influence of the Antique for the figure
on the far left of the group of Muses — the
orientation of whose head is changed in the
fresco itself. A drawing in a similar technique
for the Muse next to her, perhaps Calliope,
is in the Albertina in Vienna. There the pose
is borrowed directly from the famous classical
sculpture of *The Sleeping Ariadne.*

space of the *School of Athens* and the almost as careful landscape of the *Disputa*, there is an open space which no longer has the rigid structure of linear perspective.

The identification of the eighteen poets that surround the central group, made up of Apollo and the nine Muses, is still debatable. It is permissible to think, as André Chastel does, that each one of the Muses should correspond to one classical and one modern writer. On the left behind the outcrop, yet on the same high level, is a group of poets — Homer flanked by Dante and Virgil. Beneath

132 *Studies of heads for the Parnassus.* Detail. 1510–11. Pen and ink. 265 × 182 cm. Windsor, Royal Library.

Detailed studies for the figures of Homer and Dante in the upper left part of the *Parnassus,* and for that of the character sometimes identified as Anacreon in the lower left corner near Sappho. Again the influence of the Antique is in evidence: the head of Homer is derived from that of *Laocoon.*

133 *The Virtues.* 1511. Fresco. Base 660 cm. Vatican, Stanza della Segnatura.

The last of the Stanza della Segnatura murals to be executed shows three of the cardinal virtues: from left to right, Fortitude, with the oak of the della Rovere family; Prudence, with the double face, looking into a mirror; and Temperance, who holds a bridle and reins. The fourth Virtue, Justice, is represented on the ceiling above.

134 *Study for Trebonianus delivering the Pandects to Justinian.* 1511. Brown wash with touches of pen and ink. 36 × 21.5 cm. Frankfurt, Städelsches Institut.

Difficult to assess because of its condition, the fresco for which this is a study is the pendant on the other side of the window under the Virtues to *Gregory IX delivering the Decretals.* The use of wash is bold and dashing, exactly fixing the forms in the light.

them, in a group of standing figures, are Petrarch, perhaps Pindar and a young person with long hair who has been identified as Horace and as the Thebean poetess Corinna. Opposite them in the foreground sits Sappho, whose name is written on the scroll she holds in her hand. On the right the poets are arranged in a descending curve, beginning with the Muses and coming down towards the window. From the top to the bottom they are possibly Antonio Tebaldeo (or Baldassare Castiglione, or even Michelangelo), Boccacio, perhaps Tibulle, Ariosto and Sannazaro. The man seated in the foreground and who points authoritatively at the spectator is usually identified as Pindar; the young poet with outspread hands with whom he is talking could be Horace. An early sketch which we know through an engraving by Marcantonio shows the essentials of the composition with a few variations in the attitudes and spacing. Some of the most powerful features of the fresco, such as the two seated figures in the foreground or the Muse with her back turned towards us on the right, are not yet present. The attitude of Apollo, similar to those of *Justice* and *Philosophy* on the ceiling, is different from that which Raphael finally chose, and five winged *putti*, flying amidst the leaves of the tree, brandish the laurel wreaths that they are about to award; but these *putti* are perhaps an addition by the engraver. A second stage in the preparation of *Parnassus* is documented in a copy of a Raphael drawing at the Ashmoleun Museum in Oxford, where the figures are portrayed as nudes. The figures of the upper section vary only very slightly from, and already have the attitudes and the groupings of, the final painting. The two groups in the lower section on either side of the doorway were finalized only at a later stage, in particular the figures of Sappho and Pindar, on either side of the window, who encroach upon its painted frame in twisting attitudes, almost provocative in their foreshortened appearance. The sinuous Sappho twists and turns like a reptile. She is a happy inclusion in that she imbues the composition with an elliptical rhythm which includes the five seated figures in the center, Apollo and the surrounding Muses, Sappho and Pindar, and gives an energetic three-dimensional effect allowing one to forget at least in part the intruding window.

The standing figures emphasize this movement and echo it on a larger scale. Carried out at different stages in the preparation, the drawings of the details display another type of work. They form a beautiful group, highly coherent in style. All these drawings in Lille, Windsor, Oxford, London and Vienna are executed in pen and all are faultless in their accuracy and precision; they comprise drapery, hands, heads or entire figures as in the famous drawing in Vienna for the half-reclining figure of a Muse, perhaps Calliope, and directly inspired by the ancient *Ariane* in the Vatican.

When compared to the other frescoes in the room, *Parnassus* gives the impression of a work of abundance and freedom, full of joyous rhythm — a tribute to feminine beauty. The whole work is outstanding in its diversity of fabrics, variously draped, billowing, folded, falling and gathered up; and for the complexity of the colors which have assumed a bloom like that of fruit, in shades of pink,

135 *Pope Gregory IX delivering the decretals.* 1511. Fresco. Base 220 cm. Vatican, Stanza della Segnatura.

Placed under the fresco of the *Virtues* and next to that of the *Disputà,* the work illustrates the theme of canon law. Gregory IX is shown with the features of Julius II, the cardinal nearest him with those of Giovanni de' Medici; the two other cardinals behind him may be Alessandro Farnese and Antonio del Monte. Now in poor condition, the fresco may have been partly executed by Raphael's assistants. There is a beautiful pen and ink drawing for the right hand side of the work in the Städelsches Institut in Frankfurt.

orange and soft blue. It is difficult to picture in the *School of Athens* or the *Disputa* such sumptuous and rare harmonies as the purplish-blue, the orangey-yellow and the jade green in Homer's clothing between the pink of Dante and the dark green of Virgil. The nonchalant attitudes, unrestricted by any architectural line, are governed by the fluid rhythms in which there is a deliberate sense of vagueness of space. Even the treatment of the objects renders them softer, bathed in a light that lessens the emphasis of the outlines. One has only to compare the pen drawing for *Apollo* in the Lille Museum, clear and compact in its anatomical study, and the cor-

136 *The Massacre of the Innocents.* About 1511. Pen and ink. 23.3 x 37.6 cm. London, British Museum.

137 *The Massacre of the Innocents.* About 1511. Black chalk. 24.8 x 41.1 cm. Windsor, Royal Library.

This drawing was made from another of the same size, in pen and ink, now at the British Museum, in which the figures are all nude. The pen and ink drawing was traced through onto the sheet in Windsor and Raphael worked over it, modifying the figures, adding others and draping the female figures.

138 Marcantonio Raimondi. *The Massacre of the Innocents.* About 1511-12. Engraving after Raphael. 28.3 x 43.4 cm.

This composition, one of Raphael's most complex, is basically frieze-like yet at the same time exploits all the expressive possibilities of the third dimension, most spectacularly in the figure of the woman in the center, running out towards the viewer. The juxtaposition of the study for one of the executioners in *The Massacre of the Innocents* with a study for *The Judgment of Solomon* on the ceiling of the Stanza della Segnatura shows the origin of the artist's interest in the theme.

responding figure in the fresco whose form seems almost limp by comparison until one recognizes in the glowing slightly softened light the same muscular shapes.

The *Parnassus* is also, like the *School of Athens* but in a gently lyrical way, the best illustration of a revived antiquity that has both conviction and warmth. It is a genuine renaissance of this antiquity, gentle and sympathetic, where the classical and modern poets casually converse, and where even Apollo plays a modern instrument, the *lira da braccio*, a kind of violin with nine strings, whereas Sappho and the Muses hold instruments found in Roman sculptures.

The fresco of the *Virtues*, painted in 1511, has quite a different character, that of a lunette, which was dictated by the difficult surface to be decorated. The three figures, all on a larger scale than that of the characters on the other walls, are depicted sitting on a simple stone bench that spans the whole length of the painting above a sturdy entablature of painted architecture. They stand out against the background of the sky, appearing to be raised high above it. In this use of perspective, the work is distinct from the other frescoes in the Stanza della Segnatura with its illusionism and elaborate use

139 *Study for one of the Sibyls in the church of Santa Maria della Pace.* About 1511. Red chalk. 27.9 x 17.2 cm. Vienna, Albertina.

The influence of Michelangelo's Sistine Chapel figures upon the art of Raphael may be seen in the vigorous forms of this drawing, the sharpness of contrast between light and shade and the sense of tension in the movements.

of decoration, as it traces in the space of a rounded pediment, the clear and winding motif, devoid of any depth, of a vast bas-relief.

From left to right the figure of *Strength*, in armor and helmet, subdues a wild beast and bends the trunk of a young oak tree; an obvious allusion to the della Rovere family. In the center is *Prudence* with two faces looking in a mirror. Finally there is *Temperance* who is holding a bit with reins. Winged putti rhythmically bind the three principal figures in a counterpoint of energetic little curves. These three can be interpreted as the personification of theological Vir-

tues, complementing the cardinal Virtues — the putto picking the acorns from the oak tree represents *Charity*, the one approaching the torch *Hope*, and the one pointing towards the sky *Faith*. *Justice*, the fourth of the cardinal Virtues, features, in one of the small medallions on the ceiling, the one that dominates the fresco in which her companions are portrayed and with whom she is thus associated. This is because the whole of the wall including the frescoes of *Trebonianus Consigning the Pandects to Justinian* and *Gregory IX Approving the Decretals* is dedicated to the Laws, and as first among the four *Virtues*, *Justice* dominates. And it is well known that for Plato, and later St. Augustine, Justice was the most important of all the virtues.

In the center of the fresco, on a higher level and seen as it were, more *di sotto* than her neighbors, *Prudence* must surely represent one of Raphael's most poetic creations, with her play of masks and faces; an exquisite and mysterious profile of a young girl is reflected in the mirror, while the silhouette of an old man is outlined against her neck and a Gorgon-like head beats against her breast. The figures of *Strength* and *Temperance*, seated symmetrically, invite comparison. The former appears sturdy and powerful, rather Michelangelesque, as she displays her strength with the little putto bending the young tree. In this way the young woman fits into the tight arch of the vault. Averting her gaze, the figure of *Temperance* seems to show Raphael's response to Michelangelo. The twisting movement of the body is similar to that of the figure of *Strength*, but it is relaxed and supple, more flowing and inviting in its form which basks in the space rather than concentrating it. The beautiful, strong arms hold the reins in a languid yet lively rhythm, ready to be unleashed like a fisherman casting his nets. The comparison of the robes of the two figures is striking: the long and supple folds of *Temperance* contrast with the more sculptural folds of the more complex and irregular design of *Strength*.

When it is placed next to the *Disputa*, the damaged fresco of *Gregory IX Approving the Decretals* illustrates canon law, whereas the symmetrical fresco to the left of the window illustrates civil law. The scene depicted is a contemporary one since the Pope bears the features of Julius II, and it has been possible to identify some of the cardinals surrounding him, in particular, Giovanni de Medici. This is the first example of one of the transpositions, which will become more frequent in the *Stanza di Eliodoro*, where the reigning pontiff is portrayed in the place of one of his predecessors, or intervening in person in a sacred scene. Restricted to an even smaller space yet comprising the same architectural setting, *Trebonianus Consigning the Pandects to Justinian* has become a very difficult painting to assess. It has been damaged, restored, or perhaps it was even left unfinished at the outset. It is almost certain (and also possible in the case of *Gregory IX*) that other painters were involved in its creation.

Two painted bas-reliefs on either side of the window beneath the fresco of *Parnassus*, from which they are separated by a wide painted moulding also in *trompe l'oeil*, carry the fresco decoration on this wall from the base of the room upwards to the same level as the paintings on the other walls. The subjects of the two paintings, *Augustus Preventing Virgil's Executors from Burning the Aeneid* and *Alexander the Great Ordering the Works of Homer to be Placed in Achilles' Tomb*, clearly correspond to the room's function as a library. The vigorous and supple strength of the forms and the liveliness of the rhythm depend on the nature of the grisaille and its decorative function. They were already to be found in the *Baglioni Predella*. There is no reason then why these two small frescoes should be dated so long after the rest of the frescoes in the *Segnatura*, as has been done by dating them to 1514. And there is even less reason to say that it was not Raphael who carried out this admirable work, probably in 1511 after the *Parnassus*, but Gianfrancesco Penni or Perino del Vaga.

It was around 1510 that Marcantonio Raimondi arrived in Rome from Bologna and Venice. This was important because he undertook to collaborate with Raphael. Marcantonio's engravings,

like those of his assistants, Marco Dente da Ravenna and Agostino dei Musi (known as Agostino of Veneziano), were widely distributed after 1515, spreading the fame of Raphael's compositions far beyond Rome. *The Massacre of the Innocents*, from the engraving by Marcantonio after Raphael, is the most famous, the most beautiful and by rare good fortune the only one whose preparation for the composition we can follow since several of Raphael's drawings have been preserved. One of these drawings, in the Albertina in Vienna, which contains studies in red chalk for the group on the left, is to be found on the back of a study for *Astronomy* on the ceiling of the *Segnatura*. Another page, also at the Albertina, brings together the pen studies for the executioner on the left of the engraving and for the false mother in the *Judgement of Solomon* painted on the same part of the ceiling proof that they were prepared at the same time, probably between 1508 and 1509. The artist seems to have moved naturally from one violent theme, the *Judgement of Solomon*, to that of the *Massacre of the Innocents*. Two splendid drawings for the whole composition, one in pen in the British Museum and the other in red chalk at Windsor, give a fascinating insight into Raphael's working methods. The pen drawing in which the figures are all shown nude is repeated on the second sheet of the same size where the female figures are clothed; other figures are added and certain poses altered. There can be no doubt that *The Massacre of the Innocents* with its figures locked in violent action is a deliberate attempt on Raphael's part to rival Michelangelo's *Battle of Cascina*. Raphael's drawings, used by Marcantonio for his engrav-

140   *The Sibyls.* About 1511. Fresco. Base 615 cm. Rome, Santa Maria della Pace.

With the fresco of *The Prophets* above it, *The Sibyls* decorates the wall above the entrance arch of a chapel; hence its unusual shape. The scheme was commissioned from Raphael by Agostino Chigi. The individual identification of the Sibyls depicted is problematic. *The Sibyls* bear certain resemblances to *The Virtues* in the Stanza della Segnatura and they were probably painted in the same year, 1511, and not 1514 which is the date most often suggested.

ings, still survive. There is a hurried sketch in ink of *Adam* at Oxford dating from the end of his stay in Florence and which was also used for the engraving of *Original Sin*, and the highly finished silverpoint study at the British Museum which was engraved with a few variations as *Venus and Cupid*. But there remain no preparatory drawings for works, as important as they are famous, such as *Dido* or *Lucretia* which were very likely painted from drawings by the master and which, like the *Massacre of the Innocents*, would appear to be contemporary with the paintings of the *Segnatura*.

When he was nearing completion of his work in the *Segnatura* Raphael painted two important frescoes for the banker Agostino Chigi whose interests were closely associated with those of the Pope. The fresco of the *Sybils* and the *Prophets* in the Roman church of Santa Maria della Pace was, like the *Galatea*, commissioned by Agostino Chigi for his chapel in the church. It occupies two spaces, one above the other, on the same wall. One is a long, rectangular space, narrowing considerably in the center due to the opening of an arch below, which contains the figures of the four Sybils, four angels and three putti; further up, on either side of the high window, are the four Prophets joined by two angels. The very shallow architectural space of the area lends coherence to the two frescoes. The identification of the different Sybils is problematic and a subject of much controversy. Each is accompanied by the angel carrying an inscribed tablet or scroll. The two Sybils to the left of the arch are writing on tablets held by the angels. Those on the right are reading what an angel indicates on the tablet. The strongly Michelangelesque quality of the full, powerful figures has often been emphasized for the whole of the fresco and particularly for the upper section containing the Prophets. But the composition of the Sybils, with their relaxed and pliant gestures, the confidence of the figures that lean along the lines of the architecture in curving poses, are in their rhythmic and psychological unity completely Raphaelesque.

The fresco presented the same type of problem encountered in the *Virtues* of the *Segnatura* — the depiction of seated female figures in a very unusual and restrictive area. Here Raphael adopts a decorative approach that is as light as it is rich thanks to the delicacy of the dark curtain placed at the back of the shallow recess where the figures are seated and where he has traced a lively motif on to a dark background with sharply outlined arabesques. All the while the trio of the Virtues with their slower movement flow from one gentle color to another. A lightly drawn pen sketch at Oxford for the right section of the fresco can be found on the back of a study for the *School of Athens*. This shows that by 1509 or 1510 Raphael already had this project in mind. Several magnificent large drawings preserved in London, Oxford and Vienna are individual studies for each of the figures.

Vasari's date of 1511 is confirmed by a sketch in Oxford and by the style of the painted work. One can thus confidently abandon the date of 1514 or later, which was only ever intended as a general indication.

The *Triumph of Galatea* is Raphael's first great secular painting. It was painted as a fresco in a room on the ground floor of Agostino Chigi's villa in Rome overlooking the Tiber, later called the Villa Farnesina, at the end of 1511 or more probably at the beginning of 1512. The subject is based on a poem by Poliziano and depicts the nymph Galatea in her seaborne chariot drawn by two dolphins and guided by the child Palemon in the foreground. She appears unaffected by the arrows of the three *amorini* that fly through the sky (unlike her companions the Nereids who are struggling with Tritons) and turns round to look at one, half hidden by a cloud, holding arrows in its hand symbolizing platonic love. Thus the work deals with an idea that was popular during the Renaissance of a noble, true love that was opposed to purely sensual appetites.

It is clear that he drew inspiration from antiquity both in the mythological subject matter and in the direct borrowing of Greco-Roman motifs. The *Galatea* is one of his most frequently imitated works and one cannot begin to count the paintings of naval victories that have been inspired by it, especially in France — balanced, harmonious paintings of the seventeenth century and the gracious, delightful works of the eighteenth. The Farnesina fresco is impressive for its dancing vitality, full of rhythm and energy. The figures, bursting with life, robust and healthy, stretch themselves out, stirring the space with their broad gestures. They do battle with good humor in a bright, almost blinding light where the tones of amber and pink, the sea greens and steely blues contrast with a few dark patches, especially the astonishing Pompeiian red, so superbly discordant, of the nymph's clothing. The composition is brought to life by a strong, oval giratory movement whose thrust is derived from the arched body of Pelemon at the bottom, and is completed at the top by the bodies of the three *amorini*. In the center Galatea turns on herself in a spiraling movement, supple in rhythm, that echoes the more open and violent rhythm of the chaste St. Catherine in London. This balanced and symmetrical aspect of the composition tempers the fiery course of the chariot towards the right, with the clothing and hair billowing tempestuously, swept horizontally by the wind. The freedom in the poses of the *Galatea* is similar to that of the *Virtues* in the Segnatura and of the Sybils in Santa Maria della Pace. But the expansive movements, the complexity of some of the groupings and also the release of lyrical feeling recall the *Heliodorus* which could in part be contemporary.

141   *The Triumph of Galatea.* About 1511-12. Fresco. 295 × 225 cm. Rome, Villa Farnesina.

This was the first major commission Raphael received from Agostino Chigi who together with the Pope was to be his principal patron. It is in a large ground-floor room of the banker's villa which Sebastiano del Piombo was decorating at the same time. Unlike her companions, who are succumbing to the arrows of earthly love fired by the little cupids, Galatea aspires to celestial love, looking up towards the cupid who holds back his arrows, in the upper left part of the composition.

The Madonnas painted at the same time as the *Stanza della Segnatura* show the same concern for fullness and lyrical feeling as the frescoes. The *Mackintosh Madonna* (National Gallery, London) has in the past been so damaged that all one can now make out is the symmetrical impact of the triangular composition and fine oval face whose cast-down eyes were to delight Ingres and the balance between, on one side, the Child's body and on the other the Virgin's arm weighed down by heavy folds of cloth. The preparatory cartoon at the British Museum gives a better idea of the power of Raphael's conception through its simplification of the human forms outlined in the chiaroscuro hatched graphics with an assurance unrivalled except, perhaps, in Fra Bartolomeo's small drawings. The joyful radiance of the two figures, so tenderly intimate, again evokes the *Cowper* and *Tempi* Madonnas and allows us to suggest a date quite close to Raphael's arrival in Rome, probably 1509.

143 *Studies of heads for the Virgin and Child.* About 1508-9. Metal-point on pink prepared paper. 14.3 x 11 cm. London, British Museum.

One of the drawings in which Raphael uses metal-point to achieve the most delicate and masterly effects. It has been related to several Madonnas of the end of the Florentine or beginning of the Roman period. Note the points of similarity with the *Mackintosh* and *Aldobrandini Madonnas.*

142 *Study for the Virgin and Child in a landscape.* About 1508-9. Pen and ink. 18.6 x 14.6 cm. Vienna, Albertina.

Datable from the study for the *Disputà* on the verso, this rapid, spiralling drawing is somewhat reminiscent of Leonardo.

The little *Aldobrandini Madonna*, a triangular composition similar to the *Mackintosh Madonna* and painted one or two years after, is also in the National Gallery. It was the last time the artist painted a half length Madonna on a small scale, a precious painting for a collector, in the manner of Leonardo. With its double-arched opening on to a luminous landscape, this little painting in London is a final transformation and revival of the *Madonna of the Carnation* in Munich, painted in rare and sumptuous colors which have often, quite erroneously, led people to doubt its authenticity. It is in fact a glorious masterpiece painted with a supple, yet firm brush, a pattern of rhythmic curves drawn towards the sinuous line formed by the stem of the carnation in the center. There is an infallible unity in the artist's work; the Virgin's face, like that of a shy girl, recalls the preparatory drawing in the British Museum for the *Norton Simon Madonna.*

136

The *Madonna di Loreto*, one of Raphael's best known and most frequently copied compositions, thought to have been lost since the eighteenth century, has recently been discovered at the Musée Condé at Chantilly by Cecil Gould who identified it as a painting which until now had been considered a copy. Having been scrupulously studied by Cecil Gould and Sylvie Béguin, the *Madonna di Loreto* can now take its place in the work of Raphael. To assess it properly one has to disregard the figure of St. Joseph, added later and which hides a curtain and a window. The painting is unusual for the large amount of space around the figures which allows them to breathe and spread out their broad, expansive gestures. Fabrics comprise a large part of the composition; a sheet and white cushion on which the child is resting constitute a powerful foreground, the blue robe cast over the Virgin's arm and the transparent triangle of the veil.

The treatment of the head and the raised arm recall the sculpted forms of antiquity. These broad, powerful shapes are treated in a light, caressing, almost sketchy way, with coloring in which the pearly white, vermilion and luminous pink of the carnations are enhanced by the blue of the cloak and green of the background. One wonders whether the rapid treatment, exceptional in itself, is not proof of the particular influence of the fresco painter's technique. In any case the painting, whose similarities with some of the work in the *Stanza della Segnatura*, especially the figure of Justice on the ceiling, are remarkable, must be dated fairly early, to around the beginning of Raphael's period in Rome — 1509 or 1510. These somewhat elongated limbs of the *Madonna di Loreto*, the expansive movements of the arms and shoulders, are to be seen again in two Madonnas, both painted a little later, probably in 1511.

The *Alba Madonna*, which belonged to the Alba family in Madrid during the eighteenth century, continues in its circular format the theme of the *Virgin and Child with the Infant St. John*, set in a landscape, which was often featured in Raphael's famous works from his stay in Florence and of which one is particularly reminded by the plants in the foreground. The figures are organized in a pattern of concentric rhythms with both the hair and headdress responding in flowing waves to this movement. The muscles in the bodies have become more elastic and have assumed a new strength. The Virgin's neck leans firmly forward and to one side, the arm on which she leans is taut and the Child supports Himself by leaning on His outstretched leg. The complexity of the poses, both tense and relaxed, and the rich, supple, voluminous folds of the drapery so nobly arranged recall the sculptures of antiquity as much as the work of Michelangelo. The *Taddei Tondo* must surely be mentioned at this stage. The coloring, which is both bright and gentle without being insipid, contrasts the different tones of pink and blue.

At the Lille museum one of Raphael's most famous drawings comprises on both sides studies for the composition in Washington. On one side the drawing of a man shows how the study of nature can generate ideas on form and how much the circular shape, already chosen for the final painting, dominates even in a prepara-

tory drawing. On the other side a study for the whole composition arranges the figures inside the circle in a rapid sketch of unparalleled fluency and energy.

Less well known than the *Alba Madonna*, often misunderstood and even recently suspected of having "studio assistance," is the *Madonna of the Diadem*, clearly the work of a single hand and probably painted in the same year — 1511. This rare masterpiece can equally be compared in its breadth of style and similarity of subject to the *Madonna di Loreto*, as to the *Alba Madonna*, which adopts something of the same pose. But all the minor constraints that stem from the direct influence of Michelangelo in the *Alba Madonna* have in the sturdy yet delicate *Madonna of the Diadem* been discarded, thus enjoying a greater freedom. Air moves around the group like a hoop

144   *The Virgin and Child,* cartoon for the *Mackintosh Madonna* About 1509. Black chalk with touches of bodycolor. 71 x 53.5 cm. London, British Museum.

The corresponding painting, which is in the National Gallery in London, is in a very poor state. Powerful in its contrasts of light and shade and its rapid, free execution, the cartoon differs somewhat from the painting, in which the Virgin's draperies are more complicated. But the pricks by which the design was transferred do correspond with the contours of forms in the painting.

145   *The Aldobrandini Madonna*, sometimes known as *The Garvagh Madonna*. About
1510-11. Oil on panel. 39 × 33 cm. London, National Gallery.

In Rome in the Aldobrandini then the Borghese collections, and afterwards in London in the Day then the Garvagh collections, the picture relates compositionally to
certain Madonnas by Leonardo da Vinci. The vivid and highly contrasted coloring
has led some commentators wrongly to doubt whether it is an autograph work.

146   *The Loreto Madonna*, also known as *The Madonna of the Veil*. About 1510. Oil
on panel. 120 x 90 cm. Chantilly, Musée Condé.

Cecil Gould's discovery of the original *Loreto Madonna* which had passed unnoticed
in spite of being on show at the Château de Chantilly represented a major contribution to our knowledge of Raphael. The work was probably given by Pope Julius
II to the church of Santa Maria del Popolo in Rome. It was next in the Borghese
collection, then in that of the Prince of Salerno, father-in-law of the Duke of Aumale
who left his pictures to the Institut de France. The title comes from a copy, considered in the 18th century to be the original, which was then in the basilica of the
Santa Casa in Loreto.

147 *The Alba Madonna.* About 1511. Oil on panel, transferred to canvas. 95 cm. diameter. Washington, National Gallery.

Commissioned by Paolo Giovio for the church of the Olivetans at Nocera, the work remained there up to the end of the 17th century. It was acquired by the Marquis del Carpio, Viceroy of Naples, who took it to Spain; then it belonged to the Duke of Alba. It entered the Hermitage in 1836 and, like the *St. George,* was sold by the Soviet government in 1937 to A. Mellon who bequeathed it to the National Gallery. The tension in the closed-in forms and the fluid treatment of the draperies place the work at about the time of the last frescoes in the Stanza della Segnatura, the *Parnassus* and *The Virtues.*

148 *Sheet of studies for the Alba Madonna* (recto). About 1511. Red chalk and pen and ink. 42.2 x 27.2 cm. Lille, Musée des Beaux-Arts.

A first sketch of masterly freedom for the *Alba Madonna*, showing a number of variations from the design finally realized in the painting. The two pen and ink sketches in the upper left part of the drawing are first ideas for the *Madonna della Sedia* or *The Madonna of the Curtain*.

149 *Study for the Alba Madonna* (verso). About 1511. Red chalk. 42.2 x 27.2 cm. Lille, Musée des Beaux-Arts.

A life study, made from a male model, for the *Alba Madonna*.

150 *The Madonna with the blue diadem,* also known as *The Velo Madonna.* About 1511. Oil on panel. 68 × 44 cm. Paris, Musée du Louvre.

Acquired by Louis XV from the collection of the Prince of Carignan, this work has often been attributed to a Raphael pupil, Giulio Romano or Penni, working from an original design by the master. But the quality of the execution, the refinement and brilliance of the colors point to an autographed picture from around the end of the period of work on the Stanza della Segnatura. The landscape, solidly constructed by means of broad planes of shadow with milky effects of light playing over the distant background, is close to that of the *Aldobrandini Madonna.*

151 *Portrait of a Young Man.* About 1511. Oil on panel. 72 × 56 cm. Formerly Cracow, Czartoryski Museum.

This marvelous portrait, bought in Venice by Prince Adam Czartoryski in 1807, remains little known. It seems to have disappeared during the Second World War. The mastery of spatial effects shown in the broad movement of the arms, and the elegance of the composition, suggest a date around the time of the *Alba Madonna,* shortly after the Prado Portrait of a Cardinal.

143

and a series of oblique screens standing out against the light lead into the distance and integrate the figures into the space of the landscape.

This landscape, which can be directly compared to that in the *Aldobrandini Madonna*, is one of Raphael's most poetic inventions, one of his purest meditations on the ruins of ancient Rome. This archaeological element must be emphasized. The painting is really, and this is a new theme, the Virgin of the Ruins, and the classical flavor of the young woman's clothing emphasizes this delightfully. The coloring is an exhaustive study of the different shades of purplish or cerulean blues and the nuances of pink and pale yellow.

Several copies, of which the finest comes from the Duke of Westminster's collection and is now in the Princeton University Museum, provide us with an idea of the original appearance of an important painting by Raphael (now lost) of the *Virgin and Child with the Infant St. John in a Landscape*. The theme of the Virgin lifting the veil that covers the child and the grouping of the figures, seated or crouching in a rhythmic circle, are direct reminders of the *Alba Madonna* and the *Madonna of the Diadem* and, in view of the full-bodied figures and strong similarity of the laughing face of the infant to St. John in the *Niccolini-Cowper Madonna*, one could suggest a fairly early date during Raphael's period in Rome, even before the painting in Washington or Paris, of 1509 or 1510. This type of composition was greatly admired, as is demonstrated for example, in a tondo by Penni that represents a Holy Family in the Museum of the Abbey of Cava de Tirreni at Naples.

There is a cool air of distinction in the contemporary portraits, the hard, simplified forms that characterize the *Alba Madonna* and the *Madonna of the Diadem* and in particular, the *Portrait of a Cardinal* in the Prado. What could be more simple than this painting which is simultaneously so lean, hard and compact? It is a red bust, with a brilliant white sleeve and an unforgettable presence in the sitter's gaze. This is the period when more than ever Raphael takes an interest in sculpture. The figure stands boldly in front of a dark background, solid as a rock but softened by the moiréed fabric. This is an important moment in the history of portrait painting, when the apparent relationship of the painter to the sitter and vice-versa manages to reproduce the feelings and sensibilities of both. Later this relationship was occasionally captured by Van Dyck and Degas and more frequently by Velazquez.

The *Portrait of a Young Man* possibly dates from the same year — 1511. Lost since the last war but formerly in the Czartoryski museum at Cracow, it was thought for a long time, perhaps because of its youthful charm and "artist's" costume, to be a self-portrait of Raphael. Admirable in his studied, haughty elegance, yet far from indifferent, he is lively and determined with an unerring gaze and the hint of a smile. This young man from Cracow heralds a whole genre of seventeenth-century French portraiture. In their portraits of young men, Bourdon or Le Sueur, for example, were to emulate the same carefree aristocratic air through similar effects of costume and in particular the voluminous white shirts.

It is revealing that the young Van Dyck, when in Italy between 1621 and 1624, made a sketch after this painting whose "dandy-like" subject was well suited to him. The tone, almost pre-romantic in its intensity, shows the influence of Sebastiano del Piombo, and indeed the entire Venetian School. The elements in the composition, the rich almost tactile quality of the shirt, the fur and the hair are all Venetian in spirit, and almost Flemish. The broad setting, with the spectacular position of the arm and shoulder in the foreground, a Parmigianino-like distortion, is related to the *Alba Madonna* or the *Madonna of the Diadem*. The fairly late dating for this picture of between 1516 and 1518 can be brought forward appreciably. It could have been painted around 1511, a short time after the *School of Athens* and the *Parnassus* where, moreover, there are figures which bear a striking resemblance to the sitter.

The *Portrait of Fedra Inghirami*, Julius II's librarian, can perhaps also be given an appreciably earlier date than that of 1514 generally ascribed to it. It may be dated around 1511-1512. It is the antithesis, with its broad stocky shapes, of the *Cardinal* in the Prado, equally red but lean and gaunt. The body turns away and the head is raised at a curious almost imbalanced angle, accentuated by the cast in his eye, and which seems to make the shape of his body sway. But the horizontal plane of the stone tablet in the foreground, with books and other objects arranged in perspective, reassuringly anchors the painting. Two versions of this picture exist; one is in the Gardner Museum, Boston and the other is in the Palazzo Pitti in Florence, both variously considered in turn to be the original. The Florence portrait, more imposing and rounded and more precise in its subtlety of mood, is to be preferred to the one in Boston.

During the sixteenth century the *Portrait of Julius II* (National Gallery, London) hung as a pair to the *Madonna di Loreto* on two columns in the church of Santa Maria del Popolo in Rome on official occasions. The portrait of Julius II was considered to be one of the copies of the lost original until recently when Cecil Gould and Konrad Oberhuber confirmed that it was the original itself. The position of the sitter in the armchair, the angle of the head, the three quarter length format, appear completely free of affectation — this is one of the greatest creations in the history of portrait painting. The Pope is seated quite simply, without sinking back in the chair or sitting too rigidly, in a natural pose. In earlier portraits the hands would either rest on the arms of the chair or on a ledge, as if they defined the limits of the picture. Here they are placed freely in space, no longer merely the lower limit of the bust. They are now part of the physical activity of the painting. In their

152 *Portrait of a Cardinal.* About 1511. Oil on panel. 79 × 61 cm. Madrid, Prado.

In spite of the many names that have been suggested, the identity of the sitter has not been established. With its stark simplicity and the perfect expression of character through form, this represents one of Raphael's greatest successes as a portraitist.

154 *Study for the Portrait of Julius II.* 1511-12. Metal-point on prepared paper. 36 × 25 cm. Chatsworth, Devonshire Collection.

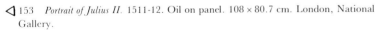

153 *Portrait of Julius II.* 1511-12. Oil on panel. 108 × 80.7 cm. London, National Gallery.

Rediscovered by C. Gould and K. Oberhuber after having been considered an old copy, this picture was given by the sitter to the church of Santa Maria del Popolo where it was on display at the same time as the *Madonna of Loreto.* It entered the National Gallery as part of the Angerstein collection in 1824. Impressive for its authority and its simplicity alike, it established a pattern for papal portraiture that was to last two centuries.

155 *Portrait of Tommaso ('Fedra') Inghirami.* About 1511-12. Oil on panel. 91 x 62 cm. Florence, Pitti Palace.

There are two versions of this portrait; the other, which comes from the Inghirami family in Volterra, is in the Gardner Museum in Boston. The Florence version seems to be the earlier of the two. The realism of the image of the librarian, busy writing, and the still life in the foreground recall portraits of German and Flemish humanists.

relationship to his handkerchief and the arm of the chair the Pope's hands express an energy and a tension almost greater than that of the face which appears somewhat resigned. In this way the entire body of the sitter can be registered in one glance that takes in the whole of the picture. The handling of the paint is highly finished, even extravagant, fitting for such an important commission. The softness of touch is striking, particularly on the face. All the components of the painting are shown with their inherent qualities — the shining fabric of the cherry-red shawl, touched by his thick, fine-haired beard, the twisting, golden tassles that hang from the shining knobs on the chair and the tight ripples of the pleats of his surplice.

The painting can be dated exactly to the winter of 1511–12, since we know that at that date the Pope had a beard. It is important to examine the relationship between the painting of the Pope and the *Madonna di Loreto* when in Santa Maria del Popolo. They were perhaps given together to the church by Julius II, and one wonders whether they were actually painted for him to hang as a pair. The grouping of red, green and white in each of the paintings tends to support this hypothesis. However, the different dimensions, the richer, more lavish composition of the portrait and the more mature style would suggest that they were brought together at a later date.

The importance of the portrait of Pope Julius II was immense. This powerful depiction of the sitter in a three-quarter length format, cut off below the knees, arms leaning on either side of the chair with hands to the fore, was to be used by generations of painters, especially for portraits of Popes. It can be seen in the work of Sebastiano del Piombo in his portraits of Clement VII (in Naples; a version in Vienna). Titian, to whom a copy of the National Gallery picture in the Pitti is often attributed, was inspired by it in his portrait of Pope Paul III, also in Naples; and the most brilliant of interpretations is by Velazquez in his portrait of Innocent X.

IV. Rome 1512–1516: The Universal Painter

Attempts to divide up the different stages in a painter's career are always based on somewhat arbitrary judgements. This is especially true in the case of Raphael whose Roman projects were large and complex and pose a great number of problems. Such a division into stages by definition seems to be an oversimplification but it can, by clearly marking them out, help to assess to what extent Raphael's art was transformed by constant effort. The transformation and its consequences are hardly less important in the ten years between 1510 and 1520 that separate the *School of Athens* from the *Transfiguration* than in the period from 1500–1510, from the *Altarpiece of St. Nicholas* to the *School of Athens*. It would appear that after a brilliant period which marks a gentle climax in his abilities and corresponds with the execution of the frescoes in the Stanza della Segnatura he gained both fame and fortune at a moment not only of maturity but also perhaps of doubt, a moment when he was seeking answers to important questions about the nature of painting, enlarging his field of interest and seriously studying other works of art.

Julius II died in February 1513. In the following month Giovanni de Medici, son of Lorenzo the Magnificent, was elected Pope and chose to call himself Leo X. Renowned as a peaceful man of letters, he was also a lover of the arts in the tradition of his family. Leo X, through politics and patronage, was even more determined than his predecessor to glorify the church of Rome. Under his pontificate Raphael became a universal artist of European fame. He diversified his artistic activity, embarking on various aspects of the decorative arts — antique grotesques, designs for mosaics and sculptures, cartoons for tapestries and even stage design, as a correspondence of March 1519, mentioning designs by Raphael for the *Suppositi* by Ariosto, attests. After the death of Bramante in 1514 he became the architect of St. Peter's and the Vatican; the following year he was also named keeper of the antiquities of Rome, responsible for directing archaeological excavations. In 1519 Raphael sent the Pope a report, drafted by Baldassare Castiglione, concerning the conservation of ancient monuments in the city, together with a plan of classical Rome.

His talents were in great demand everywhere and one can well understand how it came about that his studio assistants executed large parts of the frescoes and paintings for which he was respon-

sible. But all his various activities converged in one coherent optimistic vision of the building of a new Christian Rome at one with classical Rome. Thus, Raphael the painter, architect and archaeologist were all pursuing the same goal. And his passionate, absolute love of the city and its great past became increasingly apparent in his pictures; the decoration of the Logetta and papal apartments and that of the Farnesina show that for Raphael antiquity was not a static model to which artists had constant recourse, but a familiar living ideal reinterpreted with sympathy and feeling.

The decoration of the second of the Vatican Stanze, known as the Stanza di Elidoro after one of the frescoes, lasted from the latter part of the summer or the autumn of 1511 until the summer of 1514. After the works in the Stanza della Segnatura, appropriate to a private room reserved for study and meditation, the decoration of the Stanza d'Eliodoro, a semi-public room, showed historical subjects, events in the history of the Church. Each of the four wall frescoes contains an episode illustrating the granting of divine aid to the Church in difficult times; the subjects of the four ceiling paintings, taken from the Old Testament, are related to the paintings on the walls. The dado displays in a bold conception illusionistic caryatids supporting a lintel above which are the large compositions; the conception and preparatory drawings are certainly by Raphael but the execution is probably by Perino del Vaga.

Raphael's interest in dramatic action was already apparent in the square ceiling compartments in the Stanza della Segnatura, in several of the figure groups in the wall frescoes in the same room, and again, at about the same date, in the beginnings of the works in the Stanza di Eliodoro and the *Galatea*; now for the first time it could be deployed over a large area. The *Galatea* comprises, like the *Virtues* or the *Sybils* but in a rather more complex manner, a group with hardly any depth, a construction of warm-toned, twisting forms clearly delineated like a cameo in an almost abstract way against a cool-toned background. The paintings in the Stanza d'Eliodoro set out to convey something completely different: a drama, a story told clearly so that the spectator understands it at once, a true story in which the role of each participant, active or

149

not, is clearly defined, every personality is revealed in the subject's participation in or reaction to the central event.

And this is in effect the basis of all Raphael's work, from the *Altarpiece of St. Nicholas* down to the simplest Madonnas. There is a certain emotional link between the characters, a sensitivity conveyed in precise techniques. This is what is called — to use an overworked, rather academic but nevertheless useful term — history painting. The four wall frescoes in the Stanza d'Eliodoro allowed Raphael, for the first time, to include in a vast fresco grand historical subjects, themes involving dynamic action. In fact, few of Raphael's works before the Segnatura frescoes were of this type. The *Resurrection* in San Paolo perhaps, the two panels of the predella of the *Mond Altarpiece*, *The Road to Calvary* of the *Colonna Altarpiece*, and the small paintings of St. George and St. Michael; and we must add to these small paintings the early but ambitious *Borghese Deposition*.

The fresco of the *Expulsion of Heliodorus from the Temple* shows Heliodorus, the Syrian General who has profaned the Temple at Jerusalem and stolen its treasure, thrown to the ground by three angels, one on horseback, who have answered the prayer of the high priest Orias, who can be seen in the center of the background, kneeling in front of the altar. The theme can be related to the inviolable nature of the territories of the Church and constitutes, in 1511, an allusion to the French invasion, repelled by Julius II in the following year. There is also an allusion to a particular event concerning the Church, the treachery of those Cardinals allied to the French who tried to convoke a council at Pisa, an attempt which failed at the end of 1511.

The first stage in the preparation of the fresco is documented by a drawing sometimes attributed to Beccafumi in the Albertina at Vienna, which is a copy of a drawing by Raphael, and does not yet include the group of the Pope and his carriers on the left. Few drawings survive for this fresco or the others in the room; however, a double-sided sheet in black chalk at Oxford, which contains studies for the two kneeling women towards the left, ranks among the artist's most lively and dramatic drawings. Three fragments of the cartoon are preserved — two angel heads in the Louvre and the head of the angel's horse at Oxford, all bold pictorial statements, impressive in their vigor and fiery elegance. A comparison between the cartoons and the corresponding sections of the fresco shows that when he turns to painting, the artist displays more dramatic power. The horse's eye is larger, his mouth open wider and the faces of the two angels are more robust.

The design of the fresco with its symmetrical, basilical architecture, its paved foreground from which the background is raised by only one step, recalls the layout of *The School of Athens*. On the left emerging from the contemporary world is the group of Pope Julius II carried on the *sedia gestatoria*, which has a monumental grandeur emphasized by the powerful triangle it describes. Since Vasari's time, attempts have been made to identify the bearers; perhaps the engraver Marcantonio Raimondi, even Giulio Romano, or Raphael himself. The solid authority of this group deliberately contrasts with the rest of the composition. Elsewhere all is turmoil and violence; the very paving with its large octagons takes on a savage, broken quality. The central space, based as we have seen on the compositions of *The School of Athens* and the *Disputa*, here becomes immense and appears even more empty. In the background the high priest and the altar to which the lines of perspective lead seem almost isolated by the movements of the recoiling women on the left and the diagonal thrust of the angels on the right. And in this space the effect of the angel's shadow is remarkable, a black pool in the center of the picture which, as if by deflection, seems to project the angel even further. The movement and the drama are everywhere, intertwined like scarves in the wind: the group with the horseman and Heliodorus writhes and turns, a face, mouth wide open, shrieks in terror.

These powerful images have influenced painters for centuries. Light is used to full dramatic effect: great cavernous shadows, brooding darkness; and white, which in the Stanza della Segnatura imposes order on the architecture and tempers the colors of the draperies, here appears in strident bursts and stormy glows. The coloring includes mute shades of grey and indigo, tones of copper and glowing embers. The style of the picture responds to all this and becomes more "painterly." Nothing in Raphael's work before the *Heliodorus* is as clearly set out and legible. After 1512 dark areas begin to creep into certain sections of the paintings, the draftsmanship becomes less sharp, some forms are harder to discern and outlines are blurred. There are difficulties concerning the authorship of these frescoes. After the Stanza d'Eliodoro frescoes, a significant part of Raphael's mural painting is usually ascribed to his pupils, following their master's designs. On the other hand these changes may be manifestations of a new method of painting in which the forms are less clearly delineated and which appears for the first time in the *Parnassus* — a deliberate change of course and not a lapse on Raphael's part. Peremptory judgements are often made about the "quality" of these works which should be revised, and such judgements are also applied to the oil paintings.

From this date until his death few of Raphael's works escape critical suspicion. The generally accepted touchstone for judging the quality of Raphael's frescoes is *The School of Athens*. But in the

156 *The Expulsion of Heliodorus from the Temple.* 1511-12. Fresco. Base 750 cm. Vatican, Stanza d'Eliodoro

On the right, Heliodorus, who attempted to steal the treasures of the temple, is beaten down by the three angels who have intervened. In the background the great priest Orias is at his prayers. On the left, the crowd reacts to the event and Pope Julius II, impassive, carried in his papal chair, seems almost to be sitting in judgment on Heliodorus and dictating his punishment. The theme is probably an allusion to the Pope's struggle against the French invaders, whom he managed to expel in 1512. His carriers are possibly identifiable as Marcantonio Raimondi in the foreground and Raphael himself on the right. It has sometimes been suggested that the figure in the foreground on the extreme left is also Raphael.

157 *Head of a Horse,* fragment of the cartoon for *The Expulsion of Heliodorus from the Temple.* 1511-12. Black chalk on yellowish paper. 68.2 x 53.3 cm. Oxford, Ashmolean Museum.

Only three fragments of the cartoon for *The Expulsion of Heliodorus from the Temple* survive, two *Heads of Angels* in the Louvre and this *Head of a Horse;* that of the third angel, in Oxford. They may have belonged to Francesco Masini of Cesena, whom Vasari records as the owner of certain fragments of the cartoon. All three count among Raphael's most beautiful drawings. They combine monumental power and controlled lyricism.

158/159 *The Expulsion of Heliodorus from the Temple.* Detail of illustration 156.

Stanza d'Eliodoro Raphael is exploring a different mode and paints accordingly. There can be no doubt that Raphael had studio assistance in painting the Vatican frescoes but it is unthinkable that the *Heliodorus*, one of the artist's most brilliant and freely executed works, is a studio painting. The execution of a fresco has rarely been so painterly — each stroke, each touch of the brush, has a specific importance. One can see these brushstrokes throughout the work, cutting through the light and shadow with broad, powerful modeling. The effect of gold on the armor, and helmet of the angel on horseback, the two arches, also of gold, the interior of the temple, the glowing candles, the reflections and shadows, are all without precedent in their freedom of technique and lavish appearance in

160   *Head of an Angel,* fragment of the cartoon for *The Expulsion of Heliodorus from the Temple.* 1511-12. Black chalk on yellowish paper. 26.8 x 32.9 cm. Paris, Musée du Louvre.

161   *Study of a woman holding two children.* 1511-12. Black chalk. 398 x 259 cm. Oxford, Ashmolean Museum.

This sheet contains particularly free and expressive studies, on both sides, for the women on the left of the composition watching Heliodorus's punishment.

154

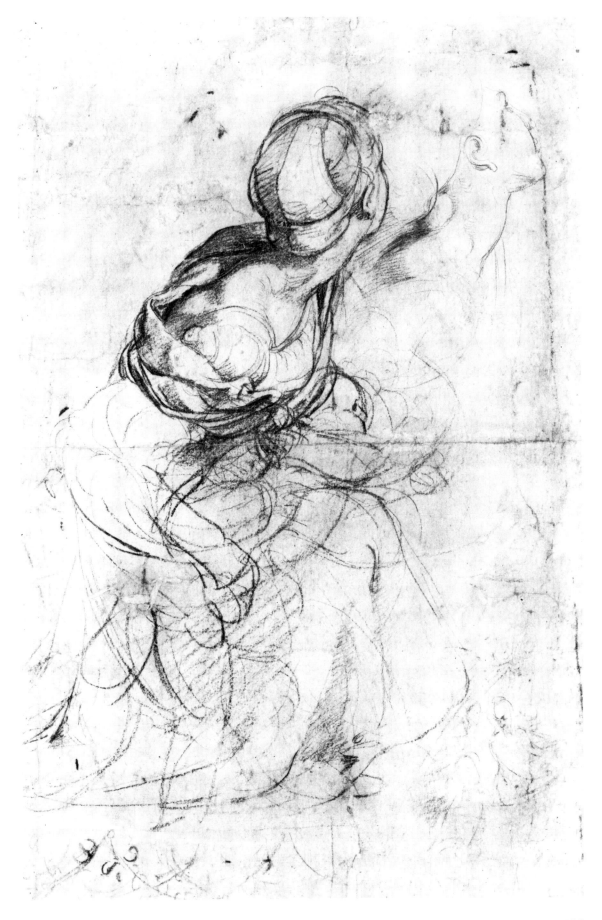

the art of the fresco. It is paradoxical that this technique rivals the art of oil painting without losing its inherent quality.

The fresco of *The Mass at Bolsena*, painted in 1512 after the *Heliodorus*, illustrates a miracle that occurred in Bolsena in 1263: a poet celebrating mass, on doubting the divine presence manifested in the Host, had a vision of it covered in blood. Pope Urban IV instituted the feast of Corpus Domine in 'the following year as to celebrate this miracle. It is known that Julius II held in particular veneration the blood-stained napkin in a reliquary at the Orvieto cathedral where he went in 1506. As in the *Parnassus* the area to be decorated was complicated by the intrusion of a window. This one is also off-center, considerably increasing the problem.

A copy at Oxford of a lost drawing by Raphael shows the first idea for the composition, in which the arrangement of the group is already present, with the priest alone in front of the altar, placed over the lintel of the window which appears to form a dais upon which it stands. The priest dominates the assembled group in which

162/163   *The Mass at Bolsena*. 1512. Fresco. Base 660 cm. Vatican, Stanza d'Eliodoro.

The fresco shows a miracle of the 13th century during the pontificate of Urban V, when a priest who doubted the truth of the Transubstantiation saw the Host emit blood and stain the altarcloth while he was celebrating the Mass. We know that Julius II was especially devoted to the relic of the altar cloth which was preserved in Orvieto. He is shown on the right, kneeling opposite the priest. Raphael incorporates the top edge of the window into his design as part of a stepped platform which he extends to the right to balance for the off center position of the window. The altar is placed on the platform on the central axis of the composition.

164 *Study for The Deliverance of St. Peter.* About 1512. Pen and ink, brown wash and black chalk, heightened with bodycolor. 25.7 x 41.7 cm. Florence, Uffizi.

Though damaged at the top and on the right, this drawing is a precious record of work on *The Deliverance of St. Peter.* It establishes the composition—although the fresco was to have yet more dramatic power.

165 *The Deliverance of St. Peter.* About 1512. Fresco. Base 660 cm. Vatican, Stanza d'Eliodoro.

Like a medieval painter, Raphael combines three episodes of his story in one design; they are separated by the very shape of the fresco and the lines of the architecture. In the center the angel appears to St. Peter, on the right he conducts him out of the prison between the sleeping guards, and on the left the guards awake. The light is the element that gives the work its unity and drama. The supernatural aura of the angel and the glow of the moon and the torches light up the darkness of the night.

the Pope is merely another participant. The fresco itself modifies and improves upon this arrangement. The dais is extended to the right, making it exactly central in the composition, while the altar is moved to the center of the dais away from the position above the window it has in the drawing. The closed apse of the drawing is replaced by an open architectural space with sky visible behind. But a semi-circular wooden screen encloses the area of the dais. Pope Julius II, shown kneeling opposite the priest, is at the same level on the other side of the altar. The inclusion of contemporary figures in a painting celebrating a historical event is managed in a more subtle and convincing manner than in the *Heliodorus.* The fresco is divided in two by an invisible wall which coincides with its symmetrical axis. On the left side, that of the historical event, everything moves in a powerful diagonal rhythm. The figures, some

anxious, some joyful, surge forward like waves about to break over a rock. On the right, as if reflected in a mirror, calm and solemn, are the pontiff, the cardinals, the Swiss guards and the porters, most of them looking towards the Host. The color scheme is designed to make the reds shine out, contrasting with both dark and pale greens, and there are dashes of white and gold throughout to further unify and enliven the composition. It has been suggested that the richness and harmony of the color scheme results from the collaboration with Raphael of Venetian painters then in Rome, perhaps Sebastiano del Piombo or Lorenzo Lotto. The treatment of certain faces, their relatively loose structure and agitated expressions, are certainly reminiscent of Lotto. But the sheer mastery shown in the rendering of light effects and the textures of materials can only be Raphael's.

Opposite *The Mass at Bolsena*, *The Deliverance of St. Peter* occupies a position corresponding to that of the *Parnassus*. Reflecting Julius II's special devotion to St. Peter, the subject is probably an allusion to the departure of the French from Italy in June 1512 and the fresco may have been painted during the second half of that year. Three episodes are represented side by side, as in a medieval painting: in the center, St. Peter in prison being awakened by the angel; on the right, the angel guiding St. Peter past the dozing guards; on the left, the guards waking up. As a preparatory drawing in the Uffizi shows even more clearly than the final work, the general layout of the composition closely resembles that of *The Mass at Bolsena*, with the main action raised up above the window frame as if on a stage and the rest taking place on two flights of steps at the sides. Each scene has its own light source, the angel in the center and on the right, the crescent moon on the left. And it is the lighting — an icy gleam on the guards' armor, a reddish tinge spreading over the stonework — that creates the mood of drama. Only Piero della Francesca had treated a nocturnal subject with such power and feeling in *The Dream of Constantine* in Arezzo — and Piero had actually painted this very same wall. For those, like Malraux, who "have little idea what liberty is but know everything about libera-

tion," *The Deliverance of St. Peter* remains the greatest image of freedom ever created by a painter. Like the final chorus of *Fidelio*, it is a work of optimism, joy and gratitude towards those personified by the angel, who come to the enchained prisoner in the night of his despair and open up the world for him.

The fourth wall of the Stanza d'Eliodoro, like that of *The Mass at Bolsena*, once bore frescoes by Bramantino. It shows *The Meeting of Leo I and Attila*, an event of the fifth century in which Pope Leo the Great went out to meet Attila's army near Mantua. St. Peter and St. Paul appeared in the sky and the Huns were routed. In the fresco the scene is changed to just outside Rome and Roman buildings are recognizable in the background. The artist's first idea

166/167 *The Meeting of Leo I and Attila.* About 1513. Fresco. Base 750 cm. Vatican, Stanza d'Eliodoro.

The last to be executed and most dramatic of the murals in the Stanza d'Eliodoro shows the encounter between Pope Leo I and Attila, who had brought his troops to the outskirts of Rome in the middle of the 5th century. The apparition of St. Peter and St. Paul in the sky armed with swords caused a rout among the Huns. Pope Leo X, recently elected, was the model for the features of St. Leo.

for the composition is known from a copy made after a preparatory drawing now in Oxford. On the left of the drawing, the papal entourage enters slowly as if in procession, the Pope on the *sedia gestatoria* surrounded by attendants with the airborne figures of St. Peter and St. Paul above. On the right in front of the army of barbarians are two horsemen, the more centrally-placed of whom is Attila himself, apparently transfixed by the sight of the Pope and the cross carried in front of him. A second stage in the working out of the composition seems to be indicated by a drawing in the Louvre, which is of the highest quality but is generally attributed to a pupil. The whole right side of the composition is almost identical to that of the fresco itself but moved towards the center. So too are the figures of the saints. But the left side is completely different, featuring soldiers and horsemen reacting to the celestial apparition. The Louvre drawing is a very coherent composition, the magnificent dramatic unity of which is somewhat lost in the fresco because of the replacement of the left side group by the Pope and his cardinals. In the Oxford drawing the pontiff is recognizable as Julius II, evidently after August 1511 since he is shown wearing a beard. In the Louvre drawing the papal group is barely visible in the left background. In the fresco the features of Leo the Great are unmistakably those of Leo X and it seems reasonable to suppose that the

composition seen in the Louvre drawing was altered at the Pope's request in order to include him in the guise of his predecessor. As in *The Expulsion of Heliodorus*, the pontiff and his entourage are set apart from the action, forming a kind of counter-balance to the drama and violence in the rest of the scene. It is not Leo whom Attila is looking at here but the two saints above. The man with the lance in the central foreground was originally in the Louvre drawing pointing to the papal suite arriving in the far distance. Now the Pope's unexpected entry upstage, which in the *Heliodorus* was so unrelated to the rest of the action as to throw it into more powerful relief, almost like a donor portrait, is less satisfactorily resolved.

The *Attila* fresco remains fascinating in its sheer strangeness. The tumultuous figure-groupings, the background with its raging fires, and the opening of the heavens behind St. Peter and St. Paul, create the most startling contrasts of light and dark. As in *The Deliverance of St. Peter* it is the fitfullness of the lighting, its fire-and-brimstone quality, that makes the work so effective. Also as in *The Deliverance of St. Peter*, the fictive arch across the top is lit as if from within the scene itself.

The ceiling of the Stanza d'Eliodoro had originally been decorated by Baldassare Peruzzi with small scenes in grisaille. He had divided the area into eight compartments separated by

168 *Compositional study for the Meeting of Leo I and Attila.* About 1513. Metal-point, brown wash and bodycolor on parchment. 36.2 x 59.2 cm. Paris, Musée du Louvre.

This drawing shows the coherence of the composition planned by Raphael before the addition of the group of the Pope and cardinals on the left was imposed on him. Its authenticity has been contested but the sheer quality and delicate richness of the drawing are worthy of Raphael.

169 *The Prophet Isaiah.* About 1512-13. Fresco. 250 × 155 cm. Rome, Church of Sant'Agostino.

The work was commissioned by the Papal Protonotary Giovanni Goritz and the Greek inscription is a dedication to the Virgin signed with his name. It forms an ensemble with the sculpture of *St. Anne, the Virgin and Child* by Sansovino. Raphael is here clearly indebted to the figures of prophets by Michelangelo on the ceiling of the Sistine Chapel which had just been unveiled.

radiating bands of ornamentation consisting of arabesques against a gold background. Raphael keeps to the idea of splitting the ceiling up by means of diagonal divisions but reduces the number of compartments to four. Each of them is occupied by a fictive tapestry painted as if stretched and attached to the surface at points around its edges. Like the use of mosaic backgrounds on the ceiling of the Stanza della Segnatura, this device makes it unnecessary for Raphael to represent his figures *di sotto in sù*, as if seen from below. It also means that the figures do not seem glaringly out of scale with those on the walls. The subjects depicted are *Moses and the Burning Bush*, *Jacob's Dream*, *God's Command to Noah* and *The Sacrifice of Isaac*, each of which can be interpreted as a prefiguration of the subject of the large fresco above which it is placed. The figures occupy a shallow pictorial space and are often set against a flat, vivid blue background, which along with the touches of gold, both emphasize the tapestry-like nature of the frescoes and play down the sense of agitation about some of the gestures. The ceiling has been thought to be the earliest part of the decorative scheme of the room. Yet the obvious influence of Michelangelo in the tense, complex poses of the figures and the linear style of painting, so different from that of the *Heliodorus* and *The Mass at Bolsena*, point to a later date after the unveiling of the Sistine Chapel ceiling in October 1512. In fact, the works date from 1514 after the frescoes on the walls below. This is confirmed by a pen-and-wash drawing in the Uffizi, in which among other sketches of that date, there is a study of Parmigianinesque elegance for the angels in *Moses and the Burning Bush*. The actual execution of the frescoes, which are in a poor state of repair, is sometimes given to Peruzzi but may well be Raphael's own.

The paintings in the Stanza d'Eliodoro lead on naturally to a consideration of *The Plague of Phrygia*, commonly known as the *Morbetto*, a fine composition of Raphael's, familiar as one of the most beautiful of Marcantonio Raimondi's engravings. The engraving was made from a pen-and-wash drawing in the Uffizi, the bad condition of which makes a definite attribution to Raphael problematic. The style, close to *The Deliverance of St. Peter* in the chiaroscuro of the architecture, suggests a date of around 1512-13. At Windsor there is a highly poetic landscape drawing, executed in silverpoint heightened with white on pink paper, that relates to the right side of the scene as engraved.

A minor project in comparison with the Stanze, the fresco of *The Prophet Isaiah* at Sant'Agostino in Rome was commissioned by Johannes Goritz, Head Chancellor of the Papal Court, to complement Sansovino's sculpture of *The Virgin and Child with St. Anne* (1512) which occupies a niche in the lower part of the same pillar. The unstable, dynamic pose of the seated figure, its monumentality and the treatment of the musculature invites comparison with the *Sibyls* and *Prophets* of the Sistine Ceiling. But the graceful harmony of the design, the modeling by means of a fluid light, and the melancholy sweetness of the face with the eyes sunk in shadow are purely Raphaelesque, showing none of the *terribilità* of Michelangelo — even though Raphael probably actually intended the work as something of a Michelangelesque pastiche. The fresco could be a

little later than the *Virtues* in the Stanza della Segnatura — it recalls the similarly Michelangelesque figure of Fortitude — and could therefore date from 1512 or the beginning of 1513.

It was customary on ceremonial occasions to hang real tapestries over these — before Raphael's they were brought out from the papal storehouses. The production of enormous tapestry series was a longstanding papal tradition. It is known that great series were executed in the Carolingian period for the Roman basilicas. Another factor behind the commission must certainly have been the attitude of Leo X as a member of the Medici family, whose splendid and lavish patronage had extended to the commissioning of a great deal of tapestry work. The Raphael Tapestries represent four episodes from the life of St. Peter, *The Miraculous Draft of Fishes*, showing his conversion, *Christ's Charge to Peter*, also called *Pasce Oves*, *The Healing of the Lame Man* and *The Death of Ananias*; and six episodes from the life of St. Paul, *The Blinding of Elymas*, *The Sacrifice at Lystra*, *Paul Preaching at Athens* and *The Martyrdom of St. Stephen*, at which Paul was present, holding the martyr's clothes, *The Conversion of St. Paul* and finally *St. Paul in Prison*. The original arrangement of the tapestries can be deduced by considering their dimensions, their borders, the direction of the lighting in the scenes depicted and the precedence that would have been given to St. Peter or St. Paul according to the placing to the left or right of the altar of the scenes from their life.

The commission was in all likelihood given by the Pope in 1514. The payments to the painter date from June 1515 and December 1516. One of the tapestries was finished in Brussels by July 1517 and seven of them were shown in the Sistine Chapel at the end of December 1519. The three last ones, *Paul Preaching at Athens*, *St. Paul in Prison* and *The Sacrifice at Lystra*, probably arrived a little later.

A comparison between the cartoons and the tapestries shows the scrupulous attention the Brussels weavers paid to their models, and at the same time the degree of freedom they allowed themselves in translating them into tapestry. They not only made "decorative" additions, plants on the ground or embroideries on the fabrics, but changes in the tonal relationships that considerably distort the overall effect of the original designs. One senses what an effort it must have been for Raphael to have to submit to the conventions of tapestry. The cartoons had to show the design that was to appear in the final work in reverse. Moreover, the medium of tapestry demands a high degree of clarity in the drawing, chiaroscuro and composition, an almost schematic approach that avoids effects of depth — and this was hardly congenial to the painter of the *Attila* and *The Fire in the Borgo*.

170   *God the Father and the Planets*. 1516. Mosaic decoration in the cupola of the Chigi Chapel. Rome, Santa Maria del Popolo.

Both the architecture and the decoration of the chapel were undertaken by Raphael whose cartoons for the cupola were executed in mosaic by Luigi de Pace. He also designed the statue of Jonah executed by the sculptor Lorenzetto. Only a few drawings for the mosaics survive. The study for God the Father was made from a live model violently foreshortened by the viewpoint. The verse of the sheet contains another study in a comparable manner.

171 *Study for God the Father for the Chigi Chapel.* About 1513-15. Red chalk. 21.4 × 20.9 cm. Oxford, Ashmolean Museum.

Study of an angel for the planet Jupiter in the Chigi Chapel. About 1513-15. Red chalk. 19.7 × 16.8 cm. Oxford, Ashmolean Museum.

The decorative element is especially pronounced in *The Miraculous Draft of Fishes*. The figures, relatively few in number, dressed in strong colors, are lined up across the center of the composition and boldly outlined, by the play of shadows, against the background of lake and sky. Above and below are strips of land and nearly-silhouetted birds, which, like the fish that fill Peter's boat, form abstract shapes of a richly ornamental kind. The combination of humility and ruggedness in the figures of Peter and Andrew in front of Christ recalls that of St. Sixtus interceding for mankind in the Dresden Madonna. Perhaps inspired by certain works of antiquity, they embody an emotional state that was to be the stock-in-trade of religious artists for years to come.

More central to Raphael's career than his work in Sant'Agostino is the Chigi Chapel in Santa Maria del Popolo which was commissioned by Agostino Chigi as his own funerary chapel in 1512 or 1513. Raphael was to design both the chapel itself and the decorative scheme. For the architecture he drew upon antiquity, especially the Pantheon, and upon buildings by Bramante. For the decoration of the dome he provided sketches that were realized in mosaic by a Venetian, Luigi de Pace, who finished and signed his work in 1516. The subject-matter is a blend of Christian and pagan. The cupola is treated as a metaphor for the vault of heaven. In the central roundel God the Father, surrounded by angels, directs the movement of the planets with a broad gesture of both arms. The planets are represented in a series of compartments by the classical gods

and goddesses with whom they are associated. Above these are angels, positioned on the appropriate segments of the zodiac who guide the movement of the astral bodies. Seven compartments are dedicated to the planets, the eighth to the stars.

The use of such an iconographic program in this setting has been explained in terms of the Neo-Platonic idea that the human soul originates in the celestial regions and returns there after death, an idea found in the writings of Bembo and Castiglione which would have been familiar to both Raphael and Chigi. It is not impossible that the altarpiece Raphael had in mind for the chapel was an *Assumption*, perhaps to have been elaborated upon from two sketches by him of that subject in Oxford and Stockholm. The altarpiece that was actually installed there, Sebastiano del Piombo's *Birth of the Virgin*, dates from much later. The violent gesture of the Creator imparts a sense of motion to the whole cupola which seems to turn like a wheel. The blue of the sky serves as a unifying background in all the compartments, giving them a degree of illusionism that contrasts sharply with the gilt ornamentation of the architectural surroundings.

The ten "Raphael Tapestries" of the Acts of the Apostles made in Brussels for the Sistine Chapel and today in the Vatican Museum stand alongside the Stanze as the artist's most important essays in history painting. The numerous copies of them woven in Italy, England and France made Raphael's designs widely known. Of all his works they were the most influential upon European art as a whole, from the 17th to the 19th century. By rare good fortune, seven of the ten cartoons have come down to us. Bought in 1623 by the future Charles I of England, they are today in the British Royal Collection and on show at the Victoria and Albert Museum in London. The accident of their survival has brought about a paradox in that we today, with our devotion to the "original" work created by the artist's own hand, tend to pay more attention to these simple working designs for the weaver than to the tapestries themselves. In fact, it is the tapestries woven at great expense in the workshop of Pieter van Aelst that constitute the definitive works and therefore deserve to be considered the true originals.

John Shearman's admirable study shows clearly how the tapestries of the Acts of the Apostles should be regarded not as independent works but in relation to the positions in the Sistine Chapel for which they were designed, having been conceived as a response to Michelangelo's ceiling above. As Shearman says, they were intended to embody "the eloquence of Raphael as a complement to the *terribilità* of Michelangelo in the first chapel of Christendom." The chapel, then called the Capella Palatina or the Capella Magna, was indeed, along with St. Peter's, the setting for the principal ceremonies of the papal court. We know that it had been completely decorated in fresco. The ceiling had just been finished by

172 *Study of an Angel for the Planet Jupiter in the Chigi Chapel.* About 1513-1515. Red chalk. 19.7 x 16.8 cm. Ashmolean Museum, Oxford.

Michelangelo (1508-12) and the middle area of the walls had, since the campaign of 1481-82, borne large history paintings: *The Life of Moses* to the right of the altar and *The Life of Christ* to the left. The lower area contained fictive tapestries with the heraldic arms of Sixtus IV.

Two preparatory drawings for this work lead us to consider the part played in the design and execution of the cartoons by Raphael's pupils. One of these, in the Albertina and attributed to Giulio Romano, may reflect a first idea for the composition. The other, in the Royal Library at Windsor and correctly attributed to Penni, is more problematic. Is it a copy of a Raphael drawing in which even his *pentimenti* have been faithfully recorded? Or does it actually show Penni elaborating on Raphael's original idea and making suggestions that the master in the event approved? Whatever the case, the collaboration with Raphael of his pupils from 1514 seems to have consisted of more than simply the execution of parts of the paintings from the master's drawings. It involved the pupils in the creative process right from its earliest stages. And it is sometimes difficult to say whether Raphael has used a pupil's design or if the design was in fact a fleshing-out by the pupil of Raphael's own rough outline sketch. Given the overall coherence of the series and the similarity of the pupils' styles, all formed under the influence of the same master, it is extremely difficult, perhaps futile, to try to distinguish individual hands.

The other cartoon with a landscape setting, *Christ's Charge to Peter*, appears at first sight to be a simple frieze-like composition. But the apostles reacting in their different ways to the event, as in Leonardo's *Last Supper*, form an extremely subtly orchestrated group with lively, varied poses, leaning increasingly forward the closer they are to Christ. St. Peter kneels in a springy, slightly twisted position, pulled forward as if magnetically attracted by Christ. The latter, His arms outstretched in a symmetrical gesture with His forefingers pointing to the symbolic sheep and to Peter, whom He is charging to feed them, stands immobile, but it is the immobility of the dancer pausing before a leap.

173 *The Miraculous Draft of Fishes.* 1514-15. Painted on several sheets of paper glued together and mounted on canvas. 319 × 399 cm. London, Victoria and Albert Museum.

The very legible, contrasted forms and the importance given to the vegetation and the birds are in keeping with the decorative function of the work. The corresponding tapestry was placed in the Sistine Chapel to the right of the altar.

174 *Christ's Charge to Peter.* 1514-15. Painted on several sheets of paper glued together and mounted on canvas. 343 × 532 cm. London, Victoria and Albert Museum.

This cartoon, like *The Miraculous Draft of Fishes,* is striking for the luminosity of the vast landscape. The figures of the apostles, arranged in a frieze-like group, become progressively more animated as they approach Christ. The red chalk drawing in the Louvre is just a fragment from a large drawing recorded in the form of a copy at Windsor. It shows a study for Christ from a live model in a pose Raphael changed for the final design.

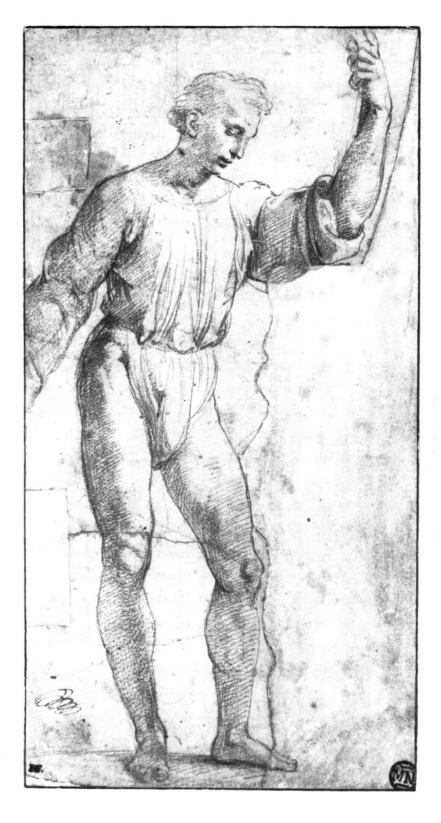

175 *Study of a standing male figure, for Christ's Charge to Peter.* 1514-15. 25.3 × 13.4 cm. Paris, Musée du Louvre, Cabinet des Dessins.

This study is only a fragment of the large drawing, a copy of which is at Windsor. The figure in Raphael's final drawing is quite different from the studio model.

The clear and lively color scheme, featuring much use of white, is in keeping with the glorious landscape, one of the most ample and true Raphael ever painted. The figures again stand out boldly against the background — and against each other, thanks to the device of separating and outlining the areas of light, dark and middle tonality. Their legibility is thus emphasized — one is reminded of Seurat's idea of "simultaneous contrast." The *modello* for the composition, now in the Louvre, has occasionally been attributed to Giulio Romano or Penni, but as Shearman and Oberhuber convincingly maintain, is by Raphael himself. A fine study in red chalk, made from life models, some of them half nude, is at Windsor. Perhaps already damaged, the sheet from which it comes was cut up and the figure of the model posing for Christ, his arm raised in a different gesture from the one finally adopted, is now in the Cabinet des Dessins at the Louvre. Two smaller fragments bearing the heads of apostles are in private hands. In the drawing the chalk is handled with an unprecedented freedom and delicacy, suggesting the very movement of the light and a sense of palpitation and anxiety in the bodies and faces.

The two tapestries with outdoor settings from the life of St. Peter must have been intended for a position close to, and on the right of, the chapel altar. Balancing them on the left were the first two episodes from the life of St. Paul, also outdoor subjects, *The Stoning of St. Stephen* and *The Conversion of St. Paul.* The cartoons for these have disappeared. The tapestries have animated and dramatic compositions which deliberately contrast with the serenity of the two scenes from the life of St. Peter, the only comparable element being the fishermen drawing up nets in *The Miraculous Draft of Fishes.* In *The Stoning of St. Stephen* the executioners throwing the stones seem to represent different stages of the same movement in an almost

cinematic fashion. The effect is like that of the youths who bend over Euclid in *The School of Athens*, but with the kind of broad movements seen in *The Fire in the Borgo*.

The Healing of the Lame Man, the third episode from the life of St. Peter, shows the apostle with St. John, healing a cripple at the entrance to the Temple in Jerusalem. The twisted columns are copies of those from the old church of St. Peter's, which were traditionally believed to have come from the Temple. The tripartite divisioin of the design by the columns recalls earlier, similarly divided predella panels such as *The Presentation in the Temple* from the *Oddi Altarpiece*. But here it is used to its full dramatic potential. Though crowded, and open more on one side than the other, the composition is still basically contained (like the Stanze frescoes) within a semi-circle. The twisted masses of the columns convey a

sense of muffled, rumbling energy that relates both to the dynamic poses of the children, which are echoed in the sculpted putti playing among vines on the columns, and the bodily contortions of the unfortunate cripples.

Among Raphael's most striking creations, the two cripples are more than just touches of realism — the idea for which has inevitably been attributed to Giulio Romano. In fact, they are recollections of Leonardo. It is not sufficiently realized that whenever Raphael painted old age or physical deformity, it was to Leonardo that he referred. The violent oppositions of light and shade, the dark shadows cast by the columns, the deep folds in the draperies and the pronounced musculature of some of the figures all help give clarity to the image. It should be noted, however, that the Brussels weavers did not always respect Raphael's intentions, showing light on St. Peter's profile, for example, when he wanted it to be in shadow.

The tapestry of the *Blinding of Elymas*, which was placed opposite *The Healing of the Lame Man*, is also composed symmetrically within an architectural setting, in this case a Roman basilica. It shows Elymas struck down with blindness by St. Paul as a punishment, which leads the Roman Proconsul, Sergius Paulus, seated in the center, to be converted to Christianity. The conversion is the real subject of the work, as the central inscription makes clear. The compressed and agitated effect of *The Healing of the Lame Man* is replaced by a calmness and solemnity enhanced by the architectural element and the monumentality of the side figures. The generally rhetorical nature of the poses is especially evident in the great triangle of gestures that links the three protagonists, St. Paul, Elymas and the Proconsul, across the empty space in the center.

A very complete and finished drawing by Raphael for the composition survives at Windsor. The lower part of the tapestry in the Vatican has been destroyed but other tapestry versions give a fairly complete idea of its original appearance. On the right, behind St. Paul, it is extended to include a good deal more architecture, with a niche containing a statue of a draped female figure for which there is a study by Raphael in Oxford. The addition of this part was necessitated by the nature of the space in the Sistine Chapel that the tapestry had to fill, and it explains why the perspective of the cartoon is off-center, especially in the tiling on the floor.

178/179   *The Healing of the Lame Man.* 1514-15. Painted on several sheets of paper glued together and mounted on canvas. 342 × 536 cm. London, Victoria and Albert Museum.

St. Peter, accompanied by St. John, cures a cripple at the entrance to the Temple in Jerusalem. The twisted and sculpted columns were inspired by those of the old basilica of St. Peter, which were traditionally believed to have come from the Temple. The violent and miserable realism seen in the figures of the cripples bears witness to an often unrecognized aspect of Raphael's genius.

The Death of Ananias features St. Peter striking dead a member of a Christian community who had kept some of its communal goods for himself. The cartoon is one of the most powerful of the whole group, largely because of the bold swinging lines of the design, with its kneeling, turning and leaning figures forming an arc below the inflexible horizontal of St. Peter and his companions. In its simple symmetry, the sense of presence about the elegant, sensitive figures and their easy inter-relationships, the strong but subtle alternation of forms, light against dark and dark against light, this cartoon was among the most admired of the series and so was the tapestry that was based on it. Two of the foreground figures were especially well liked, that of Ananias with its bold foreshortening and that of the young man on one knee recoiling from him in terror.

Though far more dynamic in feeling, the composition of *The Sacrifice at Lystra* returns to the same frieze-like format as *Christ's Charge to Peter*. It represents an episode in which St. Paul and St. Barnabus miraculously cured a lame man upon which the people took them for Mercury and Jupiter. They wanted to offer up a pagan sacrifice but St. Paul managed to prevent it. The cartoon shows the preparation for the sacrifice, with the executioner squaring up to strike the animal, and on the right, the crowd groveling before the saint in adoration, making a complex and animated group, the rounded forms of which seem to unfurl as they move from right to left. A young man in the center, convinced by the protestations of St. Paul, holds out his arm to stop the executioner's stroke. Clearly, the work was inspired by antique reliefs showing sacrificial scenes. The little sculpted altar placed obliquely in the foreground and the vista beyond, along which the eye is led by the perspective of the architecture, help create a sense of space between the crowd and St. Paul, offsetting the rather unrelieved compactness of the figure group.

There survive two drawings for *The Sacrifice at Lystra* in the same technique, silverpoint heightened with white on gray paper — a delicate study for St. Paul at Chatsworth, and a large study from life models for the whole right side of the composition which was recently acquired by the Cabinet des Dessins at the Louvre. This, the principal drawing, had previously only been known through a copy in the Uffizi. It shows the main elements of the design as in the cartoon, but the drawing is generally more pathetic and tender, and more accurate in the rendering of movements, than the final composition. An example of this is the gesture of the young man stopping the executioner, whose arm is correctly rendered in the drawing but out of proportion in the cartoon. In the drawing the figure group forms a subtly animated whole, coherent in its rhythmically organized masses. The cartoon gains in forcefulness and legibility but loses the charm and nervous elegance that makes the Louvre drawing one of Raphael's most beautiful.

The *St. Paul Preaching at Athens* must be considered somewhat separately from the rest of the tapestries. It was hung on its own, not in the part of the Sistine Chapel reserved for worship and the Church dignitaries but that set apart for the laity. Its theme, the dissemination of the Word of God among the faithful, is therefore appropriate to the function of the area in which it was displayed. Its positioning also explains the asymmetry of the composition and the displacement of the vanishing point of the perspective to the right of center. The aspect that makes it the boldest, most innovative work of the series is Raphael's use of the steps to isolate and elevate St. Paul, leaving a large area of the foreground virtually blank in front of him. The lines of the steps also emphasize the off-center perspective and direct the eye towards the audience arranged at a lower level around the preaching figure. The color is held together in a wonderful harmony, with reds and pinks opposed to greens. In the foreground the figures of Dionysius and Damaris, who are being converted by St. Paul's words, are cut off at half length, a spectacular innovation which extends the pictorial space out to include the spectator himself. This revolutionary device is not yet adopted in the magnificent preparatory drawing now in the Uffizi, where the positions of six of the figures are established in few supple lines of red chalk. Dionysius, standing rather than kneeling, places one foot on the steps and moves up towards St. Paul. Almost the whole contour of his figure is thus included. Only later did Raphael think of the powerful effect he could achieve, making the outline of the saint more impressive and allowing the spectator to imagine himself part of the assembly of Athenians, if he showed Dionysius and Damaris kneeling and boldly cut off by the edge of the design.

The cartoon of *St. Paul in Prison*, last of the tapestries of the life of St. Paul, is lost. The tapestry, very narrow because of the position it occupied in the chapel, is as exceptional in its subject and style as in its proportions. The moment depicted is when St. Paul's jailors were terrified by a miraculous earthquake. This is personified by a gigantic figure in the pose of a wrestler who bursts out of the ground, breaking it up with his fists. A silverpoint drawing in a private collection in New York shows that the inspiration for this figure was a detail from an antique relief of *The Judgement of Paris* in the Villa Medici. What may seem strange, incoherent or at worst naive about *St. Paul in Prison* could, in fact, tell us much about Raphael's aim in the work, that of expressing a precise idea as effectively as possible in a language comprehensible to the public at large. It is a somewhat embarrassing image and has often, not surprisingly, been excluded from the Raphael canon and conveniently attributed to Giulio Romano. This artist is a veritable repository for figures that do not fit our preconceptions about Raphael. Numerous other disturbing creations have been attributed to him, including the screaming figure in the *Heliodorus*, the cripples in *The Healing of the Lame Man*, the devil in the Louvre *St. Michael* and the epileptic boy in the *Transfiguration*. They are figures — and there are others — that refuse to conform to our too selective, too idyllic view of Raphael. Our views must be modified in order to include them.

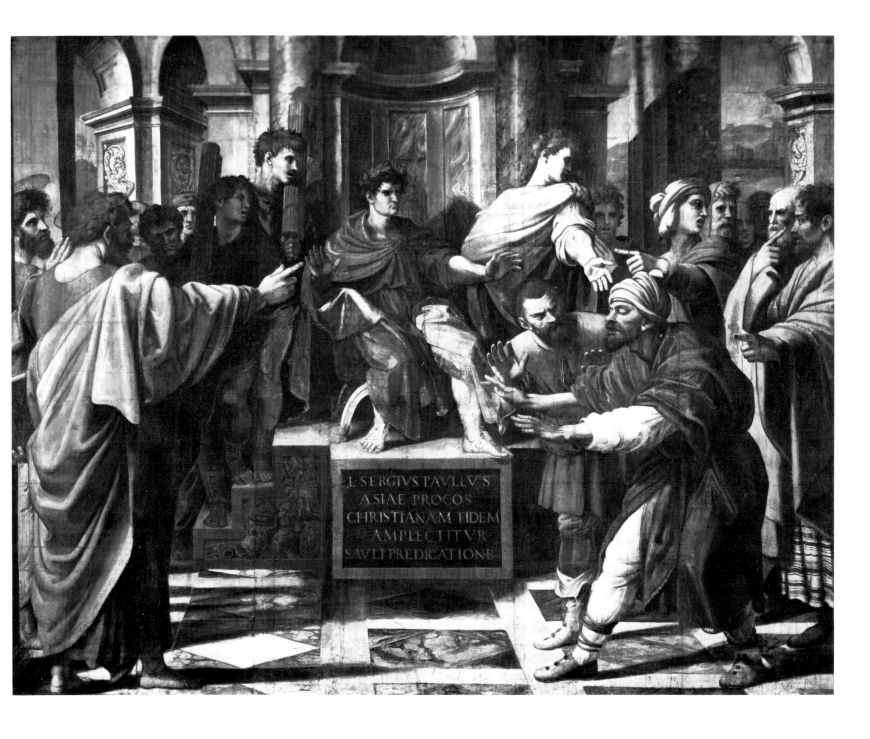

180 *The Blinding of Elymas*, also known as *The Conversion of the Proconsul*. 1514-15. Painted on several sheets of paper glued together and mounted on canvas. 342 × 446 cm. London, Victoria and Albert Museum.

The scene shows St. Paul striking Elymas down with blindness as a punishment. The Proconsul of Asia Minor, Sergius Paulus, seated in the center, is overwhelmed by the miracle and converted to Christianity. The architectural setting and the symmetry of the composition give the work a special air of authority. The corresponding tapestry was placed in the Sistine Chapel opposite that of *The Healing of the Lame Man*.

The Stanza dell'Incendio was painted by Raphael and his pupils between the middle of 1514 and the middle of 1517. The ceiling had been painted by Perugino, at the time his former pupil was at work in the Stanza della Segnatura with four dull roundels. These Raphael allowed to remain, whether out of affection for his old master (as Vasari says) or merely to reduce the amount of work to be done. In the other two Stanze, the part played by Raphael's collaborators is either non-existent or very limited; in the Stanza dell'Incendio it is self-evident. The iconographic program, highly political in flavor, was almost certainly devised by Pope Leo X who seems to have used the Stanza as his private dining-room. The historical events depicted are episodes from the lives of two of his predecessors, also called Leo: the ninth century Pope Leo IV is shown miraculously quelling a fire that was destroying the Borgo district of Rome simply by making the sign of the cross, then at the rout of Arabs who had attacked the papal flotilla at Ostia; Leo III is shown crowning Charlemagne in the year 800, then taking an oath to deny the false accusations made against him by the nephews of Hadrian I.

The dado, probably painted by Giulio Romano, bears fictive reliefs and sculptures like that of the Stanza d'Eliodoro. But whereas the architectural severity of that earlier work serves to emphasize the depth of space in the frescoes above, here the richness of the design, which includes statues of the Catholic kings painted in

trompe-l'oeil as if made of yellow cameo and placed between fictive caryatids, competes with that of the large historical compositions above. The entire wall surface is thus articulated and animated.

The fresco of *The Fire in the Borgo* was probably painted from 1514 on and is the most impressionistic of all the works in the room that bear its name. It is also the one in which Raphael gave most fully of himself. The main dramatic incident is pushed right to the back

181   *The Death of Ananias.* Tapestry. 490 x 631 cm., including the border at the sides. Vatican Museum.

The comparison between one of the tapestries and its cartoon shows the transformation wrought by the Brussels weavers on Raphael's design. The modification of the balance of light and shade is particularly apparent here in the clothes, faces and background drapery.

182   *The Death of Ananias.* 1514-15. Painted on several sheets of paper glued together and mounted on canvas. 342 × 532 cm. London, Victoria and Albert Museum.

St. Peter, in the center, inflicts capital punishment upon a member of one of the first Christian communities who had appropriated some of the community's funds to himself. The dramatic power of the composition, with its opposition between the immobility of the apostles and the violent movements of the members of the community, has been widely admired, notably by French painters of the 17th century.

where the Pope is miraculously stopping the blaze. The foreground features three groups: on the left inhabitants of the Borgo fleeing from the flames, on the right others who are bringing water to put the fire out, and in the center a group of distraught mothers turned towards the background. The most important role is played by the architecture, the plunging lines of which, strongly reinforced by those of the paving and the colonnade seen from the side, converge towards the central door of the Church of St. Peter. The horizon line coincides with the top of the steps, where at the spectator's eye-level, a crowd of people beseech the aid of the Pope in his loggia. The whole power of the fresco comes from the deliberate disparity between the two figure groups. Completely different in scale, one embracing the other, they define two clearly distinct planes, close up and distant, with no real middle ground in between. They are linked only by the subtle device of the mother and child going up the stairs in the background, who relate thematically to the mothers and children in the central foreground.

183 *The Sacrifice at Lystra.* 1514-15. Painted on several sheets of paper glued together and mounted on canvas. 347 × 542 cm. London, Victoria and Albert Museum.

St. Paul, at Lystra with St. Barnabus, miraculously healed a lame man, at which the people took the two apostles for Mercury and Jupiter and wanted to make a pagan sacrifice to them — which St. Paul managed to prevent. The work is based on depictions of sacrificial scenes on Roman reliefs.

184 *Study for The Sacrifice at Lystra.* About 1514-15. Metal-point, heightened with white, on grey prepared paper. 24.8 × 39.3 cm. Paris, Musée du Louvre.

Very close in technique and spirit to the Chatsworth study for the figure of St. Paul in the same cartoon, this study from live models which was recently acquired by the Louvre is for the left hand side of the composition. It is reproduced here thanks to the generosity of the curators of the Cabinet des Dessins at the Louvre, particularly Roseline Bacou, Catherine Monbeig Goguel and Françoise Viatte.

The disposition of the main figures corresponds to a circle filling the fresco's surface to its full height, the diameter of which coincides with the horizon line. This shape is emphasized by the body and left leg of the male nude hanging from the wall to the left. Meanwhile, the group of the son carrying his father on his back, and the woman carrying an urn, act as "wedges" that stabilize the composition to left and right. The inspiration of Roman antiquity is more obvious than ever, both in the figure types, nude and draped, and in the architecture. Raphael, it should be remembered, was at the time director of the archaeological excavations being carried out in the city. The whole scene evokes the burning of Troy rather than the burning of medieval Rome, and the group on the left recalls the figure of Aeneas carrying his father Anchises, preceded by Ascanius. The use of color is new, especially the warm tones of browns, pinks and oranges appropriate to the subject, as are the strong dark outlines and flashes of crude light.

There is evidence of collaboration in the parts which appear either too limp or too stiff: for example, the group of women in the center and the man clinging to the wall. But the fresco has been damaged in several places, making assessment difficult. The part played by Raphael himself may have been greater than previously thought. Who but he could have painted the marvelous water-carrier seen from behind on the extreme right, the group seen in close-up on the left, or the little figures in the background? But it would be presumptuous to make a final pronouncement, since the work of master and assistants appears so closely interwoven. Not one of the

185 *Study for St. Paul Preaching at Athens.* About 1514-15. Red chalk. 271 × 419 cm. Florence, Uffizi.

This drawing is a first sketch of the whole, drawn from studio models.

186 *St. Paul Preaching at Athens.* 1514-15. Painted on several sheets of paper glued together and mounted on canvas. 343 × 442 cm. London, Victoria and Albert Museum.

The tapestry corresponding to this cartoon was displayed in the part of the Sistine Chapel reserved for the laity. The composition is one of the most audacious of the group, complex both in its off-centered design and in the interplay of the different ground levels with the two figures on the right cut off by the edge. The drawing in the Uffizi shows a preliminary design for the composition, studied from live models.

preparatory drawings for *The Fire in the Borgo* seems to be by Raphael's hand, not even the lovely study in the Albertina showing the son carrying his father. Undoubtedly, several drawings have been lost. It should also be remembered that in 1514 Giulio Romano was only fifteen, so it would be difficult to ascribe to him, as has been done in the past, an essential part in the execution of the fresco.

The importance of *The Fire in the Borgo* resides in the novelty of its original scenic conception (reminding one that Raphael had designed for the theater) and also in the density and solidity of the

187 *St. Paul in Prison.* Tapestry. 478 × 130 cm. excluding border. Rome, Vatican Museum.

The cartoon for the tapestry is lost. The giant bursting out of the ground in the foreground represents the earthquake that occurred while St. Paul was in prison, and after which he converted his jailer to Christianity.

188/189 *Fire in the Borgo.* About 1514. Fresco. Base 670 cm. Vatican, Stanza dell' Incendio.

The fresco, the first to be painted in the room to which it gives its name, shows a miracle of the 9th century. Pope Leo IV stops a fire that is ravaging the Borgo district of Rome by making a sign of the Cross. The pope is visible in the distance, at a window of St. Peter's basilica. The importance of Antique statues and monuments is in evidence throughout the composition which was executed with the assistance of pupils.

figures. In *The School of Athens* Raphael had discovered structure, the interplay of human form with architectural space; in *Heliodorus Chased from the Temple* he added atmosphere and movement; in *The Fire in the Borgo* he seems to have been searching for an additional quality, that of weight. The much admired and much copied figure of the water carrier on the right represents an undulation of voluptuous form around an insistent vertical; she seems to have all the solidity of stone, of equal weight with the fluted columns in the center of the composition.

The Battle of Ostia shows a naval battle that took place in the middle of the ninth century between the Papal armies and those of the Saracens who were miraculously put to flight by a tempest. The subject was one requested by Leo X, who lent his features to the figure of Leo IV offering up thanks to the heavens, on the left hand side of the fresco, as an allusion to his own plans for a crusade against the Turks. The fresco was painted from Raphael's drawings by his collaborators, in particular Giulio Romano. Only one of the drawings has survived in the Albertina, Vienna. It is a large

190   *The Battle of Ostia.* About 1515. Fresco. Base 770 cm. Vatican, Stanza dell'Incendio.

Pope Leo IV, again with the features of Leo X, thanks God for the wreck of the Saracen fleet by a tempest during a battle off Ostia against the papal flotilla. Prisoners are brought in across the foreground. The fresco alludes to the crusade against the Turks advocated by Leo X. The execution is for the most part attributable to Raphael's pupils.

sheet of paper containing a red chalk drawing of two nude men, one of whom is a study for the soldier on the extreme left of the fresco. Raphael sent this drawing to Dürer, "to show him his style" according to the pen inscription on the sheet. In its frieze-like character, and in the heroic quality of the nude bodies foreshortened in complex poses, the fresco reveals a great debt to the works of antiquity. Like the other paintings in the Stanza dell'Incendio, contemporary personalities are identifiable here. On the left, behind the figure of Leo IV, bearing the features of Leo X, are the figures of Cardinal Bibbiena and Giulio de Medici. The date of 1515 on the drawing sent to Dürer would seem to correspond to that of the fresco's execution.

The Coronation of Charlemagne also alludes to contemporary life; this time to a precise event, the signing of the treaty between Leo X and Francis I of France which took place in October 1515. Francis I lends his features to Charlemagne who is being crowned by Pope Leo III who closely resembles Leo X, and he is described in the phrase associated with Charlemagne as "sword and shield of the church," in the Latin inscription beneath the fresco. The whole conception of this fresco is certainly Raphael's. It is the most surprising and innovatory of the four in the room in its use of perspective, with the pictorial space viewed as if from above, and squeezed

191 *Head of a Cardinal.* About 1515-16. Black chalk heightened with white on brown paper. 28.1 x 21.4 cm. Paris, Musée du Louvre.

Sketched in a beautiful energetic line that seems to be Raphael's own, this head, probably a fragment from a cartoon, is for a figure in the background of the fresco of *The Coronation of Charlemagne* in the Stanza dell'Incendio.

into a lozenge shape. It is only the alignment of white miters that gives a firm sense of structure. The composition is full of carefully-calculated and provocative imbalances, for example, in the figures of the two stooping deacons in white surplices to the left of the tribune above the door, and the truncated figures in the foreground, notably the two furniture carriers mounting the steps on the lower left hand side, whose ascending movement continues the expansive gesture of the man in armor, thereby introducing the spectator to the picture space. The device of the figures cut off by the frame in the foreground is an exploitation of a motif inaugurated in one of the cartoons for the Acts of the Apostles, *St. Paul Preaching at Athens*. A drawing of the composition in the Querini-Stampalia library in Venice is almost certainly the work of Penni, and may even be, as suggested by Oberhuber, drawn over an initial tracing by Raphael. Yet a lovely study in the Louvre for the head of one of the bishops in the background has such energy combined with gentleness that an attribution to Raphael would seem more appropriate than the more frequently proposed attribution to Penni. As for the execution of the fresco, it seems to have been mainly carried out by Penni, and in certain parts by Giulio Romano.

The last of the frescoes in the room on the window wall is the *Oath of Leo III*, which shows the Pope in the presence of Charlemagne exculpating himself from the accusations brought against him by the nephews of Hadrian I. The scene refers to the bull "Unum Sanctum" issued by Boniface VIII which had in 1516 just been promulgated once again by the Lateran Council. Most notable was its stipulation that the Pope was accountable only to God, and could therefore be neither accused nor judged by men. The strictly symmetrical composition takes up an idea seen in the *Mass at Bolsena*, that of placing the altar on a platform above a window. It is not a very innovative painting, and seems dull in execution, making the attribution to Raphael questionable. It has been suggested that Francis I is the figure seen from behind on the left hand side of the elevated platform, and that Guiliano de Medici is the corresponding figure on the right with his hand on his hip. The execution, which is difficult to judge because of the poor state of preservation of the fresco, seems to be the weakest of all the frescoes in the room, and it is thought that the majority of the work was carried out by Penni.

In 1516 at the time of the last frescoes in the Stanza dell'Incendio, Raphael was directing the decoration of two rooms in the apartment of the erudite and literary Cardinal Bibbiena. These were small bathrooms, the *stufetta*, and a loggia that had been part of a large arcade giving out onto a courtyard, the *loggetta*. The two decorative schemes were composed in the spirit of ancient Roman paintings, the "grotesques" inspired by those in the Domus Aurea of Nero. The *stufetta* was painted in wax, and given a dark color scheme dominated by Pompeiian red. The small scenes on the walls and ceilings show subjects taken from Ovid's *Metamorphoses*, dedicated to Venus and her powers. These were certainly chosen by the cardinal himself. Each of these compositions is surrounded

192 *Venus wounded by Cupid,* detail of a panel from the *Stufetta.* About 1516. Fresco. Vatican, Stufetta of Cardinal Bibbiena.

The *Stufetta,* a small bathroom, was decorated in the antique style with episodes from Ovid's *Metamorphoses.* The red and black backgrounds and the division into panels create a quite different effect to that found in the *Loggetta,* although the same artist probably carried out the work on both rooms.

by light borders of red, black or gold, bearing different motifs. Underneath them are other compartments where against a black background winged cupids are shown riding chariots drawn by snails, turtles or dragons. The free and lively execution is generally attributed to Giulio Romano, Penni and Giovanni da Udine, but it was undoubtedly Raphael who conceived the whole scheme and made drawings for the compositions. The happy spirit of invention, and the unselfconscious feeling of antique frescoes, their flavor and color, were never so well recreated as here and in the *logetta,* and they provide a unique example of a full understanding of the art of antiquity.

The second, much larger, decorative scheme is that of the *loggetta,* with its abundance of delicate grotesques seen against a white background which covers the vault and the walls. A series of shallow cornices stand out at the base of the vault. On the walls, garlands of leaves, foliated scrolls and beaded motifs create a frail, symmetrical edifice where griffons, birds and little animals play. Medallions and winged cupids provide a strong vertical axis which is anchored in position by rectangular cartouches showing mythological scenes set against a black background. Elsewhere, false niches shelter *trompe l'oeil* life-size statues of the *Seasons.* On one of the shorter sides at the end of the loggia, a lunette shows *Vulcan in his Forge* surrounded by little cupids trying out their bows.

The whole scheme is treated without any pedantry, and with a lively, eager humor. As with the *stufetta,* Raphael's collaborators, together with Penni and Giulio Romano, must have worked to the plan devised by their master who allowed them a great deal of freedom and even painted certain details here and there to amuse himself. Giovanni da Udine seems to have played an important part in the execution of frescoes.

This period, which saw the discovery of a new pictorial sense, and a new focusing of attention on human emotions, naturally led to a great upsurge of creativity in the field of portraiture. Two works which probably date from 1514 or 1515, the *Donna Velata* and *Baldassare Castiglione,* are among Raphael's greatest masterpieces. The *Donna Velata* in the Pitti Palace, Florence, is the portrait of an unknown woman in a setting rather like those of the female sitters Raphael had painted in Florence. But the *Lady with a Unicorn* and *La Muta* were distant and mysterious. Is this painting the image of a woman Raphael loved, perhaps that of La Fornarina? We do not know. The veil falls simply, calming and containing the ebullience of the forms within its gentle triangle while the sleeve in the foreground seems to burst open like a ripe fruit, unfurling the sumptuous white material and yellow braid. The relaxed, peaceful forms and the face with its pleasant reserved but unhaughty expression suggest qualities of happiness and kindness. She is an accessible being — the complete antithesis to those portraits by Leonardo whose sitters are completely immured in their solitude. The analogy sometimes drawn with the "Courtesan with a gauze veil," for this is how the *Mona Lisa* was referred to in the inventories of the Royal Collection before she acquired her present name, is only superficial. It is not impossible that the feeling of sympathy between painter and model, the velvety sense of touch, the tactile appreciation of materials and the chromatic unity of white and golden tones set against a dark but luminous background, could have come from the Venetian portraits that Raphael was able to see at the time.

The portrait of *Baldassare Castiglione* in the Louvre shines out in Raphael's work and in the entire Italian Renaissance as a miraculous painting, almost disarming in its simplicity. Castiglione, born in 1478 and a frequenter of the Court at Urbino was Raphael's friend, and one of the most cultivated men of his time. He was the author of the famous *Courtier*, where he set forth guidelines for the conduct of a true gentleman, and the canvas radiates this sense of firm friendship and cultivated ease. His gown, as elegant as it is sober, is made of fur (perhaps beaver) contrasting with black material. The picture was probably painted during the winter of 1514 to 1515 when Castiglione was an ambassador from the Court of Urbino to Rome. It could therefore be a little later than the *Donna Velata*, probably painted in 1514, and it would seem to illustrate in its bold contrasts and the authority of its outlines the role that the complicated business of making tapestry designs played in the development of painter's art, even influencing his treatment of the interplay of forms. But the monochromatic tone of the work, with its delicate grays against which the blacks gain in richness, and where the sole note of real color is in the sitter's blue eyes, seems to be an echo of Venetian painting. The pose is extremely simple; a distillation of all those developed by Raphael since his Umbrian days. The body is placed in three-quarter view, with the arm leaning along the edge of the chair, but the face is shown almost full-front. With an intentional subtlety, the hands are scarcely visible, being cut off by the picture frame as they are in the *Donna Velata* and partly hidden by the coat so as not to distract from the face. A restrained canvas, it is a unique instance of the meeting of two sensibilities: Castiglione is represented both as a man of mystery and of radiant knowledge.

The painting of two Venetian writers, *Navagero and Beazzano*, in the Galleria Doria Pamphili in Rome generally arouses little enthusiasm. It is the most austere work in Raphael's entire *oeuvre*. However, the double portrait does represent an original and daring experiment. The two half-length figures are simply aligned against a novel and daring background on the same level and with no psychological rapport between them. It is difficult to find precedents or contemporary equivalents. There are certain earlier Flemish portraits which show couples; for example, those by Memlinc (in the Louvre and Berlin Dahlem), and Mabuse (in London); or Venetian works such as the *Portrait of Two Men* in the Louvre, which is variously attributed to Bellini and Cariani. But the plasticity of the figures, their isolation and mutual independence, rather recalls the funerary portraits of Roman Antiquity, reminding us that Raphael was a great discoverer of Antiquity. The hands remain hidden so that attention is not diverted from the faces and their imperious gazes fixed upon the spectator. The only "picturesque" element is the contrast in the material of the two garments and the white shirt of Beazzano. The canvas certainly lacks the warmth and generosity of *Baldassare Castiglione* of whom Navagero on the left may have seen as an obscure and dramatized transposition, but it contains possibilities for future development. The figure of Navagero, with the black pyramidical shape of his clothing and the rigorous division between light and shadow, looks forward to Poussin's *Self Portrait* of 1650 in the Louvre. It is possible that this painting in the Galleria Doria Pamphili is the one that ended up in the house of Bembo in Padua; it was he who commented in a

193   *The Loggetta*, general view. About 1516. Fresco decoration. Vatican.

This long room was part of Cardinal Bibbiena's apartments in the Vatican and was one of the first to be decorated with grotesques based on the Antique; they are set against a white background. The execution of this lively scheme was undertaken by Raphael's pupils, Giovanni da Udine, Giulio Romano, Giovanni Francesco Penni and Perino del Vaga.

letter to Cardinal Bibbiena that Raphael had painted the portrait of the two Venetian writers during their stay in Rome in 1516.

Certain portraits from these years have disappeared, such as that of *Federigo Gonzaga*, probably painted at the beginning of 1513. The missing portrait of *Giuliano de Medici* also probably dates from 1513; there are several copies of which one, in the Metropolitan Museum, New York, has sometimes been considered as the original. This painting with its centrally placed figure shown almost full face and the importance given to the formal interplay between the hat and

194 *Portrait of a Woman,* known as *"La Donna Velata."* About 1514. Oil on panel. 85 × 64 cm. Florence, Pitti Palace.

This is undoubtedly the picture mentioned by Vasari as being in the possession of Matteo Botti in Florence and representing a woman with whom Raphael was in love. It was in the Medici family collection in 1620. In spite of the many hypotheses that have been put forward, the identity of the sitter remains a mystery. The radiant simplicity of the expression is reminiscent of the *Castiglione* in the Louvre.

195 *Portrait of Baldassare Castiglione.* 1514 or 1515. Oil on canvas. 82 × 67 cm. Paris, Musée du Louvre.

The portrait was probably still in the hands of the sitter's family in Mantua until 1630 when it was sold in Amsterdam to Lucas van Uffelen. Sold again in 1639, it passed into the collections of Mazarin then Louis XIV. The canvas was never, as is often said, cut along the bottom. This is made clear by the original black border which remains intact all around the painted surface. More than any other portrait by Raphael, the *Castiglione* bears witness to the bonds of friendship and intellectual affinity that existed between artist and sitter.

188

the garment already looks forward to the *Castiglione*, but it lacks the strength, simplicity and warmth of that picture. The portrait of the poet *Antonio Tebaldeo* is also known to us only through copies, but the original seems to have been the masterpiece whose likeness to the sitter was praised by Pietro Bembo in a letter to Cardinal Bibbiena. Probably painted towards the end of 1515, or at the beginning of 1516, it must be close in date to the *Castiglione* and it shares with that picture the reserved yet warm approach, and the device of placing the black forms of the garments and the hat against a light background. The portrait of *Cardinal Bibbiena* must also be contemporary with the *Tebaldeo*, and the Pitti Palace in Florence has an excellent example of it which has sometimes been considered to be the original.

The madonnas that Raphael was painting at the same time as the frescoes for the Stanza dell'Incendio and the Stanza d'Eliodoro are among his most popular works. One of the most famous of these

196   *Portrait of Andrea Navagero and Agostino Beazzano.* 1516. Oil on panel. 76 × 107 cm. Rome, Galleria Doria Pamphili.

This is generally identified as the portrait of these two Venetian writers mentioned as being in Padua, at the house of Pietro Bembo who noted in a letter to Cardinal Bibbiena that Raphael painted it when the two men were staying in Rome in 1516. Restrained to the point of severity, the work is in the line of unostentatious friendship portraits of which the *Castiglione* is the masterpiece.

197   *Madonna della Sedia.* About 1512. Oil on panel. 71 cm diameter. Florence, Pitti Palace.

The culmination of Raphael's work in the tondo format that was so dear to him, the picture belonged to the Medici family from the 16th century and was exhibited at the Uffizi, then at the Pitti Palace. It was in Paris from 1799 to 1815. The date usually suggested, about 1514, is probably too late.

is the *Madonna Della Sedia*, which almost defies description in that it has become a quasi-mythical object, at once a formal model for artists and a perfect image of the Virgin mother for believers. This representation of the mutual power that passes between mother and the Child caught in her embrace has become one of the best known images of the Western world. Raphael chose to depict an almost anecdotal moment with the child searching for His mother's breast underneath the shawl, but the bold placing of the design within the narrow confines of the tondo confers on it an unforgettable strength which is reinforced by the sculptural quality and dark background. The *Madonna della Sedia*, an extraordinary knot of strong, compressed forms is unique in the work of a painter who generally produced large airy canvasses. Faced with these forms, arranged like two narrowly overlapping 'U's, we are reminded of some of Picasso's paintings in the period 1931-32. Everything is swept into the circle,

198 *Madonna of the Curtain (Madonna della Tenda).* About 1513. Oil on panel. 65.8 x 51.2 cm. Munich, Alte Pinakothek.

Very close to the *Madonna della Sedia* in the basically rectangular grouping of the figures and the emphatic diagonals, the work is characterized by rather suppler, more relaxed forms and may date from somewhat later than the Florence picture.

and without the vertical baluster of the chair, the figures would appear to be carried away in a rocking movement like that of a cradle. The painting is flawless and firm, yet soft as a ripe fruit. Such work could only have been created once — or so we would like to believe — in its marvelous sense of life and plasticity of form. In fact, had he been able to choose, Raphael might have painted many more circular compositions; the surfaces of his paintings, rectangular or otherwise, often show forms whirling in a circle like a spinning top.

Amidst this mass of rounded forms there are also the subtle graphic devices of the geometrical borders of the shawl and the veil draped as a turban. The surface of the painting has a rare richness in its interplay of glossy, velvety and downy materials; particularly effective is the liveliness of the treatment of different textures: the hair, the fringe of the shawl and that on the back of the chair. The picture could have been painted as early as 1511–12, at the time of the *Mass at Bolsena*; it has a certain similarity with the group of women in the bottom left hand corner of the fresco where we see the same round heavy forms and the same emotion in the faces pressed cheek to cheek. But it is certain that the colors we see today in the painting — the warm reds, yellows and yellow-greens — are partly due to the old varnish covering it. The cerulean blue of the skirt, the pink of the sleeve, the gray-green of the shawl must once have created a cold and delicate color scheme not unlike that of the *Alba Madonna*. On the celebrated sheet of studies for the *Alba Madonna* preserved in Lille, there are two rapid pen sketches which seem to contain the germs of the first tentative ideas for the *Madonna della Sedia*. This would place the beginning of the picture's development in early 1511 which provides an argument, though not a decisive one, for giving the Pitti Palace picture a relatively early date. The *Madonna della Sedia* could therefore represent, at the end of 1511 or the beginning of 1512, the culmination of the researches into the modeling of form seen in the *Alba Madonna* and the *Madonna with a Diadem*.

The *Madonna della Tenda* in the Alte Pinakothek at Munich is very close in its origin of forms to the *Madonna della Sedia*, and it has always been considered contemporary with that picture. However, the freer forms, more relaxed design, looser and more "pictorial" treatment and more lyrical tone could indicate a significantly later date, perhaps 1513.

The *Madonna di Foligno*, very probably executed in 1512, was commissioned by the Roman church of the Aracoeli and is now in the Vatican Museum. It harks back to the tall arched shapes of the altarpieces of the painter's youth. The Virgin and Child, seated in the clouds and surrounded by a great yellow-orange nimbus, dominate the landscape. To the left are the kneeling St. Francis and St. John the Baptist; in the center a little angel holds a plaque; to the right St. Jerome presents the kneeling donor. He is Sigismondo de' Conti, secretary to Julius II, whose house in Poligno survived miraculously intact after being struck by lightning. The com-

new sensitivity to fleeting effects of light, and it reminds us that he had in the past studied the works of Sebastiano del Piombo and Lorenzo Lotto. A rich opposition of saturated colors, united with strong contrasts of shadow and light, is characteristic of Northern Italian painting, and is also reminiscent of Lotto. These two artists did, in fact, travel to Rome, Sebastiano in 1511 and Lotto in 1508, although he left the city to go and work in the Marches in 1512. The only study for the *Madonna di Foligno* is a large drawing in the British Museum of the Madonna and Child, executed in black chalk in a soft and tender style. Here Raphael used blue paper of Venetian origin, although this has faded somewhat.

The Virgin with St. Sixtus and St. Barbara in the Gemäldegalerie, Dresden was considered by the Germans at the beginning of the eighteenth century to be the most perfect embodiment of classical art. Now known as the *Sistine Madonna*, it shows a reworking of the formula of the altarpiece featuring the Virgin and Child surrounded by Saints; here, however, the complete absence of architectural elements reinforces the apparitional effect with the froth of clouds behind the Virgin almost obscuring the angels' heads. These clouds which billow upwards produce a dramatic effect emphasized by the almost frightened expressions of the Virgin, the Child and the two little angels at the base of the painting. A gust of wind from below ruffles their hair and raises the cape of St. Sixtus and the Virgin's robe and swells her veil. The horizontal ledge upon which the two angels lean, the diagonal of the falling curtain and the curtain rod above with its sliding rings, all reinforce the *trompe l'oeil* effect of the surface. The apparent simplicity of the forms, which are symmetrically arranged against a light background, with no feeling of depth, conceals the complexity of a composition full of carefully calculated folds, glides and a lack of equilibrium. The spectator is brought into the picture space by St. Sixtus who directs the gesture of his index finger towards us, and by his cope which flows forward as well as the tiara placed on the ledge at the bottom.

Also worth noting are the slightly more elevated position and contained attitude of St. Barbara whose face is yet another reference to Leonardo in Raphael's work and the graceful pose of the Virgin, who seems to move towards the spectator, the curve described by her veil balancing that of her body. The figures are linked together by strong emotion; St. Sixtus gazes intently at the Virgin, his hand on his breast. This painting, so thrilling in its combination of realism and tender feeling, has become part of the iconography of popular piety, together with the *Ecce Homo* of Guido Reni, and Murillo's *Immaculate Conception*. The fact that it was painted on canvas which was unusual for Raphael has aroused much speculation as to its original destination, and it has even been suggested that it was a processional banner. But it seems more likely that this choice of support was due to the painter's admiration for the Venetians, which we have noted before. In any case the painting was certainly commissioned by Pope Julius II, whose features are recognizable in those of St. Sixtus, probably executed at the end of 1512 or the

199   *The Foligno Madonna.* About 1512. Oil on panel, transferred to canvas. 301 × 198 cm. Vatican.

The figures adoring the Virgin and Child are on the left St. Francis and St. John the Baptist, and on the right the donor and St. Jerome. The donor is Sigismondo de' Conti, secretary to Julius II whose house in Foligno miraculously survived after being struck by a fireball. This event is represented in the background, with a richness of color and luminosity that is completely Venetian in spirit. Placed first in the Aracoeli church in Rome, the painting was later transferred to the church of Sant'Anna in Foligno. It was brought to Paris in 1797 and there transferred from panel to canvas; it entered the Vatican Museum after Waterloo. The sumptuousness of the light and color makes for an overall effect of high emotion.

position is based upon a pyramidical structure; the drapery is at once tangible and fluid, and the expressive eloquence of the poses allied to the warmth of feeling in the faces conveys a new intensity. The whole work is bathed in a changeable, diffuse light, comparable to that in *Heliodorus*, showing the effects of spring sunshine after a storm. This strangely dim landscape lit by one shaft of sunlight, which has in the past been attributed to the Battista or Dosso Dossi is a testimony with its mauve, blue and golden tones, to Raphael's

beginning of 1513, and almost certainly intended for the church of San Sisto in Piacenza.

The Madonna with the Fish, painted for the chapel of San Domenico in Naples, and today in the Prado, is an altarpiece of a more traditional structure. The enthroned Madonna and Child are surrounded by Tobias, presented by the Archangel Raphael and St. Jerome. The strong diagonal movement of the curtain in the background, the warmth of emotion uniting the figures, the simplification of the color scheme dominated by white and beige tones in opposition to greens and reds could only have been conceived after the *Stanza d'Eliodoro*, probably in 1512; the poses of Tobias and Raphael are similar to those of certain figures on the left hand side of the *Mass at Bolsena*. A striking red chalk drawing in the Uffizi shows four studio assistants posing for the group of figures in a setting which was barely modified. Another wash drawing in an English private collection shows a more highly evolved stage in the composition.

The painting generally known as the *Madonna dell'Impannata* in the Pitti Palace, which takes its name from the curtain covering the window, is the *Virgin and Child with St. John, St. Elisabeth and St. Catherine* praised by Vasari and painted for the banker Bindo Altoviti. It is widely accepted as a studio painting, although there has been some speculation as to which areas Raphael might have worked upon — the lovely head of St. Elisabeth, for example. There are two preparatory drawings in silverpoint. One for the whole composition, at Windsor, shows only the figures of the Virgin and St. Elisabeth; the other, in Berlin, shows Jesus and St. John. The elegant animated style of both drawings would place them around 1511–12, and their similarity to the *Sibyls* has often been noted. But the painting itself with its dark shadows and the vigorous musclature of St. John, fits better with the style of Raphael and his studio in later years. It is not unlikely that the earlier drawings could have been re-used in the period around 1516 to 1517.

Still in the realm of easel painting, three altarpieces, the first of which was never completed, stand out as Raphael's most ambitious undertaking in these years. In 1513 Raphael was working on an altarpiece depicting the *Resurrection of Christ* for the Chigi Chapel in Santa Maria della Pace where he had already painted the frescoes of the *Prophets* and the *Sibyls*. But he never finished the painting, and now it exists only in preparatory drawings: there are several lively pen sketches, one of which showing the whole composition is in the Musée Bonnat in Bayonne; two others are at Oxford. Nude studies for the terrified soldiers in black chalk are at Windsor, Oxford, the British Museum and in the collection of the Duke of Devonshire at Chatsworth. Their large movements, filling the picture-space, recall those of the figures in *Galatea*. The anatomical precision, the twisted postures, and the lively technique of fine hatching recall Michelangelo's drawings for the Sistine Chapel; for example, the famous study in the Metropolitan Museum for the *Libyan Sibyl*.

200 *Study for the Madonna di Foligno.* About 1512. Black chalk on grey-green paper, formerly blue, with traces of squaring-up. 40.2 x 26.8 cm. London, British Museum.

This study dates from the time in Raphael's career when he was most influenced by Venetian art and is the only example among his extant drawings of the use of blue paper so characteristic of the Venetians. The lightness and delicacy of touch in the effects of rubbing are also unique.

201 *The Foligno Madonna.* Detail of illustration 199.

194

196

But with Raphael, the light falls more softly on muscles that are less knotted, more supple and rounded. The altarpiece showing *St. Cecilia with St. Paul, St. John the Evangelist, St. Augustine and Mary Magdalene* was commissioned in 1514 by a lady from Bologna, Elena Duglioli dall'Oglio, for her family chapel in the church of San Giovanni in Monte. In the center, St. Cecilia lets her musical instruments fall to the ground and break, as she listens to the captivating sounds of angelic singing. The two types of music clearly symbolize earthly and divine love. Cecilia remained a virgin in marriage like Elena the patron who is thereby beatified. St. Paul and St. John are here representations of pure divine love; one is

202   *The Sistine Madonna*, also known as *The Madonna of St. Sixtus.* About 1512–13. Oil on panel. 265 × 196. Dresden, Gemäldegalerie.

Painted for the church of San Sisto in Piacenza, the work was acquired in 1745 by Augustus III of Saxony and has since been in the gallery at Dresden where it has enjoyed an immense reputation. St. Sixtus is shown with the features of Julius II who had personal connections with Piacenza. It has been suggested, less convincingly, that the face of St. Barbara on the right is that of Giulia Orsini or Lucrezia della Rovere, nieces of the Pope, and that the face of the Virgin is that of the artist's mistress La Fornarina.

203   *Study for The Madonna with the Fish.* About 1512. Red chalk with touches of black chalk and bodycolor. 26.8 x 24 cm. Florence, Uffizi.

This lively sketch shows Raphael's method of posing young boys in contemporary dress to help organize his composition.

204   *Madonna with the Fish.* About 1512. Oil on panel, transferred to canvas. 215 x 158 cm. Madrid, Prado.

The young Tobias, holding the fish, is presented to the Virgin by the Archangel Raphael. They are balanced on the other side of the composition by St. Jerome and his lion. Originally in the church of San Domenico in Naples, the work was bought in 1638 by the Duke of Medina de las Torres, Viceroy of Naples, who brought it to Spain where it was acquired by Philip IV. It was transferred from panel to canvas while in Paris between 1813 and 1822. The lively red-chalk sketch in the Uffizi reveals Raphael's working procedure of posing young assistants in contemporary dress to work out his compositions.

meditative, the other lyrical. St. Augustine and St. Mary Magdalene, as repentant sinners, represent victory over terrestrial love. The painting relates closely to the contemporary debate about charity and divine love.

We know that Antonio Pucci, a relative of and councillor to the patron who perhaps acted as an intermediary with her uncle, Cardinal Lorenzo Pucci, to help ensure that Raphael accepted the commission, was one of the founding members of the Confraternity of the Oratorio of Divine Love, which contributed to the movement of renewal in the Church at the time of Counter-Reformation.

198

205 *Study for the Madonna dell'Impannata.* About 1511-12? Metal-point with body color on prepared paper. 21 x 14.5 cm. Windsor, Royal Library.

The preparatory drawing in Windsor, which is of an incomparable warmth, freedom and elegance, seems to date from around 1511-12, as does another study for the *Infant St. John* and the *Christ Child* in the same technique, now in Berlin.

206 *The Virgin and Child with Saint Elizabeth, Saint Catherine and the young St. John the Baptist,* known as the *Madonna dell'Impanata.* About 1511-1512, or around 1516/1517? Oil on wood. 158 x 125 cm. Florence, Palazzo Pitti.

The rather dull surface of this work, painted according to Vasari for Bindo Altoviti, is probably attributable to the large part played in its execution by pupils.

Raphael himself, in March 1514, entered the Fraternitas Corporis Domini of Urbino, a confraternity with similar aims and interests.

This religious dimension takes on a dramatic meaning in the expression of St. Cecilia, a prototype for the ecstatic saints of Guido Reni and Domenichino. *St. Cecilia* was the painting that Bologna had been waiting for: the simple organization of the composition, enclosing five vertical figures whom the delicate obliques of St. Paul's sword and St. Augustine's crozier cause slightly to vibrate. The symmetrical arcs of the figures of St. Paul and St. Mary Magdalene define a space which expands at the top and bottom like a sheaf, and the useless terrestrial instruments seem to be conducted through the figure of the saint in ecstasy to the choir of angels singing of divine love. The figures are isolated in their rapture, contemplation and gaze fixed upon the spectator, except for St. John and St. Augustine who are looking at each other. The entire structure rests upon the diagonal design which fans out in a great butterfly shape, leading from the crossed forms of the instruments lying on the ground. But, as with the *Sistine Madonna*, *St. Cecilia* leans

towards simplicity rather than complexity of pose. Thus the figure of St. Cecilia herself is shown in a simple frontal pose, enlivened by the gentle ripples of drapery and balanced by the arrangement of the objects in the foreground. The glossy draperies of the Magdalene, with their sharply defined shadows, may already reveal a forcefulness and clarity derived from work on the tapestry cartoons.

St. Cecilia seems to be a kind of summing up, a balance sheet of a picture. We are shown different types of faces, different uses of color — brilliant for St. Paul and delicately variable for the Magdalene — and different treatments of form: light and soft in the group of angels, hard and incisive in certain areas of drapery. It seems to have been intended as a demonstration of the extent and variety of the painter's skills.

Finally, we come to *Christ Carrying the Cross*, today in the Prado, and originally painted for the church of Santa Maria della Spasimo in Palermo from where it derives its highly appropriate name *Lo*

Spasimo, meaning torment or torture. Vasari tells of the long and complicated journey made by the painting when the ship that was carrying it was shipwrecked, saved and taken to Genoa. This picture which was regarded as one of Raphael's most famous works up until the nineteenth century has frequently been underrated, its execution given to Raphael's collaborators. Recent restoration has revealed a moderate state of preservation; but given the many passages that could only have been painted by Raphael, the work must be regarded as one of the most important in the crucial period of the maturing of the painter's art.

Lo Spasimo, more than any other work, shows the influence of the tapestry cartoons on the evolution of Raphael's style, which, around 1515–16, the probable date of the painting, seems to have undergone a change, almost a transformation. The composition, complex yet clearly organized despite the animation demanded by the dramatic subject, relies upon an interplay of diagonals; we see again, though in a more complex form, the "butterfly wing" arrangement of the *St. Cecilia*. The forms are boldly defined by areas of light and shade, the figures tightly packed into groups which have a movement all of their own; the execution itself has all the freedom and decisiveness of distemper. All these factors contribute to a violent, almost schematic effect which is a long way from the curves and delicate pictorial nuances of the *Foligno Madonna*. Stylistically, it compares with the cartoons in the Victoria and Albert Museum, and the scale of the figures in *Lo Spasimo* is hardly smaller. It remains to be said that the lyrical landscape, both in its light and its execution is like that of the *Pasce Oves* and the *Miraculous Draught of Fishes*. There is much use of strongly contrasting colors in the Venetian manner, with the scale of green running from olive to turquoise opposing the reds and sparkling pinks. This is most noticeable in the banner and the clothes of the saintly women. The simply modulated contrast recalls, once again, certain cartoons — for example, *St. Paul Preaching at Athens*.

207 *Study for a Resurrection of Christ.* About 1513. Pen and ink. 40.6 x 27.5 cm. Bayonne, Musée Bonnat.

Compositional study for the unrealized altarpiece intended for the Chigi Chapel in Santa Maria della Pace. Two further preparatory drawings, in the same energetic pen-and-ink technique, are at Oxford.

208 *Study of a seated man seen from the back.* About 1513. Black chalk. 34.5 x 26.5 cm. Oxford, Ashmolean Museum.

This study, which includes repetitions of details, is for one of the soldiers in *The Resurrection,* planned for the Chigi Chapel in Santa Maria della Pace. Other similar studies, all of them suggesting comparison with the drawings of Michelangelo in spite of the greater sweetness in the handling of forms, are at Windsor, Chatsworth and the British Museum.

209/210 *St. Cecilia.* 1514. Oil on panel, transferred to canvas. 220 x 136 cm. Bologna, Pinacoteca Nazionale.

The saint, listening so attentively to the celestial music sung by the angels above that she ignores her instruments, is surrounded by St. Paul, St. John the Evangelist, St. Augustine and St. Mary Magdalene. Executed for the church of San Giovanni in Monte at Bologna, the work was exhibited in Paris between 1798 and 1815, and was at that time transferred from panel to canvas. With its emphasis on the emotions of the holy figures, within an overall design of great sobriety and control, it is a landmark of religious painting and was widely influential.

211 *Christ Carrying the Cross,* also known as *Lo Spasimo.* About 1515-16. Oil on panel, transferred to canvas. 318 × 229 cm. Madrid, Prado.

Commissioned for the church of Santa Maria dello Spasimo in Palermo, the picture was bought by Philip IV of Spain. It was exhibited in Paris at the Louvre from 1813 to 1822 during which it was transferred from panel to canvas. Though signed, the work is usually attributed to pupils, at least as far as the execution is concerned. Nevertheless, this is a key picture, showing the effect on his style of the tapestries project. It was engraved by Agostino Veneziano in 1517.

It has also been suggested that Raphael may have been inspired here by the grouping of figures in one of Dürer's wood engravings in the "Little Passion." Elsewhere, the figures in the principal group are reflected in the Flemish manner in the armor worn by the man carrying the banner; we are reminded of the armor of the small *St. George* of some twelve years earlier in the Louvre. This great dramatic poem is linked to the *Borghese Deposition* in its subject matter and in its lively poses, and the elegance of the sacred women, it looks forward to the heroic *Transfiguration.* These three paintings represent Raphael's most ambitious attempts to express deep emotion through the medium of easel painting, and they coincide with three essential stages in his career.

V. Rome 1517–1520: The Last Years

Raphael's last years are the most badly understood and by a strange caprice — a perhaps unconscious wish to reproduce in the development of the work of the greatest of all painters the cycle of the history of forms which marks the progression of every great style — archaism, maturity, decadence — the works carried out at the end of his life have been disdained as less and less in conformity with the image generally held of the painter. The collaboration in these works of his pupils who sometimes had no help at all from their master seemed proof of this decline.

We are faced with the paradoxical idea of Raphael overburdened by commissions, entrusting the execution of his works to his pupils, and no longer painting anything himself. Yet the practical functioning of his studio, about which we are ill-informed, involved an incessant coming-and-going between master and pupils in which both drawings and paintings were involved to such a point that it is often virtually impossible to distinguish the hands, and so, for all the damage it may do to our cult of "authenticity," a work partly or wholly painted by a pupil is given to Raphael. On the other hand, this man in the full vigor of his life (and there is no suggestion that he was sick or ill before he died) must have gone on doing a great deal of painting and designing himself right up to the end.

For these reasons we must look at his last works from two apparently contradictory different points of view: we must search for the creative imagination of Raphael even when his own hand is absent, and we must always look for his own hand where there is the slightest chance that it may be present. In practice Raphael's style has once again undergone a change. The shapes have become more rounded and more plastic. The experience gained in producing cartoons has been assimilated, the colors are brighter and stronger, the areas of light are placed in violent contrast to the shadows; now, more than ever before, life beats and pulsates in the bodies, sometimes as hard as marble, sometimes almost melting, and the tactile quality, present since the Umbrian paintings, takes on a new importance in works possessing an all-embracing richness of form and materials. By a remarkable paradox the hand of Raphael's favorite pupil Giulio Romano who took over the studio

on his master's death has been suspected in almost all the works of the last period of Raphael's life. Yet their dramatic manner, black shadows and almost aggressive approach are not features of Giulio's own style. This was something Giulio learned from Raphael which he went on to exploit in an altogether different spirit throughout his career. It is still difficult for us to appreciate the stylistic coherence of Raphael in these last years but we must recognize that the participation of the *garzini* of the studio with their uneven talents and inevitably diverse temperaments is a factor in the equation. And we must allow much more for the very variable condition in which these works have come down to us, so often almost defying judgement under their coating of dirty varnish and repainting.

The *Great Holy Family* in the Louvre which has slowly been stripped of its thick coating of yellowing varnish is able today to take its proper place in the same robust world, rich in colors and contrasts, as the *Loggia* of the Villa Farnesina, or the *Transfiguration*, rediscovered in all the sumptuous brilliance of the day when it was first painted. From the sixteenth to the nineteenth century, people did not look at the works of Raphael which had taken on a quasi-mythical character with our pretentious "attributionist" eye. Everybody — men of taste, artists, ordinary people — took these works to be by Raphael and admired and loved them. They were right and their eye surer than ours; and bound by our scruples, we have killed Raphael as a painter even before he was actually dead. There is perhaps some excuse, and the "cheapening" of Raphael's late style by centuries of teaching of the "Fine Arts" in France, especially since Le Brun, must carry part of the blame, with the consequence that people no longer knew — and still do not know — how to view this as the most powerful and most original style of painting the world has ever seen and as the culmination of Raphael's art. The anonymous author, who three hundred years ago wrote in *Le Mercure Galant* of November 1681 of a visit which Louis XIV had just made to the Louvre to view his collection of paintings, had a surer eye: "Among the paintings by this great master there are three which are beyond price — one represents

fruits and vegetables which underline and imitate the existing architecture of the vault. The ten pendentive subdivisions of the vaulting show the earliest episodes from the story of Psyche, with one, two, three or four large scale figures occupying most of the space; the intermediate spaces, those of the fourteen triangular "piercings," display winged cupids still against a background of sky and accompanied by animals or bearing symbols of the gods. The top of the vault, which forms a flat ceiling, is covered by two simulated pieces of tapestry, stretched between the surrounding leafy branches in such a way as to suggest a tent to keep off the sun. There are represented, without any effect of perspective, the two final episodes of the story which followed those which were planned

212 *Venus and Psyche.* About 1517-18. Pen and ink over red chalk. 10.5 x 8 cm. Oxford, Ashmolean Museum.

the *Transfiguration* and is in Rome; His Majesty owns the other two, a *St. Michael* of natural grandeur and the *Holy Family*." The opinion no doubt, of a courtier but nobody then dreamed of contesting it.

The two great decorative cycles of the final stage of Raphael's career were once again executed for his two principal Roman patrons, Pope Leo X and the banker Agostino Chigi. For the villa of the latter where he had already painted the *Galatea* Raphael conceived the ambitious scheme of decorating in fresco the vast *loggia* which opened onto the gardens at ground floor level. This *ensemble* was probably commissioned by the banker to celebrate his marriage. The overall theme, borrowed from Apuleius, is the story of Psyche. Only the vaulted ceiling begun in January 1519 was decorated, for the scenes from the earthly life of Psyche which were planned for the walls were not to be realized; all that remains of these are some preparatory drawings by Raphael. The decoration of the vault gives the impression of a large pergola open to the sky and is made up of long ribbons of greenery interwoven with flowers,

213 *Venus and Psyche.* About 1517-18. Fresco. Width about 400 cm. Rome, Villa Farnesina.

214 *Venus and Psyche.* About 1517-18. Red chalk. 26.5 x 19.7 cm. Paris, Musée du Louvre.

The preparatory drawings for the fresco showing Psyche giving Venus the vase containing the waters of the Styx, one of the ten pendentive decorations of the loggia, allow us to follow the working out of the design. The Oxford sketch, of a quivering spontaneity, represents a first idea for the grouping of the figures. The red chalk drawing in the Louvre, copied from life with great breadth and delicacy, established the positions in which they appear in the fresco itself. The execution of the fresco, with its comparatively crude, jerky modeling, could only be by assistants.

to be shown on the walls. The naked figures in the pendentives are shown against the background of the sky and placed within this constraining triangular setting out of which the painter contrives different effects, arranging figures in the shape of a bouquet, carefully placing arms or wings, making the draperies flow in the breeze and the doves hover. Several of the paintings show figures in flight and thus entirely silhouetted against the blue sky.

The "piercings" display variations which are even more complex and dizzying to the extent that the scale of the *amorini* and the angle from which they are seen varies from one section to another. And at the same time they are an excuse for some completely novel variations in the use of light, for example, in the play of shadows and reflections in the *Cupid Bearing a Shield* or the *Amorini with a Harpy*. The debt to classical sculpture which is evident in the pendentives is even more obvious in the simulated draperies of the ceiling where the composition arranges in horizontal frieze a number of close-packed but still easily identifiable figures, as in a Roman relief. But this reconstruction of antiquity is full of a robust liveliness and the nude bodies, bursting with life, owe as much to the study of living models as to that of ancient statues. The almost aggressive incongruity of solidly rounded flesh set against the blue of the sky, the ingenious realism of fruits, flowers and birds evoke in the luxuriance of their shapes and colors the wall papers of the Second Empire. This story of Cupid and Psyche, painted to celebrate a wedding, exudes a cheerful and healthy eroticism which was later misdirected by Giulio Romano into coarse pornography or turned by Parmigianino, Primaticcio and the Frenchmen of Fontainebleau in the direction of a complicated over-refinement. Rubens was the first to understand and appreciate it when less than a century later he was in Rome and greatly admired these frescoes. The *Loggia* of the Villa Farnesina was to become, more than the far less easily accessible rooms of the Vatican, the school of European painting.

Several magnificent preparatory drawings, some of which pose problems of attribution — Raphael or Giulio Romano — which are not yet resolved, bear witness to the care with which Raphael prepared the pictures. The actual execution seems to have been largely entrusted to his assistants in the studio, among them, Giulio Romano, Gianfrancesco Penni and Raffaellino del Colle. The part played by Giovanni da Udine, responsible for the garlands which constitute the "frame" of the design, and probably also for a number of the birds and flying animals, was certainly an important one. But it is often difficult, given the differing state of the frescoes, to distinguish between poor condition due to partial exposure to the elements, since several centuries passed before the *Loggia* was glassed in, and ancient restorations. It seems impossible that Raphael did not take a personal hand in so important an undertaking, and certain stronger and more subtle parts of the work can only be his; Konrad Oberhuber notes the Raphaelesque quality of much of the fresco depicting *Venus, Ceres and Juno*. And certain parts of *Mercury and Psyche*, of *Psyche Borne by the Cupids*, or of the

amorini in, for example, the *Cupid with a Bow*, seem to be by the master. We can also detect in the pictures painted by Raphael at this time echoes of this work in the *Loggia of Psyche*; a new interest in decoration, with all that this implies of the interplay of different shapes, seems to have given a decisive impulse to his painting. It is difficult to avoid seeing in paintings like the *St. Michael* in the Louvre or the *Vision of Ezekiel* in the Pitti Palace two sharp patterns of wings and outstretched arms — echoes of the Loggia compositions.

It was also very probable during these same years that Raphael, returning to and amplifying a composition which already figures in the sketches for the Stanza della Segnatura, close to the *Parnassus*, entrusted to Marcantonio the project of the engraving of the *Judgement of Paris* which was to have an immense success and where the abundance of the motifs based on reliefs or antique statues, and the grouping of figures recalls the spirit of the Loggia of the Villa Farnesina.

The original creation of Bramante who began the work which remained unfinished when he died in 1514, the architectural achievement of the *Loggias* of the Vatican was continued and completed by Raphael, who designed the decoration of the *Loggia* on the second floor, the level of the papal apartments. This long space opened up by way of great arcades, nowadays glassed in, onto the Court of St. Damasius and formed the eastern end of the façade of the palace of Nicholas III. It consists of thirteen square vaulted bays. The extremely rich and complex decoration corresponds to so many independently decorated spaces, but with a great concern for unity in the overall scheme, conceived as the *décor* of a gallery punctuated by double arches; the same distribution of *décor* reappears from one bay to the next but with subtle variations. The mural sections, the pillars, and the undersides of the arching are covered with ornament *all'antica*, stucco and fresco motifs on a light background and much damage has been caused by partial exposure to the elements and by generations of careless visitors. Their subjects are profane; the small reliefs, confined within medallions, rectangular or almond-shaped *cartouches* or Amazonian shields are symmetrically surrounded by a more luxuriant and denser *décor* than that of the *Loggetta*, and differ widely from one pillar to the next, the dominating themes being vegetation of various kinds with many birds, fishes, griffons and different figures. Almost everywhere, stucco mouldings divide, underline and enrich the *décor*, making the whole *ensemble* shimmer in the changing light of the day. In sharp contrast, painted in fresco and facing the arcades, above the pediments which surmount the windows, luxurious garlands of beautifully proportioned fruits and flowers stand out illusionistically against a background of summer sky. The overall decorative fresco scheme goes back to Giovanni da Udine, the stuccoes being the work of Giovanni himself, of Perino del Vaga, and of Lorenzetto, the man responsible for the *Jonah* in the Chigi Chapel of Santa Maria del Popolo.

215 *Scenes from the story of Moses and Joshua,* vault of the ninth bay. About 1516-19. Fresco. Vatican, Loggie.
The central square compartment is decorated with stucco. The four compositions, *Moses receiving the Tablets of the Law, The Adoration of the Golden Calf, The Column of Smoke* and *Moses showing the Tablets of the Law to the Israelites,* are presented as fictive framed pictures placed between the central compartment and the cornice. The illusionism is continued in the four corners, where *tromp-l'oeil* architecture opens to reveal a sky full of birds.

216 *Isaac and Rebecca,* detail from the vault of the fifth bay. About 1516-19. Fresco. Vatican, Loggie.

This scene from the fifth bay of the Loggie, which is devoted to the story of Isaac, shows Isaac and Rebecca embracing, spied upon by Abimelech. The power of the light effects, with the rays of the setting sun creating violent contrasts of light and shade, make this an exceptional work among the Loggie decorations. It is generally thought to have been painted by Giulio Romano.

The frescoes of the vaults make up the most ambitious and spectacular element in the program. Vivid in color and contrasts, partly illusionistic, they stand opposed to the clarity of the undersides of the arches, decorated in light relief by a dense compartmentalization of oval or square stuccos. Of quadrangular plan, each vault contains a vast square with a stucco relief at its center. The vault in the center of the gallery bears the stemma of Leo X. Four prominent paintings, rectangular in shape in most of the bays, are disposed round about, one on each side of the square at the base of the vault in the curved space of the springing of the vault. The angles which are left free are treated in a very different fashion from one bay to another. For example, the simulated architecture of a col-

217. *Joseph explaining his dreams to his brothers,* detail from the vault of the seventh bay. About 1516-19. Fresco. Vatican, Loggie.

This fresco from the seventh bay is one of those that best exemplifies the narrative intention of the whole. Joseph explains his dreams, represented by small, circular compositions in the upper part of the design, and provokes the anger of his brothers, as their expressions show. The particularly beautiful design bears the stamp of Raphael himself; the execution is often attributed to Giovanni Francesco Penni.

onnade or a building in detached perspective against the sky, a leafy pergola, material stretched out to form an imitation tent. The compositions of the *quadri ripportati* contain no elements emphasizing their spatial situation and can be considered vertical. The plan devotes thirteen bays with their fifty-two compositions to the great figures of Biblical history. It begins with the *Creation*, then *Adam and Eve*, *Noah*, *Abraham and Lot*, *Isaac*, *Jacob*, *Joseph*, devotes two bays to the story of *Moses*, continues with *Joshua*, *David*, *Solomon*, and ends with *Jesus Christ*.

The exemplary recent study by Nicole Damos has, so far as this is possible, identified the hands responsible for the frescoes. These

213

artists are named by Vasari. Giulio Romano, who was Raphael's closest collaborator in the Papal Stanze, was certainly the principal executant here and stamped his mark on numerous paintings. Gianfrancesco Penni, who was also active in the Stanze was responsible for the small signed *modelli*, very free in technique, which set the compositions in place by gathering together Raphael's ideas; but the part which Penni played in the execution of the paintings is less easy to determine.

Giovanni da Udine is probably the author of the animal scenes and his part was apparently much more modest, except for the grotesques on the walls. The identification of the part taken by Tomaso Vincidor of Bologna who is more of an individual to us nowadays is somewhat difficult. That taken by Pellegrino da

Modena was more secondary, but the role of the very young Perino del Vaga seems to have been important, above all towards the end of the undertaking. The hand of Polidoro da Caravaggio, also a very young man, can be detected in some portions. As for Vincenzo Tamagni, his seems to have been a very modest part. There are other collaborators who are not named by Vasari. Nicole Dacos identifies Raffaelino del Colle of Arezzo, Guillaume Marcilhat of Berry (best known as a master glazier) and the Spaniard Pedro Machuca.

The collaboration was certainly complex, and our grasp of it must remain weak; we know, for example, of some preparatory drawings by Penni for frescoes which seem likely to have been executed

218 *Joshua halting the sun and moon,* detail from the tenth bay. About 1516-19. Fresco. Vatican, Loggie.

The magnificent waving gesture of Joshua must surely be Raphael's own invention, although this scene has generally been regarded as the work of Perino del Vaga.

219 *The Battle of Ponte Milvio,* also known as *The Battle of Constantine.* 1520-4. Fresco. Vatican, Sala di Constantino.

Executed after Raphael's death, mostly by Giulio Romano, this enormous painting was at least conceived by the master himself. A large drawing by Penni in the Louvre gives a good impression of the original design. In the fresco, Giulio follows the letter more than the spirit.

by Giulio Romano. Raphael apparently entrusted Penni with the task of reworking his own designs so as to elaborate them in a form in which they could be reproduced as frescoes, which would explain the simultaneously concise and "pictorial" character of many of the Penni drawings which have come down to us, showing almost exactly the compositions of the whole corresponding with the actual frescoes. The frequently slight anecdotal and somewhat inchoate character of these drawings constrains us to see them as "first attempts". These traits are striking in drawings like that of *Moses Striking Water from the Rock* in the Uffizi or the *Finding of the Infant Moses* in the Victoria and Albert Museum in London. This last design seems in no respect to lead on to the cluster of beautiful, round and heavy masses of the corresponding fresco. Throughout the work the force and strength of the figures, rhythmically linked, powerfully simplified in the division between light and shadow which were to make such an impression on Géricault, belong only to the paintings and make no appearance in Penni's drawings. What actually strikes one in the small paintings of the loggias is their unity, the fact that they are all servants of the same language, that of Raphael. It may be that Raphael produced numerous drawings which are lost today. Some are known to us in the form of copies, occasionally faithful ones; where Raphael's design has been pre-

served, like that of *David and Goliath* in the Albertina at Vienna, it testifies in every possible way — movement, space, outline — to his genius and delicacy of suggestion. The creative invention behind the paintings seems everywhere to be Raphael's even if he could often only contribute a rough sketch: the small figures with their brisk movements, illuminated by contrasting strengths of dark and light, are the same as those in the background of the *Fire in the Borgo* or the countryside of *Lo Spasimo*. These small surfaces were for Raphael a "testing ground". *Moses Receiving the Tablets of the Law* in the zig-zag violence of its presentation, or the *Column of Smoke* with its sharply-outlined forms in the manner of Delaunay must be included among his most innovative creations.

And who but Raphael could have invented the marvelous undulating arms of the *Joshua Halting the Sun and the Moon,* or the finely harmonized group of three citizens listening to *Joseph Interpreting the Dreams*? Nowadays, people refuse to recognize any share by the master himself in the execution of the frescoes. Powerful and delicate sections of the *Adoration of the Golden Calf, The Finding of the Infant Moses,* and *The Flight of Lot* which we would like to attribute to him belong more probably to Giulio Romano whose personality seems to have dominated the work. This is also the case with the first of the frescoes, *God the Father Dividing Light from Darkness,* different in

215

scale and style from the other compartments which evokes the manner of the Raphael of the Stanze. But it must be said once again: the paintings of the *Loggias* form part of the *corpus* of Raphael's work. Each of the compositions is striking in its careful balance of masses, equilibrium of movements, precision of light-effects; and the colors which people used to dismiss as noisy and blatant come very close, with their lively blues, golden yellows, mauves and vermilions, to those in the paintings of the final stage of his career which have recently been cleaned.

The enterprise displays above all, and more clearly than any other of Raphael's, the narrative and didactic concern of his painting. Each section tells a story, and their combination constitutes a coherent story, the story of humankind. It is in the "serial" aspect of the *Loggias*, as Longhi called it, which seems sometimes on the verge of *naiveté*, that we rediscover the candor of the Umbrian predellas. In these small paintings with their exaggerated features, there is a whole world of "imagery" which will enchant the faithful: moving or exemplary deeds, fairyland countrysides, natural prodigies, an astonishing bestiary with camels with human eyes and the flocks of sheep of Lalanne; and the dreams which Joseph recounts to his brethren or to the Pharaoh are depicted in illustrated "bubbles." Coming after another great undertaking, that of the *Acts of the Apostles*, which had taught Raphael how to sum up an incident in an expressive action, how to play on sharp contrasts and lively colors in order to achieve "legibility," the paintings of the *Loggias* show a small number of figures with their heads out of proportion in order to mitigate the distortion of perspective and at the same time make it easier to read the expressions on their faces, their postures as sharp and striking as in some sublime puppet-show. They also assert the painter's determination to make precise statements simply and clearly: the success of the diffusion of this "Raphael's Bible" is sufficient proof that he succeeded.

Certain further undertakings by Raphael as a fresco artist should also be mentioned, but their actual execution was the concern of his studio. Two are frescoes perhaps over-neglected nowadays, which were removed from the Villa Magliana, a papal residence in a southwestern suburb of Rome, and finished up in the eighteenth century, one at the Louvre, and the other at the Narbonne Museum. The Louvre fresco, which decorates the space of a small spherical vault section, shows the *Eternal Father between Two Angels*. Its poor state makes a firm judgement impossible but the dryness of the actual execution seems to have no connection with Raphael, while on the contrary the overall conception with its fine dramatic effect and the design of each of the three figures, admirable in the handling of their taut or relaxed movements, have the stamp of the master. They hint at a style that seems closer to that of the frescoes in the Stanza d'Eliodoro (c. 1511-13) or of the first frescoes in the Stanza dell'Incendio (c. 1514-15) than to that of the paintings of Raphael's final years.

Yet it seems that the frescoes of the Villa Magliana were commissioned by Leo X in about 1517-20. Can it be that they were based on Raphael drawings of a slightly earlier date? The semi-circular second Magliana fresco, the *Martyrdom of St. Cecilia* now at Narbonne, is unhappily in a fragmentary condition; only part of the surface survives, the two lateral sections. The composition is repeated by Marcantonio in a print identified by Vasari as a *Martyrdom of St. Felicity* but which really shows the *Martyrdom of St. Cecilia*. The central portion of the print was copied in the nineteenth century to replace the missing portion of the fresco. The variations between the print and the fresco, especially the right-hand part, show that the former could have been executed from a *modello*, perhaps the very badly damaged drawing preserved at Dresden. Does the fine and dramatic conception of the surviving portions of the fresco go back to Raphael? The supple treatment of the draped figures and the strong contrasts allow a comparison with the best parts of the *Loggias*; the light which bathes the figures on the left between the white columns, distantly inspired by the *Healing of the Lame Man* in the Sistine tapestries, is especially remarkable.

Marcantonio's print, probably completed after Raphael's death, also shows some strong analogies with the "Bible" of the *Loggias* in its narrative which is acted out by shortened figures in violent postures. The execution of the Narbonne fresco with its graceful strength seems even closer to that of the last compositions of the *Loggia* series, very probably painted by the young Perino del Vaga — which would confirm a dating for the two frescoes of about 1517-1519.

Altogether more ambitious must have been the decoration of the Stanza di Constantino in the Vatican, its dimensions much vaster than those of the three *Stanze* already decorated; it was painted by Raphael's pupils after his death, foremost among them being Penni and Giulio Romano. Raphael seems to have fixed the general conception of the decorative scheme, a very ambitious one with its huge simulated tapestries and its statues (also simulated) of the Popes, framed by *Virtues*. The principal painting, *The Battle of the Mulvian Bridge*, seems in its general composition faithful to Raphael's chosen conception; a large color-wash drawing by Penni in the Louvre shows the composition as it was before Giulio Romano who executed the painting added a few ideas and drawings of his own. A nude study at Oxford for two figures crouched in a boat can be attributed to Raphael himself. The other designs which have been preserved are by Penni or Giulio and the *décor* of the whole abounding in shining rounded masses bears the mark of Giulio. The paintings in the Stanza di Constantino showing four scenes from the life of the first Christian Emperor must display in all its grandeur the realization of Leo X's ideal with its mixture of the Antique and the Christian. The references here to ancient Roman reliefs and statues are numerous.

Raphael's last oil paintings, executed in the final three years of his life, represent the greatest achievement of his career and the summit of his art. Several of them have recently been restored and stripped of the centuries-old layers of yellowing varnish which almost entirely covered them, reducing them to dull monochromes

This group was used in reverse in an engraving by Marco Dente da Ravenna. It seems to be a study relating to *The Battle of Constantine* in the Sala di Constantino. The freedom of brushwork, robustness and dynamism recall both Leonardo and Poussin.

of brown, reddish or ochre tones. We are perhaps only just beginning to take measure of these paintings and the logical and essential qualities they reveal as the consummation of Raphael's revolutionary enterprise. They both recapitulate and question the whole of his art but every great work of art questions painting as a whole. Above all, painters of the succeeding centuries looked at these paintings. To some extent, we look at the *St. Michael* or the *Transfiguration* and tend to see a less Raphaelian fullness than when we look at the *Belle Jardinière* or *The School of Athens*. It seems to be almost a betrayal.

The notion that the pictures were executed "with a considerable participation by the studio" gives us reassurance. But we must be on our guard here; these powerful, brilliant and lively-colored masses, these black shadows, this search for the exaggerated or delicate expression — all this is certainly Raphael. And there is an element of the absurd in emphasizing, in what is perhaps the greatest victory of style in all Western painting by a painter of thirty-five at the peak of his fame, the intervention of pupils of only fifteen or eighteen.

Preserved in the Louvre, *The Holy Family with St. Elisabeth, the Infant St. John and Two Angels*, generally known as *The Holy Family of Francis I* after its owner, or the *Great Holy Family*, as opposed to the *Small Holy Family* (itself too, since the seventeenth century, part of the Royal Collections), was commissioned by Lorenzo de' Medici, Duke of Urbino, at the same time as the *St. Michael*. The two pictures must have been commissioned as a diplomatic gift to

221 *The Large Holy Family,* also known as *The Holy Family of Francis I.* 1518. Oil on panel, tranferred to canvas. 207 x 140 cm. Paris, Musée du Louvre.

Signed and dated on the hem of the Virgin's garment, the work was part of the same diplomatic gift to Francis I as the St. Michael. The restoration carried out in 1982-3 revealed an unexpected brilliance of color, with the most luminous pinks and violets balanced by soft greens and oranges. The confidence and variety of the execution shows the part played by Raphael himself to have been greater than was previously thought.

222 *Study of a woman for The Large Holy Family.* 1518. Red chalk. 17.3 x 11.9 cm. Paris, Musée du Louvre.

Though occasionally given to Giulio Romano, this life study, with its powerful evocation of forms through light, could only be by Raphael himself.

King Francis I and Queen Claudia at whose court Lorenzo de' Medici was the Vatican ambassador. They were completed at the end of May 1518. *The Holy Family,* fully signed and dated 1518, is striking in its ample and monumental character. The composition looks like the culmination of the many *Madonnas* or *Holy Families* of Raphael. We need only cite three large Florentine *Madonnas,* especially the *Belle Jardinière,* where the rhythmic links which unite the two figures are developed more generously and spiritedly or the *Canigiani Holy Family* which as here creates a balance of equilibrium between two confronting forces.

But there is also the small *Holy Family with the Lamb* of the Prado, with the touching disequilibrium of its "cascade" organization, and the dynamic positioning of the Virgin, half-kneeling, half-seated in which the placing of the foot is so telling, and also the movement of her arms, holding the Child safe and secure and where the ampleness and fluidity of the folds play their part in the rhythm of the whole piece. The cradling here introduces an important rhythmic suggestion and the composition incorporates a play of balances which leads from one side of the picture to the other and recurs in the shared curve of the arms of mother and child joining the two bodies in one organic whole. An arrangement of arched shapes dynamically inclined towards each other takes the form of a vault, and this structure just like an architectural vault owes its equilibrium to the delicate balance of the forces which give it life. And the whole gains animation in an extraordinary movement which is reminiscent of the organization of the *St. Michael* and the *Transfiguration.*

The power of the elastic and muscular bodies, as if poised to spring, recalls the mythological characters of the *Loggia* of the Villa Farnesina with which they share the majestic fullness inspired by ancient marbles, and which are contemporary with them. The analogies with the simulated tapestries of the *Loggia* are particularly outstanding, especially with the *Wedding of Cupid and Psyche* in which there reappears, disguised as a mythological deity, an angelic figure in antique dress with both arms upraised ready to scatter its flowers in the same gesture as the harpist with both arms lifted up. The plastic power of the figures which spring out of the shadow and their grouping recall once again Leonardo da Vinci whose work Raphael seems to have completely grasped in his last years. This almost raw effect of light on the principal figures strikes us afresh now that the picture has been restored and has recovered the force of its contrasts and colors. The vigorous thrusting forward of shapes, achieved by the contrast of vivid lights and strong shadows, makes a deep impression: this aspect was the subject of lively criticism by Sebastiano del Piombo who wrote to Michelangelo that in the *Holy Family* and the *St. Michael* (the other picture sent to Francis I) "the figures seem to have been exposed to the smoke, or again to be shining figures of steel, all bright and all black."

The share which Giulio Romano may have had in the execution of the picture, and which is noted by Vasari, could have been confined to certain parts of the left hand side. Only Raphael could have painted the main section with a pictorial sense close to that displayed in the *Transfiguration*. The Virgin's face and draperies are reproduced with a sculptural authority, while the marvelous stooping figure of St. Joseph, his face resting alongside his hand, remains in the velvety half-shadows; the veined marbles of the flagstones are handled with an enchanting freedom of brush stroke. The colors revealed by the restoration, flesh-pink, porcelain-blue, and the pale lemon-yellow of the Madonna's robes, intentionally contrasted with dull greens and purplish-blue tones, are of a splendor and boldness which could not have been suspected, and yet comparable to those of the *Transfiguration*. Three drawings for the *Great Holy Family* also pose the problem of Giulio Romano's participation in the enterprise. It seems likely that the Louvre drawing so exact and delicate from a model posing for the figure of the Madonna and a study in the Uffizi for the infant Jesus are certainly by Raphael; the other sheet in the Uffizi showing a draped Madonna with its heavier and more insistent effects may be the work of Giulio. Insofar as this latter drawing which contains very finished drapery studies, seems likely to have served for the picture itself, one can probably infer a collaboration between the two painters which varied in intensity at different stages of the work, and discard the overly simple scheme of "the execution by Giulio of Raphael's designs."

The *St. Margaret*, also in the Louvre, was probably also painted in 1518 like the *Great Holy Family* and the *St. Michael* for the French court and in particular for Margaret de Valois, the King's sister. The idea of a lonely figure on foot in a shadowy wooded countryside calls to mind Leonardo's *St. John the Baptist*, also in the Louvre. As in these latter pictures the figure comes softly to life as it emerges from a somber background. It looks like a more calm and feminine version of the *St. Michael* whose spirit it sketchily hints at. It is very hard given the present condition of the picture which was damaged in a fire long ago to say how much of it is Raphael's work. The conception of the forms, with their fine flowing rhythm together with the delicate balancing of the stance of the Saint in contrast with the violence of the coils of the dragon, must belong to the master. Vasari indicates that the picture was executed by Giulio Romano. The stiffly arranged pleats of the clothing seem to go back to him but the painstaking and powerful execution of the dragon, still attributed to Giulio because of the exaggeration of its expression, bears some resemblance to that of the wings of the devil in the *St. Michael* and might prompt us to ask whether Raphael had a hand in the painting.

Another picture of *St. Margaret* in the Kunsthistorisches Museum in Vienna looks back one last time to Leonardo's *Leda* in a countryside itself Leonardesque in mood. We may experience some sense of doubt before this jostling play of less substantial forms, to some extent glued within the writhing coils of a dragon like the Louvre dragon, and before the slightly gratuitous gesture of the arm drawn back behind the body.

Currently misjudged, but easier to appreciate since a recent restoration which has confirmed its quality, the *St. John the Baptist*

in a Landscape in the Louvre, must take its place in the catalogue of the autographed works of Raphael even though it contains areas of wear and irreparable gaps which will never permit us to say how far this or that collaborator could have had a hand in its execution. Leonardo's influence is obvious in the gesture of the hand in the shadowy undergrowth and above all in the young man's expression, at once disturbed and delighted. The date is generally given as about 1516–1517. But the beautiful countryside with its contrasted effects of rippling light, like the elegance of the pose, at once taut and supple, so natural that it seems almost accidental, and the almost romantic tone of the piece, fit badly into the last heroic brilliant years, and more easily into the time when Raphael was most influenced by Venetianism. This was around 1513, a little later than the *Galatea* and *Isaiah* with which the *St. John the Baptist* shares the characteristic large movements which claim the space for themselves. But the Leonardesque qualities, comparable to those of the *St. Margaret*, and the provenance of the picture which comes from the collection of Adrien Gouffier, Cardinal de Boissy and the Chateau d'Oiton makes us hesitate and lean towards a late date, about 1517–18. The present poor condition of the work makes a confident modern judgement difficult. There is in any case a striking contrast with another *St. John the Baptist* in the Uffizi, also with the index-finger raised but seen full-face, which is always compared with the Louvre picture. The tension of the muscular forms, seemingly ready to spring, and the wild energy of the facial expression suggest a very late date, shortly before the painter's death, and very probably the hand of Giulio Romano.

A number of *Madonnas* and *Holy Families*, painted near the end of Raphael's life and often executed wholly or in part by his collaborators and often neglected, nevertheless deserve examination.

The *Holy Family with a Rose* in the Prado is often considered as a work from Raphael's studio. It seems that the painter himself took a major part in it: the admirable design of the two children, with Jesus' posture so energetic that it reminds one of a *putto* in an ancient bacchanalian dance, and the figure of Joseph, half-buried in shadow, are very Raphaelesque, but the figure of the Madonna herself, her body twisted, lacks fullness and amplitude, and a certain chilly sense of hardness in the face and in the too-thin body is a little disconcerting. In any case the picture lacks the radiant force of Raphael's last works.

Another famous composition cherished for its religious imagery, the *Madonna del Divin' Amore* in the Capodimonte Museum at Naples, which is reminiscent of Leonardo and Fra Bartolomeo, exploits a familiar vein of unctuous sentimentality with its soft and spiritless faces. Its execution is nowadays most often attributed to Gianfrancesco Penni, inspired by a drawing by Raphael.

223   *The Large Holy Family*. Detail of illustration 221. Photograph after restoration.

Two *Holy Families*, both in the Prado, were probably painted in Raphael's studio in about 1518 by Giulio Romano, and seem to be influenced by the *Great Holy Family* in the Louvre. The *Holy Family under a Chestnut-Tree*, commonly called in Italian *La Quercia*, which was perhaps painted with the help of Raphael's drawings, distances itself from the master in the excessive richness of its motifs and effects and the absence of any tension and rhythm in its relaxed forms. The movement of the draperies has a separate life from that of the bodies and the fine realistic passages — cradle, chestnut-tree, and above all, the remarkable overturned capital — are treated independently. The other *Holy Family*, less appealing at first sight, is in fact more interesting and more Raphaelesque. It is called *La Perla*, ever since Philip IV named it as the "pearl" of his collection of pictures. The close-packed group formed by the Madonna, St. Elisabeth, the child Jesus and the infant St. John once again evokes Leonardo's St. Anne, and the pyramidal organization echoes the Florentine compositions. Only Raphael would have conceived the beautiful knot of the sinuous forms of the Madonna and Child, and in the richness of its dramatic effects, aided by the half-darkness, the picture approaches the spirit of the master's last pictures.

225   *The Vision of Ezekiel.* About 1518. Oil on panel. 40 x 30 cm. Florence, Pitti Palace.

Vasari describes the picture in Bologna in the collection of Count Ercolani. It was in the Uffizi at the end of the 16th century, entering the Pitti Palace after a period in Paris from 1799 to 1815. The execution is sometimes attributed to a pupil, Giulio Romano or Penni, but is strong and coherent enough to be by the master himself.

224   *St. John the Baptist in the desert.* About 1517-18? Oil on panel, transferred to canvas. 135 x 142 cm. Paris, Musée du Louvre.

The picture was part of the collection of Adrien Gouffier, Cardinal of Boissy and Royal Chaplain under Francis I. It is difficult to judge in its present poor state of repair but seems to be an original Raphael of great intensity and lyricism, though perhaps executed with the help of assistants.

226   *The Small Holy Family.* About 1518-19. Oil on panel. 38 x 32 cm. Paris, Musée du Louvre.

Though generally considered to be the work of a pupil working to Raphael's design, the picture deserves reassessment; it may well be largely by the master himself. The composition, with its inter-related arcs described by the bodies of the two mothers and two children, recalls that of the *Canigiani Holy Family.*

222

227/228 *St. Michael trampling on the Devil,* known as *The Large St. Michael.* 1518. Oil on panel, transferred to canvas. 268 x 160 cm. Paris, Musée du Louvre.

The work was given to Francis I by Lorenzo de'Medici, Duke of Urbino and papal ambassador, at the same time as *The Large Holy Family.* It is signed and dated along the bottom of the archangel's tunic. The rich, refined execution, with its tones of gold, orange and blue, is Raphael's own.

Today in the Louvre, the *Small Holy Family* has the same provenance as the *St. John the Baptist* — it comes from the collection of Adrien Gouffier, Cardinal de Boissy. The execution of this tiny panel is still attributed to a pupil, Giulio Romano or quite often Penni, working from a drawing by Raphael. In fact, the authority of the forms which articulate themselves in a knot of strong curves, and which one could easily imagine inscribed within a circle like most of the late Raphaelesque *Holy Families*, can belong only to the master. There are several surprising discordances in the proportions of the Madonna's body, with its too-small foot pushed forward and its rather strong head, or again in the slightly chaotic conception of the robe with its many patches of shadow.

But such stylistic traits do evoke the contemporary undertaking in the *Loggias*, and the lively and nervous execution bears no sign of the touch of sentimentality and regularity which the hands of pupils normally introduce. The recent restoration has revealed the vigor of the brushwork and the subtle brilliance of the colors; the countryside, in particular, bears Raphael's delicate touch. We must then entertain the possibility — for the work is too vigorous for Giulio Romano and Penni's manner of painting remains difficult to pin down — that Raphael was partly responsible for the execution of the *Small Holy Family*. A fairly mediocre drawing, harsh in its execution, which is preserved at Windsor, contains a few variations from the composition of the Louvre picture, and must be a copy or a version of a lost drawing by Raphael or somebody else.

The kinship in style and execution of the *Small Holy Family* and the *Vision of Ezekiel*, in the Pitti Palace at Florence, which have the same dimensions, is striking: the rounded, thick-set bodies, strongly modeled by black shadows and lively touches of light, and the vigorous *impasto* execution, invite one to see an identical hand in both pictures — that of Penni, for Konrad Oberhuber. Others have more often thought of Giulio Romano. The *Vision of Ezekiel*, unlike the neglected picture in the Louvre, counts among Raphael's celebrated works; it is identified with a picture described by Vasari at Bologna in the house of Count Ercolani.

The group of forms, well separated and clearly distinguished against a light background, and the narrative spirit, recall equally the paintings of the *Loggias* and those of the *Villa Farnesina*. The authority of the musculature has always made people think of Michelangelo, and Vasari noted the "antique" character of the picture: "Christ with the features of Jupiter" as he described the principal figure. The plastic power of the motif, which makes one actually think of a Roman cameo, and the novelty and boldness of the representation, with a tiny Ezekiel lost in the splendid countryside, pre-romantic in its rich effects of stormy light, encourage us to accept the traditional attribution to Raphael. This would have been about 1518 despite the absence from the last years of securely autographed small pictures which alone would make possible a decisive comparison. The question as to whose hand was responsible for the Louvre and Pitti paintings is not without significance: if, as we are inclined to believe, these pictures are by Raphael, then

they reveal at the end of his life a return to such delicate little pictures of Leonardesque style, as the *Holy Family with a Lamb* or the *Esterhazy Madonna*, of which there is no further example in his corpus later than the *Aldobrandini Madonna*.

Quite different in its aims from the *Holy Families* is the *St. Michael* in the Louvre called *Great St. Michael* because of the presence in the same collection of the small early panel of the same subject which has already been discussed. Like the *Great Holy Family*, it was part of Lorenzo de Medici's diplomatic gift on his arrival as ambassador to the court of Francis I. The subject is connected with the Royal Order of St. Michael, symbol of the ties between France and the Church. It is both a religious and political picture. Like the *Holy Family*, the *St. Michael* is signed and dated 1518, and also appears to have been painted between March and the end of May of that year: like it too, it is under a cloud, suspected of having been painted not by Raphael, but for the most part by Giulio Romano. If this collaboration, difficult enough to pin down, seems certain for the *Holy Family*, for the *St. Michael* it seems to have been either minimal or non-existent. In fact, we have here, as with the *Transfiguration*, a masterpiece from the end of Raphael's career.

Of all Raphael's work, the *St. Michael* appears the most prodigiously dynamic picture, with the formidable audacity of the great oblique of the thrusting leg and the body, matching and paralleling that of the lance, and crossed by another and steeper oblique, that of the raised arm and outstretched leg. Everything would tilt to the left were it not for the turning movement which carries the play of the curves and arms and wings around the central axis of the face and gives to the whole piece the flamboyance of a sunflower. Of all the variations of articulation in the treatment of shoulders and neck, examples of which are afforded by so many figures, the *St. Michael* displays the supreme example. The body is here the center of the forces which control the organization of the picture. The great whirlpool of the forms of the upper part, displayed in the bright light, finds its response and its contrast in the convulsive curves of the devil with its crooked shapes of ram's horns, fork and wings, glittering in the shadows where one can sense the flames of Hell. But there is no disorder, no confusion: the archangel, imperious as a constellation, is almost weightless, borne up in the air by the beating of his wings, soon to climb again as his lance springs back from the ground after the stroke which will destroy the devil. Face, neck and hair are enclosed in a tight triangle, half light and

229   *Double portrait,* known as the *Portrait of Raphael and his Fencing Master.* About 1517. Oil on panel. 90 x 83 cm. Paris, Musée du Louvre.

The identification of the figure behind as Raphael is unanimously acknowledged but that of the figure turning round towards him remains problematic. It may be a pupil, possibly Polidoro da Caravaggio. The complex psychological and spatial relationship between the figures, like the use of blacks and whites, suggests comparison with the work of Venetian painters.

half shadow, and yet the powerfully structured forms have touches of Leonardesque delicacy. Above all, the *St. Michael*, among Raphael's last works, seems to be the one which most clearly illustrates how much his art had been nourished by the classical sculptures of Rome. Those ancient figures who at the same period of time people the mythological world of the Villa Farnesina also inspire in even richer fashion his great religious works, as well as the frescoes of the Vatican, the Stanza di Constantino or grotesque decorations. Whether it is the antique garments in which he clothes his sacred characters, their hair-styles inspired by imperial portraits or their architectural surroundings, everything in the late "Holy Families" revives the glory of Rome, and it was at Rome that the biblical text came to life. The relief-effect of the bodies and the draperies has a completely sculptural look, and is exactly in the spirit of Greco-Roman sculpture with its precisely-observed musculature — even in the children — and its folds sharply marked and gathered in sheaves, or flowing over the body.

In the *St. Michael* the concern for an antiquity which was relieved in its refinement and luxury and colors is even more manifest. The archaeological precision of the discoverer of antiquities allies itself with the inventiveness of a theatrical costumier in the amazing cuirass with its gilded scales, and two superimposed tunics, the complicated sandals with their grieves, the engraved sword and the knot of ribbon which divides and separates the tresses of the hair. The scarves float just as they do in the imperial reliefs, and the painter's signature unfolds itself at the bottom of the archangel's tunic in the impeccable lettering of a lapidary inscription. This appeal to ancient forms gains life from its recourse to the shapes and colors of nature, with the wide landscape so effective in its contrasted illumination, and the wings with their yellow and blue feathers, and a tactile quality which makes one almost think of the ravishing *Crow's Wing* in the Albertina, a watercolor by Dürer of six years earlier.

It is a brilliant picture, radiant yet calm, and offering proof of how false is the widespread public image of an unstable later Raphael, overcome by anxiety, the legibility of his forms drowned in a penumbra of melodrama. The picture illustrates with precision the victory of spiritual over irrational forces, and at the same time of good over evil. It represents that synthesis of Christianity and Imperial Rome desired by Julius II and Leo X, the object of whose activity was to lead the Roman Church back to the power and influence of ancient Rome. If we had to represent all of Rome in one single image, the Rome of Emperors and the Rome of the Popes, it is this picture sent to His Most Christian Majesty, that great lover of ancient forms, which we would have to choose.

The last portraits of Raphael bear witness to the unsettling nature of the questions which the painter asked himself about his art. They all display a refusal to exploit his successes as a formula, successes which must have been so much admired — the *Donna Velata*, the *Castiglione*, the *Tebaldeo*, the *Navagero and Beazzano*. Others would see to that. These pictures were to be a complete reexamination of the nature of portraiture, treatment of space, grouping of colors. In their conception they demanded an emotional participation from the viewer. The *Double Portrait* of the Louvre, traditionally entitled *Raphael and his Master of Arms*, even if it no longer enjoys the celebrity which it deserves, is numbered among the great Raphael masterpieces. It is perhaps the most gripping of the portraits which he painted at the end of his life. Two men dressed in black and white are in a half-length format in front of a uniformly gray background. One, slightly behind the other, looks at his companion with his hand resting on his shoulder; the latter turns backwards to look at his friend and points with his finger at the viewer whom he seems to be pointing out to him. We are not certain of the identity of the man in the front — can he be a pupil of Raphael? But the figure on the left, neither smiling nor stern, is most certainly Raphael, of whom we have here, along with that in *The School of Athens*, the only certain self-portrait. Thus the picture takes on a most moving dimension, that of an allegory of painting, where the finger indicates at once the mirror reflecting the two men and ourselves, the spectators, ensnared by the image. The sharp contrast of black and white shapes against a neutral background evokes in a nearly monochrome group the *Castiglione*, although here it is more lively and the well-articulated draftsmanship brings to mind Poliakoff's canvases.

But it is the unique audacity of the spatial effect that is particularly effective, the broad sweep described by the outstretched arm, the curve of the shoulders, the pivoting head, the turning gaze. This freedom in the turning, sweeping movements, handled with power and elegance, is just what we find in the figures and historical pictures of the same period, refined to an essential simplicity, in a confident work in which there is none of the stiffness and pomposity demanded by official portraits.

One might say that we have here a sort of private exercise, where the man commissioned to paint the portraits of *Leo X*, *Lorenzo de Medici* and *Joan of Aragon* reasserts the right of pure painting. Amid the rich brocades, the gold jewelry, the cascades of beautifully-cut materials, all these reds and golds, here is a picture in black and gray and white. Coming before the bloodless dummies of the mannerist school, it is a miraculous balance of strength and sanity; the *Double Portrait* in the Louvre, of all Raphael's portraits, is the one where we find most clearly stamped the influence of Sebastiano del Piombo, to whom it has sometimes been attributed, in the sense of the spectacle provided by these brusque movements, the masses sculpturally simplified in cylindrical form, the clear, cold grays. One can also compare it with the *Portrait of a Gentleman* in the Budapest Museum, the *Man in Armor* in Hartford (both c. 1515?) or the *Violinist* in a Parisian collection, long attributed to Raphael (1515?), or again with Washington's *Cardinal Sanli* (1516), or finally with the later *Anton Francesco degli Albizzi* in Houston (c. 1525?), where the authority of the forms, especially those of the sleeve-opening and of the forward-pointing hand, come close to the Louvre picture.

But this last moves away from Sebastiano with a less clear-cut softness and roundness of modeling and a calmer light-effect, and above all with its atmosphere of "good companionship," so different from that of the combative Venetian. In any case it is to venetian examples, probably via Sebastiano, that this picture carries us back in its subject and its "emotional" handling. (We might cite here the very Giorgonesque *Double Portrait* in the Palazzo di Venezia at Rome.)

And it is again to Venice that we are taken by the comparison with another marvelous *Self-Portrait*, it too thrown into a violent disequilibrium by a wide, three-dimensional movement, that of Savoldo, also in the Louvre. This is difficult to date precisely and could be later than the *Double Portrait*. Given this powerful Venetianism, given also the dates of the comparable works by Sebastiano, it looks as if the very late date of 1520 recently suggested by Konrad Oberhuber must be challenged; in the last portraits, more brilliant masses with blacker shadows are distinguished by a more vigorous sharpness than we find here. This picture could date from 1517, or even a year earlier, immediately after an artistic reconsideration, following perhaps the execution of the *Portrait of Navagero and Beazzano*. It is in any case one of Raphael's most important canvases, the equivalent in its handling of plasticity and space to that of pure sensibility in the *Castiglione*.

Following on from the series of intimate and "affectionate" portraits, from the *Castiglione* to the *Double Portrait*, there are three pictures which must be considered as "official portraits" and which present quite different problems: these are *Pope Leo X*, *Lorenzo de Medici*, and *Joan of Aragon*.

The *Portrait of Leo X*, probably painted during the winter of 1518-19, shows the pontiff seated and viewed from a three-quarter angle, a little like the *Julius II* in London but seen from slightly farther away in a larger setting with his hands resting on a small table supporting a book whose page he is about to turn. He is accompanied by two cardinals standing behind him (which completely alters the composition), his two nephews, Giulio de Medici on the left and Luigi de Rossi leaning against the back of the chair on the right. Perhaps no other portrait by Raphael ever possessed this plastic strength of forms which seem about to burst out of the space with the brutal confidence which comes near to distorting the perspective. Standing in front of these solidly-built forms, one thinks of the portraits by Fouquet, the only precedents for so much force in such simple shapes; and Nicole Reynaud aptly refers to the much-admired likeness, now lost, of *Pope Eugenius IV* which was painted by Fouquet at Rome just over seventy years earlier, and in which, like the Raphael, the pontiff was accompanied by two friends. But the importance given to pictorial effect, asserted in opposition to a Sebastiano who cared for nothing but the sculptural massing of forms in space, is underlined by the sumptuousness of a color scheme in which the reds erupt like a fanfare and by a craftsmanship which is mature and versatile and treats the different materials with care in translating them into their pictorial

equivalents — not in an allusive, Venetian manner, but with the strength of masses well-integrated in space. Thus they all fall into position, the enchanting play of velours, damasks and furs, the careful drawing of the chiselled hand-bell, the illuminated book, the seal on its ribbon. This is a moment of equilibrium but also of tension on the edge of a rupture between two concerns: the need for a formal structure and the enticement of color and craftsmanship.

The true heirs of such a picture are Ingres' *Monsieur Bertin* and Velasquez's *Innocent X*. The picture can be summed up in the gilded ball on the back of the chair (with the reflection of the window repeated, exactly, in the *Bertin*), in the joy of pure volume and of pure feeling. The necessary comparison with the *Julius II* of seven years earlier shows us a *Leo X* more dramatic, and growling with restrained energy; the draperies flutter and billow, the positioning of the table accentuates the oblique viewpoint, the reds glow with all their fire, without the counterpoint of the green background which in the London picture tempers and regulates them. Above all, the faces, with a stronger and richer modeling, are enhanced by the penumbra and betray fleeting anxieties.

Another impressive, half-length likeness shows us another aspect of Raphael as official portraitist. It is the portrait of *Duke Lorenzo de Medici*, long believed lost but rediscovered and published by Konrad Oberhuber in 1971. It is a large canvas, almost a meter in height, whose condition is not perfect but where the beauty of numerous sections, especially in the dress, points to the hand of Raphael. The positioning of the subject, the three-quarter face with the shoulder almost face-on, and the supple curves of the body are in the tradition of portraits of heads of state for which Fouquet had established a formula with his *Charles VII*, a formula which the greatest European painters, like Holbein, were to take over again at the start of the sixteenth century. The work is magnificent in its fullness, with the folded arms allowing the sumptuous and symmetrical deployment of cloth-of-gold and furs. But there is a per-

230 *Portrait of Leo X between two cardinals.* About 1518-19. Oil on panel. 154 x ▷ 119 cm. Florence, Uffizi.

The Pontiff is surrounded by two of his nephews, Cardinals Giulio de'Medici and Luigi de'Rossi. The date of execution can be placed between the second half of 1517, when de'Rossi became a Cardinal, and August 1519, when he died. The almost brutal power of Leo X's silhouette stands out against the brilliance of the reds.

231 *Portrait of Lorenzo de'Medici, Duke of Urbino.* About 1518. Oil on canvas. 99.5 ▷▷ x 81 cm. New York, Collection of Ira Spanierman.

The portrait has been reestablished as an autograph work from the end of Raphael's career by J. Shearman and K. Oberhuber. The power of the volumes, with their heightened chiaroscuro, and the sensual treatment of materials, place it close to the *Leo X*.

232 *Portrait of a young woman,* known as *La Fornarina.* About 1518-20. Oil on panel. 85 x 60 cm. Rome, Galleria Nazionale, Palazzo Barberini.

The picture has been in successive Roman collections since the end of the 16th century, those of the Countess of Santafiora, the Duke Buoncampagni, then the Barberini family. Historians have yet to agree on the parts played by Raphael and Giulio Romano in its execution, which X-rays suggest dates from several different periods. Whatever the case, this is certainly not a completely autograph work.

sistently contradictory element in this simple, almost geometrical presentation combined with a handling of space which is animated, dramatic and moving; the result is a likeness which is somewhat constrained and insecure, with a look that is anxious and not very attractive. There is a wide gap between this picture and the peace and air of calm of the *Castiglione.* We might ask whether the well-known portrait of *Francis I* in the Louvre, most often attributed to Jean Clouet, may not owe something to the *Lorenzo de Medici;* perhaps even more interesting for the angle of view and above all the large *encadrage,* is the portrait of *Odet de Coligny* by François Clouet at Chantilly.

Oberhuber has rightly emphasized this "French" character in the portrait of Lorenzo, precisely at a moment when the ties between the French and the Papal courts were especially strong. He also cites a possible connection with some portraits by Fouquet of the type of the *Jouvenel des Ursins* in the Louvre, comparable in their design. It is moreover possible that the canvas was painted on the occasion of the Duke's marriage to Madeleine de la Tour d'Auvergne in May 1518, which would give us an exact date.

We know that Raphael probably did not himself paint the Louvre *Portrait of Joan of Aragon,* commissioned from him by Cardinal Bibbiena who planned to give it to Francis I of France. Giulio Romano was sent to Naples where the young woman, the fiancée of Ascanio Colonna, lived in order to do the preparatory sketch for the picture from the life. The picture, which was once popular, is not greatly admired today for all that it is one of the most striking and attractive portraits of these years. The delicacy of the Leonardesque forms stands in contrast with the exuberance and sumptuousness of the draperies. There are persistently Raphaelesque elements: the princess' face recalls almost to the point of confusion the face of a young man, generally identified as Francesco Maria della Rovere, in *The School of Athens.*

We do not know what parts Raphael and Giulio Romano took in the composition, and in the execution of a work which seems in both respects rather superior in the firmness and generous ease of the forms to anything that Giulio could have done on his own; and we know of no comparable work by Giulio except the later (1525?) *Portrait of Isabelle d'Este* at Hampton Court, uncertain in its presentation, and apparently inspired by the Louvre picture. The background, on the left, in any case appears to be the work of Giulio alone.

The portrait of *La Fornarina,* Raphael's mistress, which hangs in the Palazzo Barberini of the National Gallery at Rome is perhaps the most famous of the painter's pictures, but heaped with opprobrium. For theoreticians of religious art of the nineteenth century, *La Fornarina* was a hated symbol of the artist's degeneration and "moral damnation"; and for art historians of the twentieth century, equally a symbol of a Raphael attempting a tenderness and *suavité* of which he was no longer capable, or of a Raphael so overcome by his own glory that he no longer had the time to paint his own pictures. This "baker's daughter" has often been identified — none too securely — with a certain Margherita who was the daughter of a Roman baker called Francesco Luti. Her armlet bears in large lettering, almost a proclamation, the words "RAPHAEL URBINAS," made all the more prominent by the pointing of the index finger of the hand on the breast; one is reminded of that portrait of the Duchess of Alba where Goya wrote his name and that of his model on the rings which she flaunts, thus confessing and cementing their *liaison.* As with so many too well-known pictures, *La Fornarina* is one of those works which one can no longer look at without difficulty and which people are perhaps too ready to exclude from the painter's oeuvre. There is here, in this portrait of a woman whom Raphael perhaps loved — even amid the difficulties which we experience when we look at it, confronted by these imperfections and this expressive intensity of the gaze, this failed gracefulness — a reflection of Raphael's art, and perhaps of his life, which was so powerful that this work, which he may not in fact have painted, must continue to take its place in his *corpus.*

One is bound to be struck by the differences between this painting and the Raphael portraits which are assumed to be contemporary with it — a weaker modeling, a less solid structure in depth,

233 *Portrait* said to be *of Bindo Altoviti.* About 1519-20 ? Oil on panel. 60 x 44 cm. ▷ Washington, National Gallery.

The picture is often attributed to Giulio Romano but is more probably by Raphael, though very difficult to place chronologically. A date around the time of the *Castiglione,* about 1514-15, seems unlikely in view of the great differences in the coloring of the two works. The powerful tonal contrasts and the rapid, sensual brushwork suggest a much later date, around the time of *The Transfiguration.* The portrait belonged to the Altoviti family, was bought by Ludwig I of Bavaria and was in the Munich Pinakothek until its purchase in 1936 by Samuel H. Kress who bequeathed it to the National Gallery in Washington.

234 *Portrait of a young woman.* About 1519-20. Oil on panel. 60 x 44 cm. Strasbourg, ▷▷ Musée des Beaux-Arts.

Acquired from an English collection for the Strasbourg Museum by Bode in 1890, the portrait is normally attributed to Giulio Romano. X-rays and visible changes in the neckline indicate that it was painted at two different times. Comparable in technique to the portraits of Leo X and Lorenzo de'Medici, it seems largely if not totally by Raphael and would date from the last years of his career.

the shadow trembling along the length of the arm, the hands a little limp, at least the hand resting on the breast. The extraordinary power of the picture owes more to the clear outlining of the figure placed in front of the dark leafy background than to a confident disposition of forms.

It is not a question of saying "This painting is not by Raphael because it presents some weaknesses," but of specifying what seems "un-Raphaelesque" in its structure, in the organization of the forms even more than in the execution of the work. Mouth, nose, and eyes are modeled with confident precision, with a lively play of light-contrasts. Against that the face itself forms a soft and less well-defined mass, a little in conflict with the impact of the black blot of the hair and the almost metallic sharpness of the folds of the odalisque turban from which Ingres was to draw inspiration. Most of all, the representation of the shoulder and the neck on the right side seems completely to contradict the language of Raphael, who loved to produce in his portraits a beautifully compact and fleshy whole in an almost unbroken sweep from ear to shoulder which keeps the neck, and with it the head, firmly on the shoulders.

The picture as a whole presents us with something which is at once both more moving and harder than the Raphael we know. Who was the painter? Raphael alone? Giulio Romano, who is brought to mind by the strong contrasts and the less robust modeling? But how then to explain the signature? Raphael "assisted" by Giulio? Or should we think of it as a picture painted after Raphael's death? And there are more questions to be asked about the sitter's identity. There is no doubt that the word *fornarina* signifies in popular speech not a baker's daughter but a lover — in a pejorative sense — and that this name was given to the picture in the Barberini Gallery in the eighteenth century just when it was beginning to cause scandal. We should also remember that a very similar picture in the Pushkin Museum in Moscow, *A Naked Woman at her Toilet*, generally ascribed to Giulio Romano, is also by a tradition which appears to be scarcely any older entitled *La Fornarina*. We know the importance which high-ranking prostitutes formerly held in Rome, where they could often play a leading intellectual role.

The portrait of *Bino Altoviti*, long in the Munich Pinakothek, now seems to us to some extent an "exile" in the National Gallery in Washington, for such is the strength of feeling it conveys with its energy concealed beneath a mask of softness that it seems to possess something of the "German Hero." This very violence, the force of contrasted light and shadow, the warm and tactile immediacy of the materials with that extraordinary fragment of neck and nape of neck, bare of clothing, where the tresses of the hair are just beginning to spread out place the picture at an altogether late date, about 1519–1520.

In its sensitivity and fire it is comparable with the figures of the apostles in the *Transfiguration*. The pose, with the head turned in the direction of the viewer, is that already sketched out in the *Navagero*. These backward movements of the head are seen throughout Raphael's work. They are his way of defining space and taking possession of it. As with others the authenticity of this fine portrait is disputed: Raphael for some, Giulio Romano for others. The hypothesis of a collaboration in one way or another between the two men seems hard to sustain, given that the picture is so much of a piece and that the execution seems to have a single source. We must choose, and plump firmly for Raphael. For a long time it passed as a work of Raphael's, and the nineteenth century saw the painter's own face in its sweet and intense features. The picture's provenance from the Altoviti Palace in Rome and then from Florence seemsd to justify its being identified with the *Bino Altoviti* of which Vasari writes: "He made the portrait of Bino Altoviti when he was a young man." The youth of the subject, emphasized by the growth of down on the cheeks, has in fact often been stressed, and different dates have been proposed to take account of this (Altoviti having been born about 1490): 1512, 1513, 1515. The proposal to place the work in the last year of Raphael's life seems contradicted by the age of a sitter who could not have been out of his twenties. Perhaps, however, Vasari's phrase ought not to be taken literally, or Raphael may have painted the handsome Aldoviti as he was "when he was a young man" and idealistically fixed his looks as they were at the age of seventeen or eighteen. The picture would then be a retrospective fiction. But, of course, this hypothesis remains a *jeu d'esprit* and it is possible that the young man in Washington represents someone other than Altoviti.

The Portrait of a Young Woman in the Strasbourg Museum, another piece often overlooked (except by Pope-Hennessy), has been reinstated by Michel Laclotte, who has suggested including it in the Raphael *corpus*. Attributed most often hitherto to Giulio Romano, the picture seems on radiographic examination to have been executed at two different stages. That Raphael is responsible for the picture, in whole or in the greater part, is something of which everybody should be satisfied from the positioning of the shoulders and the neck, and the powerful and well-articulated masses are also his. The execution of the clothes, the hand and the hair has the grand fullness of that of the *Leo X*. The face, and the eyes in particular, contain hints of a somewhat dour firmness which could belong to Giulio Romano. Should one imagine a picture by the youthful Giulio having been taken over by Raphael? It is a fragile hypothesis, given that the face here, with its tenseness and bashfulness, seems better than anything which Giulio could have painted.

Might this portrait, so much more lively and more pictorial in quality than the *Fornarina*, possibly be, as Laclotte tentatively proposed, the pendant of the *Bino Altoviti*? We are tempted in this direction by the identity of their dimensions, as by the green backgrounds and the attitudes of the figures with hand on breast, which suggest a double portrait for a wedding. Ther divergent tonalities, which are cold in the Washington picture with its bright blue clothes and warmer in the Strasbourg picture, could stand in the way of the idea. But only a physical examination of the pictures and a setting of them side by side could allow one to have a firmer grasp of the problem.

Raphael died on April 6, 1520 which was a Good Friday as had been the day of his birth. The coincidence of these dates as well as the premature nature of his death struck both contemporaries and posterity, and provided an occasion for both grief and wonderment. He truly was "the divine Raphael." We are ill-informed about the cause of his death which appears to have been swift. Vasari puts it down to amorous excesses which Raphael was reluctant to admit to his doctors who bled him too much; others speak of a chill contracted in the antique ruins, or simply exhaustion brought on by overwork. A letter addressed to Alfonso I d'Este by one of his agents, Paulucci, talks merely of a "sharp and incessant fever." Near his deathbed was set the picture on which he had been at work for some years and which he had almost finished, the *Transfiguration*.

This huge painting, over four meters high, today in the Vatican Pinacoteca, represents the high-point of Raphael's genius and the consummation of everything he strove to achieve. Once again it was a picture destined for France; it was commissioned, probably in 1516, by Cardinal Giulio de Medici for his cathedral at Narbonne of which he was bishop. We know that it never traveled to France, but was placed over the High Altar of the church of San Pietro in Montorio at Rome. We can follow the history of the work through the letters which Sebastiano del Piombo wrote to Michelangelo about *The Raising of Lazarus*, a rival commission given to Sebastiano by the Cardinal for the same cathedral at Narbonne which is now in the National Gallery, London. It seems that in July 1518 work had not yet begun on painting the great work, but it may be that various drawings and plans were already in existence. The actual execution must have been going ahead throughout 1519 and the early months of 1520. At an early stage, to judge by a very hurried large sketch in the Albertina in Vienna which is probably a copy of a lost Raphael drawing, the scene of the *Transfiguration* is set on a mountain-top with a distant landscape, just as in the *St. Michael*, but viewed from a lower angle. Christ stands erect on the ground between Elijah and Moses and is surrounded by three apostles kneeling in the foreground, with St. Justus and St. Pastor (the patron saints of Narbonne) on the right. The whole upper third of the composition is filled with a striking vision of the Eternal Father whose outstretched arms echo and emphasize those of Christ amid a tumult of clouds peopled by an angelic host. Next comes a sketch in the British Museum, again a copy of a Raphael drawing, which shows us the succeeding stage in the evolution of the whole. There are six principal figures who are shown in dancing postures within two matching and intersecting circles — a splendid piece of evidence which permits an appreciation of the whole creative process, enabling us also to read the Albertina design as itself based on two intersecting circles, one containing the group of apostles and Elijah and Moses, the other (and smaller) circle the figure of God the Father. It was only later that the scene in the foreground which shows the apostles unable to cure the child possessed of the devil despite his parents' pleas came to be introduced in conformity with the Gospel of St. Matthew, which places the incident of Christ's healing of the child immediately after the Transfiguration while making it clear that the apostles themselves had not known how to effect a cure. Three drawings contain this new element. The first is in the Louvre and is a drawing by a pupil copying a Raphael *modello*; it shows a composition with draped figures, close to that finally adopted, but with two schematic circles at a tangent, and above all less moving and lyrical. The figures of Christ, Elijah and Moses are represented standing erect on the mountain, not in a state of levitation, and the characters in the lower section form a circle which is effective enough but lacks the bold diagonal slash which in the Vatican picture divides the group of apostles from the child's family group like a wild cry.

The drawing of the Albertina version, which presents the ensemble of the composition with unclothed figures in the poses of the final picture, seems to be by Giulio Romano, perhaps superimposed on a preliminary sketch by Raphael. It contrasts with the astonishing red chalk drawing which is in the Devonshire Collection at Chatsworth, and which likewise shows the figures unclothed and in the poses which became definitive, but only those of the upper section of the work. Its delicate, lively assurance can belong to nobody but Raphael.

The sharp division between the two "registers" of the *Transfiguration* is called for by the subject. The lower scene illustrates the powerlessness of the apostles, who have lost their faith, to cure the possessed child while the gestures of the child's relatives give expression to their revulsion and the apostles' helplessness — they can only point to Christ as the one possibility of salvation. The division in the painting thus symbolizes the drama of the separation between humankind, assailed by the devil, and the heavens, the image of redemption.

235/236 *The Transfiguration.* About 1517-20. Oil on panel. 405 x 278 cm. Rome, ▷ Vatican Museum.

Commissioned in 1517 by Giulio de'Medici for the cathedral at Narbonne, where he was bishop, the picture was still unfinished at Raphael's death. It was installed in 1523 above the main altar in the church of San Pietro in Montorio in Rome, where it remained until being taken off to Paris in 1797. It was returned to Rome in 1815 and entered the Vatican collection. This and the *Borghese Deposition* are the only works taken to Paris during the Revolutionary and Napoleonic Wars not to have been removed from their original supports and transferred to canvas. It seems certain that it was virtually complete when Raphael died and that the contribution of Giulio Romano, who perhaps finished off the figures of the possessed boy and his father, in the lower right part of the design, was really minimal. Letters from Sebastiano del Piombo to Michelangelo show that Giulio de'Medici was contriving a kind of competition between Sebastiano and Raphael, having also commissioned for Narbonne the former's *Raising of Lazarus*, which is now in the National Gallery in London.

237 *Head and hand of an apostle, study for The Transfiguration.* About 1518-19. Black chalk. 36.3 x 34.6 cm. J. Paul Getty Museum, Malibu.

Study for the apostle shown in profile standing on the left hand side of *The Transfiguration.* Further similar studies of heads are at Oxford and the British Museum. This is one of Raphael's last drawings, astonishing in its sense of life and in the rendering of volume through the freest and most sensual indications of light and shade.

238 *Study for the upper part of The Transfiguration.* About 1518-19. Red chalk. 24.6 x 35 cm. Chatsworth, Devonshire Collection.

One of the last studies for the composition of *The Transfiguration,* squared up for transfer. The figures, shown nude, are in the same poses as they are in the painting itself; the figures of Moses and Christ are just slightly moved to the right. The light, vibrant lines of the drawing establish the bodies and their movements with an assurance, elegance and strength that is unsurpassable.

The composition was undoubtedly completely transformed after these early essays but the idea of organizing it in two overlapping circles was retained. One huge circle, embracing the whole expanse of the canvas, encompasses the figures in the foreground, while another, slightly smaller and higher, has as its axis the figure of Christ between Moses and Elijah and, in its lower segment, James, Peter and John. Only such a rigorously geometrical arrangement could give some sort of unity to a composition which is obviously split into two parts, without a glance directed by any of the characters from one "register" to the other — save perhaps for the frightened gaze of the child — with on the one hand a symmetrical scene of moving stillness and on the other a disturbed and variegated crowd, here a transparency of clear coloring against a white light and their brilliant and contrasting colors in a strong *chiaroscuro*. The three apostles, who sprawl beneath the figure of Christ in such a remarkable movement, are contained within an almond-shape which matches the intersection of the two circles; in their geometry, rhythm and coloring they assure the transition from one level to the other. The same is true of the three arms stretching up towards the floating figures of Christ and the two prophets, a wonderful group swimming with a masterly freedom as if in the depths of the ocean.

Among the drawings associated with this picture are several nude studies which seem too weak to be by Raphael and which may be by Giulio, or possibly are copies of lost Raphael drawings. But a red chalk drawing in the Louvre, which shows the nude figures of the two apostles leaning forward in the middle ground, is powerful and alive in its sense of control and could well be from the hand of the master himself. There are a number of large preliminary drawings at Oxford, Chatsworth or the British Museum for the heads of the apostles, which are numbered among the masterpieces of Raphael as a draftsman. There is a new sense of freedom and warmth which allows the ample, solid forms to spread out in space

and also a sensual, almost pictorial, meticulousness in the depiction of the different textures of the hair and the wrinkled or taut skin, all qualities which will be there in a magnified form in the finished canvas, "a Caravaggio of the High Renaissance" as John Pope-Hennessy has described it.

Only the composition of *The Acts of the Apostles* in its treatment of the subject and its handling of figure groups can bear comparison with the lower section of the *Transfiguration*. We can better appreciate just how much these compositions, as they unfurl in parallel schemes over the surface of the work, and their geometrical framework, must represent the conscious effort and discipline imposed by the decorative imperative whenever we stand in front of the *Transfiguration*, with the bludgeoning violence of its forms which seem to start out from the canvas. The recent restoration work has revealed a powerful use of color, and a beauty of execution which can only have come from Raphael. The colors, springing like a fountain from deep shadows, have the magical brilliance of stained glass. The amazing diversity of the pictorial effects is achieved by the soft and smooth handling of the Christ figure alongside such rich elements in the painting as the heads of the apostles and the country landscape, drawn from nature. Here already are Poussin, Guercino, and Rubens.

One might say that, for Raphael, this picture represents the staggering and entirely fresh discovery of a completely new way of depicting materials and forms. Nobody had ever before painted mankind in its totality or represented so completely man's most powerful emotions of grief and hope. Only the works of Giotto and Van Eyck could have given their contemporaries a comparable idea of painting's powers, of its capacity to create fictions as truthful as reality. *The Transfiguration* stands as the "Triumph of Painting," as the awe-stricken Romans saw it. Painting could go no further. Raphael was dead. And for three and a half centuries others would follow by one path or another in the footsteps of this master.

VI. Raphael, or the Craft of Painting

Raphael enlarged the boundaries of the painter's domain in order to encompass all categories of techniques, dimensions and functions. He provided drawings for engravers and sculptors; he created palaces and churches; and he supervised efforts to unearth antiquities in Rome and restore ruins. In this way, he established a comprehensive and coherent repertoire of forms extending to the fringes of painting. Rubens and Le Brun, who also benefited from the trust of princely patrons, are perhaps the only other artists who proposed comparable ambitions for the craft of painting. Because it has been imitated so often, the style dominating Raphael's world appears so "natural" to us that we are obliged to exert ourselves in order to appreciate its distinctiveness, namely the extent to which the painter's world reflects a system of forms and colors selected by him and belonging solely to him, regardless of whether he shaped it according to his own wishes or whether it was intended for use by others.

It seems, however, that every aspect of Raphael's art was learned and that his entire life was guided by a thirst for knowledge. He seems to have quickly absorbed the experiences gained by the leading artists of Umbria, Florence, Rome and Venice, and to have made them his own without any indications of contradictions or abrupt changes. In every case, other painters' contributions revealed a possibility of expressing the human spirit with a new vigor and harmony through forms derived from nature. Indeed, Raphael's experience with drawings, spontaneous sketches, or studies of live models quickly gave a body and a soul to the plastic solutions, patterns of lines, and formal concepts suggested by prior painters' creations and he adapted these elements easily. By assimilating the outstanding works of Perugino, Signorelli, Leonardo, Fra Bartolomeo and Michelangelo, Raphael gradually forged a peerless tool, namely his own style of drawing which was capable of the fullest expressive power in a seemingly effortless manner. If one can dare to make such an affirmation, this vigorous incorporation of another person's experience or his scrutiny of their works and of nature itself, requiring a degree of perseverance which we cannot measure, represents the very essence of Raphael's creativity. Raphael personified talent and receptivity, and he learned in the same way from a drawing by da Vinci or Michelangelo as he did from a model posing for him. Hence, it would be somewhat incomprehensible to expect to discern traces of an indecisive personality in his openness. Furthermore, when one studies an artist, it is both easy and dangerous to attempt to explain everything in terms of influences. For painters, works of art, in the same way as natural forms, serve as a source of images; sometimes they are the catalyst that provides access to images. Since the greatest painters (consider Rubens!) are precisely those who have most assiduously painted "according to the masters" without concealing their sources, it should not matter if their sources included their own contemporaries. This history of painting teems with abundant dialogues and we must sometimes leave painters to themselves, without always suspecting plagiarism, borrowing and without always being prepared to believe that their work is not "personal." Paradise for painters is not the art historian's paradise. Creativity can travel along many paths and Cézanne learning from Pissarro or Cézanne drawing according to Rubens is more "personal" than boastful Bouguereau inspired by a nude female.

It is true that in comparison with the creations of da Vinci and Michelangelo, the prolixity of Raphael's paintings, which reflect his successive "styles," is dazzling. Actually, his works reveal a continuous, coherent and intentional journey even though its trajectory is full of surprises, unexpected creations, and the "excrescences" that are always present among the accomplishments of outstanding geniuses. Thus, it is not entirely fruitless to attempt to establish positions for Raphael's paintings and drawings within a chronological continuum in order to understand the phases and detours and even the hesitations of his creative progress; then there may be a possibility of recognizing its coherence. In a comparable way, the study of the works of Picasso, despite their multiplicity and contradictions, permits us to reconstruct the artists' indissoluble unity, as if it were a mosaic. Usually, attempts are made to characterize the unity of Raphael's work by certain words: balance, clarity, gentleness, gracefulness. Nevertheless, these terms offer few contributions in terms of defining a style and they are only fitting for a carefully selected Raphael, detached from the creations of his mature years. Raphael's paintings can be described as a patient

244

239 *Study of a woman reading and holding a child.* About 1512. Metal-point on grey prepared paper, heightened with white. 19 x 14 cm. Chatsworth, Devonshire Collection.

A splendid sketch from life of models in contemporary dress, the life and freedom of which looks forward to the Carracci, this drawing has sometimes been related to the figures of mothers and children in *The Mass at Bolsena.* Another study of a mother and child in the same technique, not in Oxford, shows the same sense of domestic intimacy.

240 *Head of a child.* About 1510? Black chalk. 10.3 x 7.7 cm. Lille, Musée des Beaux-Arts.

Though crowned with leaves, this exquisite head of a child, an instant of radiant life, is more that of a young St. John than a Bacchus. The expression is reminiscent of the St. John in a lost Madonna with a veil, known through a copy in Princeton. But there are also points of similarity with the Christ Child in the *Niccolini* and *Mackintosh Madonnas.*

quest for the proper expression. They also represent tension, violence and turmoil. The surprising thing is that he did not forego anything while his expressive qualities grew more profound. A careful scrutiny of his works fully demonstrates this point. The "*Oddi Coronation*" and the "*Transfiguration,*" which are displayed beside one another at the Vatican galleries, belong to the same world: robust contours, individualization of figures, and dramatic exchanges. The second of these paintings is merely a consequence or indeed an exaggeration of the first.

Despite the gradual proliferation of techniques, a sense of the unity of Raphael's quest may be obtained more easily from studying his drawings than from his paintings. Even in the earliest drawings to have been preserved, observation of natural sources is represented by precise positioning of forms within space. These forms are always rhythmic, suggesting a vigorous and delicately executed movement of figures with a sound instinct for equilibrium in three dimensions. Furthermore, the path of the artist's instrument upon the paper, whether bold or subtle, captures living forms with a palpitation and a transparency amid a light that characterize Raphael. It is astonishing to encounter certain recurrent elements in his drawings: the admirable metal tip drawing for the "*Sacrifice at Lystre,*" recently displayed at the Louvre, has a boldness and a delicacy that situate it within the same universe as Raphael's earliest Umbrian drawings, even though there is a gap of fifteen years. Careful scrutiny of Raphael's drawings also demonstrates more fully that attribution of idealized portrayal to Raphael's figures is a dangerous myth. Observation of nature and a quest for ideal beauty are mutually compatible at a given time and do not represent two successive stages, as would occur much later in Ingres' works. Raphael's paintings developed from forms suggested by his drawings, with a stronger and more comprehensive characterization. Consequently, it was possible for a single figure to be drawn from several models. "In order to paint one beautiful woman, I need to see several," Raphael wrote to Castiglione. Elsewhere in the same letter, the frequently discussed phrase referring to a "lack of beautiful women," indicates that Raphael had to rely upon "that certain idea which arises within the mind," is possibly nothing more than the lament of a painter who cannot find a suitable model instead of a description of creative techniques.

Consider now the "pictorial" aspect of Raphael's works. In fact, as soon as brushstrokes and color come into play, that is when a painting or a fresco is being planned, the liveliness of a robust and clearly defined subject is immediately combined as if by magic with a constantly predominant vigor of design. The painter's gestures are simple, fluid and free so that forms, colors and the subject's position in relation to light are determined simultaneously. Drawing is transformed into painting. Beautiful movements turn within space, gently endowing forms with fullness. Nothing is left empty and every element grows, develops and expands. To render comprehensible the intensity and the roundness of Raphael's shapes, it is only possible to envision fruit, large pebbles worn smooth by the sea or shells. A proper harmony is established for plenitude and for open areas, while volume is brought to life with pulsations and throbs; elements are interwoven and counterbalanced, interacting as firm embraces or distant series of echoes. The painting becomes an organic whole, and harmony among forms expresses relationships among human figures whose movements recur, multiply, enter into opposition, and overlap, face to face and back to back. The bold and lively rhythm dominating Raphael's paintings has often been compared to the flowing but orderly rhythm of dancing.

His execution is so simple that few dare to describe it. There are no similarities to Leonardo's impalpable creations in which brushstrokes and colors always appear to be laid bare. Raphael's brushstrokes are decisive and at times almost abrupt, with the paint applied in an undiluted form so that there is a distinct contrast with the extremely delicate effects achieved by density or by nuances, semi-penumbras and transitions, which of course embody qualities originating from the contemplation of Leonardo's creations. The vigorous brushstrokes, underscoring the contours of shapes and facilitating their interpretation, paradoxically create through a sense of delicate transitions a certain "haziness," which, although it does not restrict the sharpness of clearly distinguishable forms, inexplicably clothes them with a languid and velvety aura like mist, as if it is nothing and everything at once.

Consider also Raphael's colors. This is an unusual endeavor in which one is inclined to proceed warily; in the early compilations of the seventeenth and eighteenth centuries in which each of the leading painters of the past was briefly described according to his individual merits, the painter from Urbino received a mediocre appraisal as a "colorist." Overwhelmed by the genius of his "draftsmanship," we have tended to go no further, as if each painting were not a combination of drawing techniques and color and had not acquired its inherent qualities from this combination or collision. Perhaps we are too deeply respectful of the engravings which have given a black and white image of Raphael for too many centuries, highlighting his graphic skills. Why does this reticence still persist? The diversity of Raphael's color schemes may have created an impression that color was a secondary concern. Nevertheless, one wonders whether his paintings are too polychromatic to be truly colorful! Throughout his career, Raphael developed, diversified and refined the varied palette of intense and contrasting colors adopted by the Umbrian painters, endowing it with increasingly expressive and dramatic qualities. His earliest paintings, such as the "*Saint Nicholas Altarpiece*," the "*Mond Altarpiece*," and the "*Oddi Altarpiece*," demonstrate how somewhat sharp contrasts among vermilion, azure, gold and black are gradually softened by employing a more delicate tonality. In the "*Oddi Altarpiece*," whites, grays, and beiges allow tempering of contrasts and it even appears that a range of colors is already subtly represented by each of the smaller compositions adorning the altar-step. In the "*Presentation at the Temple*," there is a gilded harmony with clear greens, soft reds, and pale yellow hues. In the "*Adoration of the Magi*," lively, fresh, and matutinal effects are created within a natural setting by clear blues, whites and vermilions. In turn, the "*Sposalizio*" (Nuptials) achieves a precise equilibrium through contrasts created by extremely dark and even black tones along with extremely bright and even white ones so that forms are impeccably demarcated and accentuated amid a musical

dialogue of intense colors — red, pink, orange, yellow, and honey-like tones — in contrast with cold colors such as bright or pale blues and purplish grays. This dialogue of warm and cold tones, usually resonant blues and reds, is reintroduced in many of the Florentine paintings, although contrasts are softened by the pale tones of carnations and the soft green of landscapes. It appears that toward the end of Raphael's Florentine period, his palette became more diversified and more refined. Softer and more subtle shades such as deep purples tinted with orange or soft golden tones and combined with slate-like grays, verdigris and russet greens are coordinated with bold reds in the "*Borghese Deposition*." At a later point, the London "*Saint Catherine*" was attired in blue, red, yellow and green but each color is accompanied by unusual melancholy and almost sorrowful nuances, so that the color scheme merges with the mood expressed by lines, the pose, and the face itself. The importance of frescoes in Raphael's works after he resided in Rome becomes obvious in his coloration. The "*Disputa*" and the "*School of Athens*" are distinguished by less fragmented colors with a predomination of clear, extensively developed tonalities, and particularly of white. The ongoing dialogue between warm and cold tones is represented by the red and blue garments of Plato and Aristotle in the "*School of Athens*," as well as by beige tones and bluish, coppery and azure-tinted grays. At the same time, the colors of Raphael's paintings became more intense and more uniform: the "*Virgin of Loreto*" contains vast expanses of color where white acquires a resonance comparable to that of other colors. In several of his "Virgins" completed close to 1511, such as the "*Virgin of Alba*," the "*Virgin with a Diadem*," and the "*Aldobrandini Virgin*," one encounters prodigious variations upon the pink-blue gamut, expressed by bright and mannered nuances, or, in contrast, by pale and muted nuances.

A readiness to consider Raphael's interest in color does not truly emerge until an opportunity arises for discussion of his frescoes of Heliodorus' quarters. Indeed, his paintings during the same period were characterized by a new chromatic unity derived from more somber tones, characterized by introduction of gray, violet, or brownish hues, or muted pinks adorned with pale or golden flecks. The "*Bolsena Mass*" vibrates with the boldest reds, representing the uppermost levels of the color spectrum. It has always been observed, and rightly so, that these shades played the same role in the paintings of Lorenzo Lotto and Sebastiano del Piombo which Raphael would have been able to observe during this period. At the same time, the "*Virgin of Foligno*" achieves an exaltation of blue, red and yellow, with an entirely Venetian brilliance. Clear and lively colors returned to Raphael's sketches for tapestries, reflecting a preoccupation with the distinctness that exists in contrast to the dark vastness of shadowed areas. His final creations reveal increasingly accentuated contrasts in colors and shapes within the context of a disconcerting freedom from restraint. Shadows vary to a deep black and whitish tones tend to fade amid light. The "*Transfiguration*" provides a spectacular illustration of this change: ceramic blues, bright pinks, vermilions, golden yellows and acidic greens are separated from a somber background with a burning fervor. These intense effects provide contrasts with the snowy whites of the upper portion of the painting and the conflict among colors expresses a tautness or a vigor that is comparable to that of the lines and forms derived from the subject. Instead of being superimposed upon design, color constitutes the body of the painting, providing structure and coherence. Indeed, it is possible to interpret Raphael's creations as an extended conquest of the expressive capabilities of color.

Raphael shaped a world in which design, pictorial elements and color jointly contribute to the expression of the experiences, emotions and history of mankind. His receptivity to other painters' works and his assiduous attention to natural forms permitted him to develop a style which was regarded as perfect or "definitive." Painters who imitated him did not succeed in recapturing his essential qualities: enjoyment and an understanding of life combined with sympathy for living things. Those are the attributes which initially won renown for Raphael's art. Da Vinci always evinces a detached perspective whereas Michelangelo is slightly disdainful. Hence, we encounter fluidity and harmony, although there is never an idealization of natural forms, instead of an intimate understanding and a recreation of their essence. The "beauty" of Raphael's human figures is derived from his talent for capturing these recurrent miracles which all of us experience during brief moments throughout our lives. This is the exquisite and deeply moving beauty — which is even more moving when it has gone unnoticed — of children, young women, and adolescents. It is nothing other than the radiance and plenitude of life, or life in its most lively form. Because of the exquisiteness of his soul, Raphael was exceptionally sensitive to these moments, and with unique insight and efforts he succeeded in recreating their pricelessness. More than the works of any other artist, Raphael's creations incontestably demonstrate an acute sense of the charm of young children. His love for women is also revealed in an unmistakeable way: beginning with the studies which he completed for the "*Belvedere Virgin*" and for the "*Belle Jardinière*," in which female models are depicted in a true-to-life manner, there is a proliferation of more joyful and more sensuous evocations of femininity that are most strikingly represented by the Muses of Raphael's "*Parnassus*" and by the figures appearing in Psyche's *loggia* at the Farnese library. This man with a zest for life was, nevertheless, a sincerely devout person who lived among members of the clergy and nearly received a cardinal's *biretta*. This contemporary of Luther was the creator of images evoking triumphant Catholicism, in which religious iconography was revolutionized by the introduction of a profoundly expressed affectivity and pathos in portrayal of sacred figures. Only the *Seicento* was capable of understanding and achieving this quality. A sense of the sacred is present in all of Raphael's religious works, beginning and ending with two victories of faith over the forces of evil in the "*Saint Nicholas Altarpiece*" and in the "*Transfiguration*." Raphael's faith became stronger as his career continued and this is why the climate of his final years became heavily laden with eroticism and religiosity. This is why Raphael perplexes those of us who are so prudish and have little religious devotion. The paintings of Raphael's maturity are his least abstract creations; there are few works so humanly violent and so disturbing as the "*Fornarina*" (Baker's Daughter) or the "*Transfiguration*" because we encounter something less than painting… or something more. We have preferred to admire Raphael for the "*Belle Jardinière*" and the "*School of Athens*" instead of for these somewhat fear-inspiring paintings that convey the almost biological vitality of this little man.

Hence, throughout this painter's works it is possible to discover a coherence, a logic and a persistence that identifies Raphael's style. The constant factor or the guiding element is energy coupled with restlessness rather than calmness. The important aspect is portrayal of life as a whole; it is precision of expression. The Raphael whom we must consider is the one who pursued a variety of categories although he has received insufficient admiration during the twentieth century. This artist is the Raphael who created cartoons of the deformed, the howling figure who accompanies Heliodorus, the madman of the "*Transfiguration*." This is the true Raphael, who hunted for suitable subjects and was the first to discover the great "historic" language of painting. Perhaps through studying his "scorned" creations (after "*Heliodorus*," for example) and through understanding his quest — as well as his success, which molded Western painting for nearly four centuries — it will be possible to grasp more clearly and as something new the exquisite creations of the gentle Raphael who existed prior to 1512, and lastly, to comprehend the "*Borghese Deposition*" as something other than a "stylistic exercise."

In summation, the frail native of Urbino with a feminine countenance was actually a stout-hearted man — if such an expression is permissible — capable of undertaking the greatest endeavor ever achieved by a painter. He was a discontented and restless person who continued to the outermost limit, thereby creating painting. After having embraced the universe of forms and colors that fills his works, and after becoming aware of its almost monstrous vastness, therein he pursued his path like a lightning bolt, one must conclude that Raphael is painting personified. He is the destination to which everything flows and the source from which everything begins, until the fragmentation emerging in our own century. Raphael's ambition was to transform painting into a language capable of expressing every aspect of mankind: beauty, ugliness, faith, sadness and the rage to live. His message will be transmitted. It will be understood that his role was inimitable. The word "charm" has always been used to describe the quality that his creations joyfully radiate, with exceptional modesty. No better word could be chosen. This was his supreme gift, and it was combined with precise and powerful expressiveness. Why should anyone fear that painting can be overwhelming *and* felicitous, like love itself?

Bibliography

General Works

F. Antal, *Raphael zwischen Klassizismus und Manierismus*, Fulda 1980.

J.H. Beck, *Raphael*, New York 1976.

A.M. Brizio, "Raffaello", *Enciclopedia Universale dell'Arte*, XI, Venice-Rome 1963.

E. Camesasca, *Tutta la pittura di Raffaello*, Milan 1956.

G.B. Cavalcaselle and J.A. Crowe, *Rafaello, la sua vita e le sue opere*, Florence 1884–1891.

P.L. De Vecchi, *Raffaello, La Pittura*, Florence 1981.

L. Dussler, *Raffael, Kritisches Verzeichnis der Gemälde, Wandbilder und Bildteppiche*, Munich 1966; English edition: *Raphael, A Critical Catalogue of his pictures, paintings and tapestries*, London-New York 1971.

O. Fischel, *Raffaels Zeichnungen*, I–VII, Berlin 1913–1941.

O. Fischel, *Raphael*, London 1948; German edition: Berlin 1962.

H. Focillon, *Raphaël*, Pais 1926.

V. Golzio, *Raffaello nei documenti, nelle testimonianze dei contemporanei e nella letteratura del suo secolo*, Vatican City 1936.

W. Kelber, *Raphael von Urbino*, Stuttgart 1963–1964; 2nd edition: Stuttgart 1980.

E. Müntz, *Raphaël, sa vie, son oeuvre et son temps*, Paris 1881.

K. Oberhuber, *Raphaels Zeichnungen*, IX, Berlin 1972.

K. Oberhuber, *Raffaello*, Milan 1982.

A.P. Oppé, *Raphael*, New York 1970.

S. Ortolani, *Raffaello*, Bergame 1942.

J. D. Passavant, *Raphel von Urbino und sein Vater Giovanni Santi*, Leipzig 1839–1858; French edition: *Raphaël d'Urbin*, Paris 1860.

J. Pope-Hennessy, *Raphael*, The Wrightsman Lectures, New York 1970.

P. Pouncey and J.A. Gere, *Italian Drawings... in the British Museum; Raphael and his Circle*, London 1962.

M. Prisco and P. De Vecchi, *L'opera completa di Raffaello*, Milan 1966.

A.C. Quatermère de Quincy, *Histoire de la vie et des ouvrages de Raphaël*, Paris 1824.

S. Ray, *Raffaello architetto: linguaggio artistico e ideologia nel Rinascimento romano*, Rome 1974.

M. Salmi (under the direction of), *Raffaello, l'opera, le fonti, la fortuna* (notably: L. Becherucci, "Raffaello e la pittura"; A. Marabottin, "I collaboratori"; A. Forlani Tempesti, "I disegni"; G. Marchini, "Le architetture"; G. Becatti, "Raffaello e l'antico"; V. Golzio, " La vita", "La fortuna critica"; L. Bianchi, "La fortuna di Raffaello nell'incizione"), Novare 1966; English edition: *The complete work of Raphael*, New York 1969.

W. Schöne, *Raphael*, Berlin-Darmstadt 1958.

G. Vasari, *Le Vite de' Più Eccellenti Pittori, Scultori ed Architettori*, 1550 and 1568; G. Milanesi, edit., Florence 1906 ("Vita di Raffaello da Urbino", v. IV, p. 311)

H. Wagner, *Raffael im Bildnis*, Berne 1969.

H. Zerner and P. De Vecchi, *Tout l'oeuvre peint de Raphaël*, Paris 1969; 2nd edition 1982.

Umbria

L. Becherucci, "Il Vasari de gli inizi di Raffaello", *Il Vasari storiografo e artista, Atti del Congresso Internazionale nel IV centenario della morte*, Arezzo 1974.

S. Béguin, "Un nouveau Raphaël: un ange du retable de saint Nicolas de Tolentino", *Revue du Louvre*, 2, 1982.

P.L. De Vecchi, *Lo Sposalizio della Vergine di Raffaello*, Quaderni di Brera no. 2, Florence 1973.

R. Dubos, *Giovanni Santi, peintre et chroniquer à Urbin*, Bordeaux 1971.

S. Ferino, "A Master-painter and his pupils: Pietro Perugino and his umbrian workshop", *Oxford Art Journal*, I, 1979.

S. Ferino, "Raphael's activity in Perugia as reflected in a drawing in the Ashmolean Museum, Oxford", *Mitteilungen des Kunsthistorischen Institutes in Florenz*, 25, 1981.

S. Ferino, *Disegni umbri del Rinascimento da Perugino a Raffaello*, catalogue d'exposition, Florence, Cabinet des Dessins des Offices, 1982.

R. Longhi, "Percorso di Raffaello giovine", *Paragone*, May 1955, p. 8.

K. Oberhuber, "The Colonna Altarpiece in the Metropolitan and Problems in the early style of Raphael", *Metropolitan Museum Journal*, XII, 1977 (1978).

E. Panofsky, "Raffael und die Fresken der Dombibliothek zu Siene", *Repertorium für Kunstwissenschaft*, 27, 1915.

R. Wittkower, "The young Raphael", *Allen Memorial Art Museum Bulletin*, Oberlin College, XX, 1963, p. 150.

Florence

A. Chastel, *Art et humanisme à Florence au temps de Laurent le Magnifique*, Paris 1959.

L. Ferrara, S. Staccioli, A.M. Tantillo, *Storia e restauro della Deposizione di Raffaello*, Rome 1972.

E. Panofsky, "Herkules am Scheidewege", *Studien der Bibliothek Warburg*, 1930, p. 37.

C.L. Ragghianti, *La Deposizione di Raffaello*, Milan 1947.

F. Sangiorgi, "La Muta di Raffaello, considerazioni storico-iconografiche", *Commentari*, IV, 1973, p. 90.

J. Shearman, "Raphael at the court of Urbino", *Burlington Magazaine*, CXII, 1970, p. 72.

Rome: Frescoes and Decors

N. Dacos, *Le logge di Raffaello: maestro e bottega di fronte all'antico*, Rome 1977.

H. von Einem, "Das Programm der Stanza della Segnatura in Vatikan", *Vorträge, Rheinsih-Westfälische Akademie der Wissenschaften, Geisteswissenschaften*, 169, Opladen 1971.

L.D. Ettlinger, "A note on Raphael's Sibyls in Santa Maria della Pace", *Journal of the Warburg and Courtauld Institutes*, XXIV, 1961, p. 322.

E. Gombrich, "Raphael's Stanza della Segnatura", *Symbolic Images, Studies in the Art of the Renaissance*, London 1972.

M. Hirst, "The Chigi Chapel in Santa Maria della Pace", *Journal of the Warburg and Courtauld Institutes*, XXIV, p. 161.

K. Oberhuber, "Die Fresken der Stanza dell'Incendio im Werk Raffaels", *Jahrbuch der Kunsthistorischen Sammlungen in Wien*, XXII, 1962, p. 23.

K. Oberhuber and L. Vitali, *Il cartone per la Scuola di Atene*, Milan 1972.

H. Pfeiffer, "Zur Ikongraphie von Raffaels Disputa. Egidio da Viterbo und die christlich-platonische Konzeption der Stanza della Segnatura", *Miscellanea Historiae Pontificiae*, 37, Rome 1974.

D. Redig de Campos, *Raffaello nelle Stanze*, Rome 1965.

E. Schröter, "Raffaels Parnass: eine ikonographische Untersuchung", *Actas del XXIII Congreso Internacional de Historia de Arte*, III, Grenada 1973 (1978).

J. Shearman, "The Chigi Chapel in Santa Maria del Popolo", *Journal of the Warburg and Courtauld Institutes*, XXIV, 1961, p. 129.

J. Shearman, "Die Loggia der Psyche in der Villa Farnesina und die Probleme der letzten Phase von Raffaels graphischem Stil", *Jahrbuch der Kunsthistorischen Sammlungen in Wien*, XXIV, 1964, p. 59.

J. Shearman, "Raphael's Unexecuted Projects for the Stanze", *Walter Friedländer zum 90. Geburtstag*, Berlin 1965.

J. Shearman, "The Vatican Stanze: Functions and Decorations", *Proceedings of the British Academy*, LVII, London 1972.

J. Shearman, *Raphael's Cartoons in the Collection of her Majesty the Queen and the Tapestries for the Sistine Chapel*, London 1972.

E. Wind, "Platonic Justice Designed by Raphaël", *Journal of the Warburg and Courtauld Institute*, I, 1937–1938, p. 69.

E. Wind, "The Four Elements in Raphael's Stanza della Segnatura", *Journal of the Warburg and Courtauld Institutes*, II, 1938–1939, p. 75.

Rome: Paintings

S. Béguin and C. Gould, *La Madone de Lorette* (files in the department of painting, 19), Paris 1979.

A.M. Brizio, "La Santa Cecilia di Raffaello", *Studi in onore di G. Nicco Fasola, Arte Lombarda*, IX, 1965, p. 99.

D.A. Brown and K. Oberhuber, "Monna Vanna and Fornarina: Leonardo and Raphael in Rome", *Essays Presented Myron P. Gilmore*, Florence 1978.

H. von Einem, "Die Verklärung Christi und die Heilung des

Besessenen von Raffael", *Abhandlungen der Wissenschaften und der Literatur*, 5, Mayence 1966.

H. von Einem, "Bemerkungen zu Raffaels Madonna di Foligno", *Studies in the Late Medieval and Renaissance Painting in honor of Millard Meiss*, New York 1977.

B. Fredericksen, "New Information on Raphael's Madonna di Loreto", *J. Paul Getty Museum Journal, III,* 1976.

S. Freedberg, F. Mancinelli, K. Oberhuber, *A Masterpiece Close-up: The Transfiguration by Raphael*, Cambridge 1981.

E. Gombrich, "Raphael's Madonna della Sedia", *Charlton Lecture*, London 1956.

C. Gould, *Portrait of Pope Julius II. The Reemergence of the Original*, London (1970).

K. Oberhuber, "Vorzeichnungen zu Raffaels Transfiguration", *Jahrbuch der Berliner Museen*, IV, 1962, p. 116.

K. Oberhuber, "Raphael and the State Portrait: I, The Portrait of Julius II; II, The Portrait of Lorenzo de'Medici", *Burlington Magazine*, 1971, p. 124; p. 436.

M. Putscher, *Raphaels Sixtinische Madonna. Das Werk und seine Wirkung*, Tübingen 1955.

D. Redig de Campos, "Restauro della Transfigurazione di Raffaello: nota sulla sua autografia", *Colloqui del Sodalizio*, 2, 5, 1975–1976 (1977).

J. Shearman, "Le Portrait de Baldassare Castiglione par Raphaël", *Revue du Louvre*, 4, 1979.

Index of Works

Index of locations of paintings

Index of names of people

Photo Credits

We wish to thank the following musuems and libraries for giving us permission to reproduce the photos in this book. The numbers refer to the illustrations.

Photo material has been gathered by Ingrid de Kalbermatten.

Bayonne, Musée Bonnat 207 (photo Réunion des Musées Nationaux, Paris)
Bergame, Accademia Carrara 12 (photo Anderson-Giraudon, Paris)
Berlin, Staatlich Museen Preussicher Kulturbesitz, Gemäldegalerie 13 (photo Bildarchiv Preussicher Kulturbesitz, Berlin); 11, 76, 93 (photos Jörg P. Anders, Berlin)
Bologna, Pinacoteca Nazionale 209, 210 (photos A. Villani & Figli, Bologna)
Boston, Isabella Stewart Gardner Museum 37
Brescia, Pinacoteca Tosio Martinengo 5, 50, (photos Fotostudio Rapuzzi, Brescia)
Budapest, Fine Arts Museum 99 (photo Interfoto MTI, Budapest)
Chantilly, Musée Condé 54, 90, 146 (photos Lauros-Giraudon, Paris); 115 (photo Giraudon, Paris)
Chatsworth, collection Devonshire 154, 220, 237, 239 (photos Courtauld Institute of Art, London); 238
Cracow, Czartoryski Museum 151
Dresden, Gemäldegalerie 202 (photo Pfauder, Staatlich Kunstsammlungen, Dresden)
Edinburg, National Gallery of Scotland 91, 94
Florence, Department of Drawings, Uffizi Gallery 18 (photo Guido Sansoni, Florence); 19, 56, 58, 69, 77, 98, 164, 185, 203 (photos Alinari, Florence); 104 (photo SCALA, Antella)
— Uffizi Gallery 40, 71, 72, 88, 230 (photos Alinari, Florence)
— Pitti Palace 73, 78, 102, 103, 155, 194, 206, 225 (photos Alinari, Florence); 197 (photo SCALA, Antella)
Frankfurt, Städelsches Kunstinstitut 116, 134 (photos Ursula Edelmann, Frankfurt); 47
Leningrad, Hermitage 75, 89
Lille, Musée des Beaux-Arts 16, 42 (photos Giraudon, Paris); 2, 61, 148, 149, 240
Lisbon, Museu Nacional de Arte Antiga 28
London, British Museum 15, 41, 65-68, 96, 107, 136, 143, 144, 200
— National Gallery 22, 35, 48, 49, 53, 106, 145, 153
— Victoria and Albert Museum 173, 174, 178-180, 182, 183, 186
Madrid, Prado 97, 152, 204, 211
Milan, Pinacoteca Ambrosiana 124
— Pinacoteca di Brera 44, 45
Montpellier, Musée Fabre 118, 119 (photos Claude O'Sughrue, Montpellier)
Munich, Alte Pinakothek 92 (photo Blauel-Bavaria, Gauting); 100, 198 (photos Bayerische Staatsgemäldesammlung, Munich)
Naples, Galleria Nazionale de Capodimonte 4 (photo Sprintendenza per i Beni Artistici e Storici, Naples)

New York, collection Ira Spanierman 231
— Metropolitan Museum of Art 26, 27, 36, 83
Oxford, Ashmolean Museum 3, 8, 9, 17, 20, 21, 24, 33, 43, 51, 62, 82, 108, 111, 126, 127, 131, 157, 161, 171, 172, 208, 212
Paris, Bibliothèque Nationale 1, 138
— Musée du Louvre 77, 223 (photos ACRACI, Paris); 6, 55, 57, 85-87, 105, 150, 160, 168, 175, 184, 191, 195, 214, 222, 224, 226-229 (photos Réunion des Musées Nationaux, Paris); 221 (photo Lauros-Giraudon, Paris)
Pasadena (California), Norton Simon Museum of Art 14
Pérouse, Church of the Monastery of San Severo 52 (photo Soprintendenza Monumenti et Gallerie, Pérouse)
Raleigh, North Carolina Museum of Art 29
Rome, Church of Santa Maria della Pace 140 (photo Anderson, Rome)
— Church of Santa Maria del Popolo 170 (photo Alinari, Florence)
— Church of Sant'Agostino 169 (photo Anderson, Rome)
— Borghese Galleries 39, 63, 64, 70 (photos P De Antonis, Rome)
— Doria-Pamphilj Galleries 196 (photo ARTE FOTOGRAFICA, Rome)
— Galleria Nazionale, Barberini Palace 232 (photo ARTE FOTOGRAFICA, Rome)
— Villa Farnesina 141, 213 (photos P. De Antonis, Rome)

São Paulo, Museu de Arte 10
Stockholm, National Museum 31
Strasbourg, Musée des Beaux-Arts 234
Vatican, Palace of the 109, 112, 113, 117, 121, 123, 128, 129, 133, 158, 159, 162, 163, 165, 167, 188, 192, 193, 201, 215-219 (photos Monumenti Musei e Gallerie Pontificie, Vatican); 118, 122, 130, 135, 156, 190 (photos P. De Antonis, Rome); 166 (photo Anderson-Garaudon, Paris)
— Picture Gallery 23, 34, 176, 177, 181, 187, 199 (photos P. De Antonis, Rome); 25, 30, 32, 60, 235, 236 (photos Monumenti Musei e Gallerie Pontificie, Vatican)
Urbino, Galleria Nazionale delle Marche 74 (photo Alinari, Florence)
Vaduz, collection of the prince of Lichtenstein 38 (photo Walter Wachter, Schaan)
Vienna, Albertina 81, 95, 114, 125, 139, 142 (photos Österreichische Nationalbibliothek, Vienna)
— Kunsthistorisches Museum 80, 84
Washington, D.C., National Gallery of Art 59, 79, 101, 147, 233
Windsor, Royal Library Frontispiece 46, 110, 132, 137, 205